"The third edition of *A Guide to Practicum and Internsh*
continues and expands its influence on the professional development of school counselors. As a distinct mental health- and education-focused profession, school counseling requires unique expertise and training experiences. This guide aids not only those of us in counselor education programs, but also the professionals in the field who are mentoring our next generation of school counselors. With a unique focus on what many students understand to be the most significant aspect of their education—the field experience—Drs. Studer and Oberman provide a connection between the university classroom, the school environment, and the school counselor and bring the profession to life for the ultimate benefit of the students and families they serve."

Janna L. Scarborough, PhD,
Professor of Counseling,
East Tennessee State University

"*A Guide to Practicum and Internship for School Counselors-in-Training* is a game changer for school counselors-in-training, site supervisors, and counselor educators. This guide delivers practical activities and insights to help school counselors-in-training successfully navigate the clinical experience, apply the ASCA National Model, and transition into the profession with a clear professional identity. It has given me a new perspective on practicum and internship supervision. I won't teach another internship course without it."

Kimberlee Ratliff, PhD,
Professor of School Counseling,
American Public University System

A Guide to Practicum and Internship for School Counselors-in-Training

The ideal resource for school counseling field experiences, the updated and expanded third edition of *A Guide to Practicum and Internship for School Counselors-in-Training* covers all aspects of the practicum and internship experience from the initial contact with supervisors to detailed descriptions of students' different roles.

Readers will gain an awareness of school culture and the understanding needed to develop an individualized philosophy of school counseling. Each chapter contains activities, case studies, worksheets, and images to facilitate understanding, and all material is consistent with both the Council for Accreditation of Counseling and Related Educational Programs (CACREP) 2016 Common Core and School Counselor Entry-Level Specialty Areas and the school counselor standards identified by the American School Counselor Association (ASCA). Specific focus is given to strategies for implementing the ASCA National Model (4th edition) as a part of clinical experiences.

This text can be used by faculty, students, and supervisors alike to support and enhance the school counseling knowledge base used to meet the needs of all students.

Aaron H. Oberman, PhD, is an associate professor at The Citadel, and coordinator for the counselor education programs. His scholarly work focuses on school counseling and the ASCA National Model.

Jeannine R. Studer, EdD, is a professor emerita from the University of Tennessee, Knoxville. She has written numerous articles and texts surrounding the role of the school counselor.

A Guide to Practicum and Internship for School Counselors-in-Training

Third Edition

Aaron H. Oberman and Jeannine R. Studer

Routledge
Taylor & Francis Group

NEW YORK AND LONDON

Third edition published 2021
by Routledge
52 Vanderbilt Avenue, New York, NY 10017

and by Routledge
2 Park Square, Milton Park, Abingdon, Oxon, OX14 4RN

Routledge is an imprint of the Taylor & Francis Group, an informa business

© 2021 Taylor & Francis

The right of Aaron H. Oberman and Jeannine R. Studer to be identified as authors of this work has been asserted by them in accordance with sections 77 and 78 of the Copyright, Designs and Patents Act 1988.

First edition published by Routledge 2010

Second edition published by Routledge 2016

Library of Congress Cataloging-in-Publication Data
Names: Oberman, Aaron H., author. | Studer, Jeannine R., author.
Title: A guide to practicum and internship for school counselors-in-training / Aaron H. Oberman, Jeannine R. Studer.
Description: Third edition. | New York, NY : Routledge, 2020. | Includes bibliographical references and index. |
Identifiers: LCCN 2020012907 (print) | LCCN 2020012908 (ebook) | ISBN 9780367217877 (hardback) | ISBN 9780367217884 (paperback) | ISBN 9780429266089 (ebook)
Subjects: LCSH: Educational counseling. | Student counselors–Training of. | Internship programs.
Classification: LCC LB1027.5 .G836 2020 (print) | LCC LB1027.5 (ebook) | DDC 371.4–dc23
LC record available at https://lccn.loc.gov/2020012907
LC ebook record available at https://lccn.loc.gov/2020012908

ISBN: 978-0-367-21787-7 (hbk)
ISBN: 978-0-367-21788-4 (pbk)
ISBN: 978-0-429-26608-9 (ebk)

Typeset in Galliard
by Swales & Willis, Exeter, Devon, UK

We dedicate this book to school counselors-in-training and practicing school counselors. Your unique, essential role in schools make a huge difference in the lives of school-aged youth.

Aaron and Jeannine

Contents

Acknowledgments

We would like to thank all the individuals who have made this book possible. The expertise and talent of the contributors to the current edition of this book have enriched the knowledge base of the readers. We are grateful to Carolyn Stone, Jolie Ziomek-Daigle, Brittany L. Pollard, Sibyl Cato West, Kaitlyn Figurelli, Michael Bundy, and Caroline Baker, as well as the previous edition's chapter authors, Cyndi Crawford, Melinda Gibbons, Kristi Gibbs, Jennifer Jordan, Amy Kroninger, Robin Wilbourn Lee, Jay Manalo, and Shawn Spurgeon.

We are exceptionally appreciative of the support and encouragement from the editorial group for bringing this book to completion. Although there are numerous individuals behind the production of this project, we would like to give special acknowledgements to editor Amanda Devine, editorial assistant Grace McDonnell, production editor Abigail Stanley, project managers Adam Bell and Tamsin Ballard, and copy-editor Huw Jones.

About the Authors

Aaron H. Oberman, PhD, NCC, is an associate professor and program coordinator for the Counselor Education programs at The Citadel. He earned his doctorate in counselor education from the University of Tennessee, Knoxville. Aaron focuses his scholarship on the role of the professional school counselor, the ASCA National Model, best training practices, and supervision. He regularly publishes and presents on the role of the professional school counselor, and serves as an editorial board member for the *Professional School Counseling Journal.*

Jeannine R. Studer, EdD, is a professor emerita from the University of Tennessee, Knoxville. She was also a high school counselor and a professor at Heidelberg University and California State University, Stanislaus. Jeannine has written numerous articles surrounding the role of the school counselor and is an author of six texts. She is currently retired.

About the Contributors

Caroline A. Baker is an associate professor of School Counseling at the University of Wisconsin River Falls, where she teaches cultural and ethical foundations of school counseling, career counseling in schools, school counseling practicum, and the introduction to school counseling courses. Prior to her work in higher education, for the previous ten years Caroline worked as an elementary school counselor in Tennessee. Her scholarship focuses on teaching and learning in graduate-level counseling programs.

Michael Bundy, PhD, NCC, is a professor emeritus of Counseling at Carson-Newman University (CNU), where he currently serves as Coordinator of School Counseling Internship Field Experiences. He earned an advanced degree in counselor education and supervision from the University of Tennessee in 1989. Before becoming a counselor educator at CNU, Michael was a school counselor for over 25 years in a variety of elementary, middle, and high school settings in East Tennessee. He has delivered over 75 professional presentations at local, state, and national counseling conferences, and has published over 25 articles on counseling and related topics. Among his professional leadership roles, Michael served as 1987 president of the Tennessee School Counselor Association and 2013 president of the Tennessee Counseling Association. He was the recipient of the Tennessee Counseling Association Lifetime Achievement Award in 2017.

Kaitlyn M. Figurelli is a graduate student in the Department of Counseling at Indiana University of Pennsylvania. She graduated with her MEd in School Counseling in the fall of 2019. Kaitlyn completed her practicum experiences in both public and private school settings, working with diverse student populations in the Pittsburgh area. She most enjoys working with adolescents in the secondary school environment. She looks forward to making an ongoing difference in the field of counseling.

Brittany L. Pollard is an assistant professor at Indiana University of Pennsylvania (IUP), where she coordinates their Pittsburgh-based master's-level counseling programs. She teaches across both the Clinical Mental Health and School Counseling tracks, as well as in IUP's Counselor Education and Supervision doctoral program. Before joining the IUP faculty in 2015, Brittany worked in Knoxville, Tennessee, counseling individuals newly diagnosed with HIV and advocating for equitable public health services for her clients. Brittany's primary research interest involves the experiential training of master's-level students on niche areas of counseling, namely group work, human sexuality, and grief. She also enjoys studying the intersection of culture and student/supervisee development and exploring how counselor educators can use experiential learning methods to help students conceptualize and approach diversity issues in new ways. Brittany currently co-chairs the

Association for Specialists in Group Work's Special Initiatives Committee and presents regularly at the international, national, regional, and state levels.

Carolyn Stone is a professor of Counselor Education at the University of North Florida, where she teaches and researches in the area of legal and ethical issues for school counselors. Prior to becoming a counselor educator in 1995, Carolyn spent 22 years with the Duval County Public Schools in Jacksonville, Florida, where she served as a middle school teacher, elementary and high school counselor, and supervisor of 225 school counselors. Carolyn was the 2016 distinguished professor for the University of North Florida, the 2006 President of the American School Counselor Association (ASCA), the longest-sitting Ethics Chair now entering her 17th year; recipient of the American School Counselor Association's Lifetime Achievement Award in 2010, and recipient of the Florida School Counselor Association's Lifetime Achievement Award in 2012. Carolyn was the chairperson for the last three revisions of the ASCA Ethical Standards and served the court as an expert witness in eight cases involving school counselors. Carolyn has delivered over 600 workshops in all 50 US states and 23 countries, and guest lectured for 18 colleges and universities. Her professional path has prepared her with first-hand experience and understanding of the professional world of school counselors.

Sibyl Cato West is an associate professor of Counselor Education and Supervision at Indiana University of Pennsylvania, where she teaches in the School and Clinical Mental Health Counseling programs and the Counselor Education and Supervision PhD program. Prior to becoming a counselor educator, Sibyl worked as a professional school counselor in Tucson, Arizona. Sibyl is also the co-director of the Frederick Douglass Institute, which is an interdisciplinary program that serves as a resource for information and advocacy on issues related to equity and diversity for undergraduate and graduate students. Finally, Sibyl works closely with the Ruling Our Experiences (ROX) non-profit organization, which focuses on issues relating to girls, as research consultant and facilitator trainer.

Jolie Ziomek-Daigle, PhD, LPC is a professor at the University of Georgia. She received her doctoral degree in Counselor Education from the University of New Orleans. Jolie has been a licensed professional counselor since 2003 in both Louisiana and Georgia. She has published two edited textbooks, 27 peer-refereed journal articles, and 16 book chapters. Her areas of research include the clinical preparation of school counselors and incorporating evidence-based practices in the delivery systems of comprehensive school counseling programs. Her work is validated by external funding, and she has secured over $3,000,000 from the Health Resources and Services Administration to expand and enhance the behavioral health workforce. Jolie is the recipient of the 2014 ACES Counseling Creativity and Innovation Award and a Fellow with the American Counseling Association.

Preface

Since the inception of the school counseling profession, the role of the school counselor has been a source of confusion among parents, students, teachers, administrators, and even school counselors themselves. Although various school counseling models and role descriptions have been proposed throughout the profession's history, it was not until the American School Counselor Association (ASCA) took a vigorous stance and developed the ASCA National Standards, later renamed Student Standards, and now retitled Mindsets and Behaviors for Student Success, that students took center stage on school counselor contributions to student achievements. The ASCA later developed the ASCA National Model with the intention for school counselors to more thoroughly answer the questions "What do school counselors do?" and "How are students different as a result of what school counselors do?" These prototypes serve as a foundation for school counselors to create a program that harmonizes with the philosophy and beliefs of a comprehensive school counseling (CSC) program. In line with this systematic change was an endorsement to standardize the title from that of "guidance counselor" to "school counselor" to express more accurately express our role in the schools and to be more reflective of our education and our training.

The ASCA continues to advocate for and validate the growth of students who participate in a CSC program, which has led to stakeholders to more thoroughly understand the school counselor's role and contributions to enhanced student growth. As the needs of the profession, education, and students change, a fourth edition of the ASCA National Model was released in 2019, and the changes within the model are noted within each text chapter.

The contents within this text are primarily focused on enabling the school counselor-in-training (SCIT) to better understand the clinical experiences. However, counselor educators, program supervisors, and school site supervisors are also able to benefit from the information in this text. A description of how all individuals involved in the supervision process can benefit is given below.

For School Counselors-in-Training

This text is designed to help you understand the clinical experiences of practicum and internship. These are pivotal field-based opportunities in which you will be supervised under the vigilant eyes of a school site counselor supervisor and program supervisor. We encourage you to take advantage of the supervision you receive, take risks, and explore new areas of personal and professional growth. The guidance and advice you receive from your supervisors at this time are especially critical, as this will most likely be the last time you will receive feedback on your clinical skills before you completely transition into the profession. As you read the information in the chapters and engage in the Conceptual Application Activities and Student

Activities that are provided, you will have opportunities to appreciate your role as a leader of a CSC program.

As the school counseling profession undergoes a renewal in perspective, you, as a SCIT, are instrumental in clarifying this new era of school counseling. With your newly acquired skills and knowledge, you will be an influential voice for communicating your role, building on the foundations established by our predecessors, and acting as a change agent who more directly contributes to greater student development.

For School Counselor Site Supervisors

A "dirty little secret" of the profession is that most school counselor training programs do not offer training in supervision which leads to school counselors having little preparation in the "how to" of supervision, other than to model the supervision received as trainees. Ironically, an ASCA ethical responsibility is to provide supervision to students entering the profession. The question then becomes, "How do I receive training in supervision?" School counselor training programs often offer classes in supervision, and this information can also be found through books, conferences, and/or workshops. However, professional development workshops that focus on supervision of school counselors are sometimes difficult to find, particularly for school counselors who are located in remote areas. The materials in this text will assist you in gaining information regarding your role in supervision, issues surrounding this practice, models of supervision, and activities to help your supervisee learn about the school counselor's leadership role in the ASCA National Model.

For Faculty Program Supervisors

This text provides students with information about the clinical experiences of practicum and internship. Standards of the Council for Accreditation of Counseling and Related Educational Programs (CACREP) are identified to address student learning and strategies for gaining an experiential understanding of the ASCA National Model which will assist in reaching your program standards. Through our experiences as clinical instructors, students in these classes often struggle to apply concepts, theories, and techniques they may have already acquired in previous classes, or those they will obtain in future classes. Although school counseling curricula often require specific courses in professional orientation and ethical practice, social and cultural diversity, human growth and development, and helping relationships, supplemental knowledge surrounding these areas is included in this text to facilitate students' conceptual application in their clinical classes.

This text is revised to reflect the ASCA National Model Fourth Edition, which does not change any of the previous information, but does mirror the more current language of educational reform. The component of Foundation was changed to *Define*, Management was substituted by *Manage*, Delivery was replaced with *Deliver*, and Accountability is now labeled *Assess*. Furthermore, the themes of leadership, advocacy, collaboration, and systemic change are no longer shown at the boundary of the model, but are instead integrated within the four major components, and these concepts are incorporated throughout the chapters in this text.

Each chapter contains hypothetical situations, activities, case studies, and worksheets intended to facilitate students' understanding of the profession and responsibilities, knowledge, and skills as a school counselor. Conceptual application activities are intended to facilitate professional development, and student activities are presented as interventions that can be adapted in work with students. The chapters and content are outlined below.

Part I, "The Practicum and Internship Journey"

Chapter 1, "Getting Started in Your Clinical Experiences," includes a glossary of supervisory terms, various perspectives surrounding school counselor identity, practical views of the clinical experiences of practicum and internship, professional counseling organizations, what to expect from supervision, materials that will be needed for supervision, factors to consider in working with a site supervisor, and concrete activities that are designed to help you think about your personal identity in the profession. As you engage in a rudimentary grasp of the supervisory process, understanding the educational milieu is the next step.

Chapter 2, "Understanding the School Culture," includes topics to facilitate your understanding of the school environment with explanations of the school culture and climate, federal and state initiatives, and responsibilities to stakeholders and other professionals. After you have had an opportunity to gain a basic appreciation for school-related concepts, your attention is then turned to a review of theories most frequently used by school counselors.

Chapter 3, "Applying Counseling Theories during Your Clinical Experiences," offers a summarization of the more widespread approaches for counseling students in schools. Although you have probably already had a class in counseling theories, clinical school counseling students often express a need to review some of the more popular theories that are used with children and adolescents. This need becomes particularly relevant because the nature of the clinical experiences requires application of theory to actual counselees with real concerns. In addition, creative counseling strategies such as art, play, and music, as well as additional considerations for working with school-aged youth, can be found in this chapter.

Chapter 4, "An Overview of Supervisory Practices," provides the SCIT with information on making an initial contact with the school site supervisor, appropriate dress, school policies and procedures, introducing yourself to stakeholders within the boundaries of the school policies, and considerations for making a contribution to the school site and the profession. Furthermore, wellness as an integral, philosophical, professional component and attention to self-care are described. As you are apprised of the logistics surrounding supervision, your next step is to have an awareness of how supervision works, not only as a novice, but later as an established, experienced member of the profession. For site supervisors and program faculty, the information in this chapter will provide practical guidance on the supervisory process.

Chapter 5, "Supervision as a Developmental Passage," provides insight into developmental models of supervision with examples of supervisor roles and expectations. At times, supervision is not a smooth progression, as there are various challenges such as multicultural issues, anxiety and resistance, parallel processes, and dual roles that could impair the process. As a student training for the school counseling profession (and later on, when you are an experienced member of the profession), an awareness of these issues can assist in preparation for supervision. For site supervisors, the information described will reveal the epigenetic growth you will achieve as you gain experience as a supervisor.

Part II, "The ASCA National Model (4th ed.) as a Structure for Understanding the Role of the School Counselor"

Chapter 6, "The ASCA National Model as a Supervisory Guide," summarizes the ASCA National Model and the school counselor's role in leading a comprehensive school counseling program. Although it is likely that you have already been introduced to the ASCA National Model, the revised model is summarized in this chapter with a description of empirically based studies that support this type of programming. Furthermore, the school counselor standards are discussed and the recommended percentages of time school counselors are to spend on various direct and indirect activities are outlined.

Chapter 7, "Understanding How to Define Your School Counseling Program Using the ASCA National Model," provides activities for you to apply the ASCA Mindsets and Behaviors in your school counseling action plan and to crosswalk identified standards within the curriculum. Furthermore, the school counselor professional competencies and standards give you an opportunity to assess your personal goals from the novice stage of the profession and throughout your career. Although Chapter 11 more thoroughly provides information on the ASCA Ethical Standards, activities to assist you in your own moral development are encompassed in this chapter, in addition to a discussion of personal values and ethical and legal standards.

Chapter 8, "Understanding How to Manage Your School Counseling Program Using the ASCA National Model," contains practical suggestions for organizing and administering school counseling tasks throughout the academic year. Considerations such as the school counselor's office arrangement and space, assessments, and tools that facilitate these tasks such as management agreements, the advisory council, the use of data, action and lesson plans, and calendars are discussed to aid in your understanding of how the school counseling program can be best organized.

Chapter 9, "Understanding How to Deliver Your School Counseling Program Using the ASCA National Model," reviews direct student services in the form of instructing students directly in small groups or individually. Direct services also include working with students to assess their abilities, interests, skills, and achievements, and helping students make sound decisions in regard to these data. Indirect student services include referrals, consultation, and collaboration in which students are impacted through school counseling stakeholders.

Chapter 10, "Understanding How to Assess Your School Counseling Program Using the ASCA National Model," includes a discussion of program and school counselor performance assessments and data analysis techniques. Types of research, a summary of the MEASURE program, and specific types of assessment instruments are discussed in this chapter. Acquiring procedures for revealing best practices in counseling to document the contributions of the school counseling program to the academic mission of the school is paramount. Through these efforts, school counselors are better equipped to engage in direct activities that support student growth.

Chapter 11, "Applying the ASCA Ethical and Legal Standards in Your Clinical Experiences," reviews the principles of counseling ethics and provides an acronym (COMPLICATIONS) as a model for making ethical decisions. The school counselor is often placed in a precarious decision-making position due to his/her unique status in the school, as well as the paradigm differences that exist between this profession and the school administrators. Numerous legal cases and statutes are outlined for consideration in recognizing the difficulty in reconciling the disparities that exist between ethical stipulations and legal provisions.

Part III, "Diversity and Developmental Issues among School-Aged Youth: Guidelines for School Counselors-in-Training"

Chapter 12, "Cross-Cultural Competence in the Schools," provides information related to working with different groups of school-aged youth. A self-assessment of awareness, knowledge, and skills in relation to working with diverse populations while in your training program is summarized. Highlighted in the chapter are culturally and ethnically diverse students, those with special needs, gifted students, gender differences among youth, students who are lesbian, gay, bisexual, transgender, and queer (LGBTQ), English language learners, socioeconomic differences among students, and students with multiple exceptionalities. School counselor responsibilities in working with these students are also discussed.

Chapter 13, "Developmental Issues of Students," offers school counseling students a summarization of the cognitive, physical, affective, and behavioral issues of students at various grade levels. Discussions of childhood obesity, asthma, autism spectrum disorder, attention-deficit hyperactivity disorder, learning disabilities, and the role of the school counselor are also provided.

Part IV, "Completing the Clinical Experiences"

Chapter 14, "Transitioning from Clinical Experiences to a Professional School Counselor," presents suggestions for terminating your internship experiences. At this stage in your professional development, you will have mixed feelings of sadness and anticipation. Useful strategies for terminating relationships with the individuals with whom you worked are included, as are considerations for taking the next step in your professional journey as you apply for a position as a professional school counselor.

Part I

The Practicum and Internship Journey

1 Getting Started in Your Clinical Experiences

Aaron H. Oberman and Jeannine R. Studer

CACREP Standards

Foundations

1. history and development of school counseling

Chapter Objectives

- provide an understanding of the school counseling practicum and internship experiences
- describe clinical supervision and what to expect in these experiences
- provide you with opportunities to self-reflect on your reasons for entering the profession

Introduction

This chapter is written to assist you in understanding the *what* of the clinical experiences. In other words, as you read this chapter, you will hopefully have a better understanding of what the school counselor clinical experiences entail, what the expectations are, and what factors need to be considered during the supervisory process. You have undoubtedly already taken several courses that have provided you with a perspective on the historical developments that have impacted the professional school counselor's role and how the American School Counselor Association (ASCA) has shaped policy to address societal concerns. If you have not taken the time to reflect on your reasons for entering this profession prior to now, take time to do so. Have you had certain experiences that have led you to this career? Were school counselors that you had as a pre-K–12 student part of this decision? Or, do you have special talents that are compatible with those of people who are successful in this profession?

As counselor educators, we regularly meet with prospective school counseling students. When we question them regarding the reasons why they are interested in this profession, we have had a few inquiring students state, "I want to have time off in the summer and I know I do not want to teach, so I think this would be a good alternative." If this is one of your reasons for your career decision, perhaps you need to think in terms of whether this is the best profession for you and for those with whom you will be working. The school counselor requires skill, dedication, and energy, and as you enter the clinical experiences, you are provided with an extraordinary opportunity to scrutinize your readiness for this profession. For those of you who have already taken courses within the school counseling curriculum, you are probably already familiar with some phraseology related to supervision. Others may not have had these foundation courses and are in the process of learning professional terminology. Table 1.1 is a glossary of terms that serve as a review or introduction to the phrases common to the profession.

As you begin your clinical training, you will probably have conflicting feelings and thoughts. Not only will you be feeling a sense of excitement about putting the textbook concepts into practice, you may also be feeling anxious about beginning these new experiences. The school counseling program in which you are enrolled will provide you with specific details regarding the program requirements and policies for these experiences in a program handbook. However, this chapter will provide you with additional ideas and

Table 1.1 Glossary of common supervisory terms.

American Counseling Association (ACA)	Counseling association that represents counselors in various settings
American School Counselor Association (ASCA)	Promotes school counseling professionals and activities that support student development
American School Counselor Association National Model	A framework developed by ASCA for comprehensive school counseling programs that are preventive and developmental
Comprehensive counseling (CSC) programs	Data-driven programs based on standards that enhance student growth (ASCA, 2019b)
Council for Accreditation of Counseling and Related Educational Programs (CACREP)	Independent organization that develops standards for counseling training programs
Education Trust's Transforming School Counseling Initiative (TSCI)	A national agenda to reshape school counseling that emphasizes the use of data to promote student achievement
Mindsets and Behaviors for Student Success	Term designating the next generation of the ASCA National Standards that were originally the ASCA Student Standards
Program faculty supervisor	A practicum or internship instructor who is a member of the counselor education program and has appropriate training and experiences
Program placement coordinator	An individual who is usually associated with the school counseling training program who serves as a liaison between the program and the school sites. This person coordinates the practicum and internship placements
Site supervisor	A counseling professional in the pre-K–12 school setting with credentials in school counseling, a minimum of 2 years of experience in the school, and training in supervision
Supervision	A process by which novice professionals acquire skills under the direction of an experienced member of the profession (Bernard & Goodyear, 2019)
Individual supervision	Occurs between a counselor-in-training and an experienced member of the counseling profession
Group supervision	Takes place between experienced members of the counseling profession and more than two counselors-in-training
Triadic supervision	Occurs between an experienced member of the counseling profession and two counselors-in-training

information about school counselor identity, the clinical experiences, and your responsibilities as a school counselor-in-training (SCIT).

What Is Meant by a Counselor Identity?

The formation of a professional identity is a process that starts from the beginning of your coursework and continues throughout your professional career. As you navigate your way through the profession, you may find it disconcerting when some school counselors still refer to themselves as "guidance counselors" rather than using the title "professional school counselor," as endorsed by the American School Counselor Association (ASCA). Furthermore, it may be disheartening to learn that not all school counselors operate under a comprehensive paradigm that is supported by the ASCA, but rather one that is more traditional in structure. And you may be confused when the school administrator assigns tasks to the school counselor that often have little resemblance to the counselor's education and training.

Throughout the decades, counseling professionals have made concerted efforts to define this profession. The American Counseling Association (ACA) initiated an effort known as the 20/20 Vision for the Future of Counseling, in which counseling was defined as "a professional relationship that empowers diverse individuals, families, and groups to accomplish mental health, wellness, education, and career goals" (American Counseling Association, n.d.), with the intention that this definition would be broad enough to encompass the "whole" of the profession, yet specific enough to describe the unique settings in which school counselors work. The ASCA professionals did not endorse this definition, using the rationale that the definition did not fully represent counseling in schools. However, the ASCA statements outlining the essential role of elementary, middle, and high school counselors indicate that school counselors are "educators uniquely trained in child and adolescent development, learning strategies, self-management and social skills who understand and promote success for to-day's diverse students" (ASCA, 2019a, para. 3). A major goal of the ASCA is to have all professional school counselors speak with one voice regarding the definition of school counseling and to perform tasks that are consistent with the mission of the organization that represents school counselors in all settings.

Today's school counselors evolved from what were formerly known as guidance counselors. These "guidance counselors" were trained under a traditional, reactive approach to counseling with an emphasis on counselor-initiated services and tasks rather than student outcomes. Today, due to the Transforming School Counseling Initiative (TSCI) and the ASCA National Model, the emphasis is on training school counselors as leaders of a comprehensive school counseling program based on measurable student outcomes.

Unfortunately, since the ASCA changed the title nearly three decades ago, the title "guidance counselor" is still being used throughout America (Zyromski, Hudson, Baker, & Granello, 2019). The title used makes a difference in regard to professional identity and integrity, and as a result, school counselors using this more all-encompassing "school counselor" title were more confident in their role as a leader of a comprehensive school counseling program (Zyromski et al., 2019). To further exacerbate the concern about counselor identity, there is debate regarding whether the school counselor is a practitioner responsible for the mental health of students or an educator with the responsibility of assisting teachers and other educators in the learning process. However, as future school counselors advocate for their profession through the collection, analysis, and distribution of meaningful data, support for the professional school counselor identity will eventually be an outcome. The application of knowledge to authentic school settings begins through the clinical experiences.

What Is Meant by the Clinical Experiences?

The Council for Accreditation of Counseling and Related Educational Programs (CACREP) was created to standardize counselor education programs, including the clinical experiences of practicum and internship.

Not all school counselor programs are CACREP accredited. At the time of this writing, there are 270 nationally accredited CACREP school counseling programs (CACREP, 2019). Programs that do not have this accreditation follow other standards, such as those mandated by their state board of education. Other CACREP-like programs follow the recommendations of the council and may offer clinical programs in a different format, such as combining clinical work into one experience, or in some cases even use different terms such as "fieldwork." Be certain that you are aware of your program training requirements and terminology.

What Is the Difference between Practicum and Internship?

The *practicum* provides an opportunity for the SCIT to work with pre-K–12 students for the express purpose of improving counseling skills with individuals and groups of students. During weekly individual or group supervision sessions, you will review your tapes to discuss counseling techniques and theory, and self-reflect while receiving feedback on your skills. In addition, you will have an opportunity to share case conceptualizations, receive feedback, have questions answered, and plan future sessions.

Although direct learning occurs in group supervision, vicarious learning is more prevalent. A breadth of experiences are shared, reviewed, and thoughtfully considered which provide greater insight from a broad perspective and help you see the bigger picture of the school counseling profession.

For programs that are CACREP accredited, the student will complete a minimum of 100 clock hours that include a minimum of 40 hours of direct service in individual counseling and group experiences. The remaining 60 or more hours are considered indirect hours. You will have weekly interactions of at least 1 hour per week by your site supervisor and a minimum of 1½ hours per week in group supervision, most likely by a program faculty member or a doctoral-level counseling student.

The *internship* is taken after the completion of the practicum and is designed to help you become familiar with a variety of professional tasks that are a normal part of the professional school counselor's regular responsibilities. The internship consists of a minimum of 600 clock hours, of which at least 240 are spent providing direct service to students. As in the practicum, the remaining hours are considered indirect.

Some of the experiences that may be part of the supervision include:

- role-play
- case study conceptualization
- counseling technique demonstrations
- listening to previously recorded counseling sessions
- providing feedback to peers regarding taped sessions
- discussing theory and techniques
- sharing site concerns
- brainstorming solutions to dilemmas encountered at the school

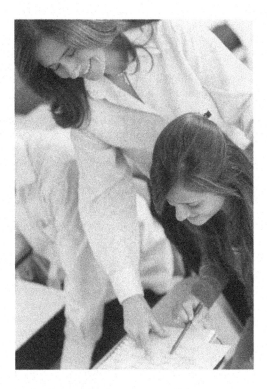

Figure 1.1 Supervisor and school counselor-in-training collaborating on a project.
Source: Shutterstock.

What Are Direct and Indirect Hours?

Students are often confused about the differences between direct and indirect service hours. How these hours are defined may vary from program to program, but generally *direct hours* refer to the activities in which there is face-to-face interaction with students such as in group and individual counseling, classroom instruction, and appraisal and advisement services. *Indirect hours* are those activities that are provided on behalf of students, such as referrals, consultation, and collaboration (ASCA, 2019b). These hours are discussed in more detail in Chapter 9, which addresses the Deliver component of the ASCA National Model.

Conceptual Application Activity 1.1

From the following list, identify those professional school counselor practicum and internship tasks, responsibilities, or activities you consider to be indirect or direct. Mark those you think are indirect with an *I* and direct with a *D*.

Planning the school-wide academic calendar for the year	Making phone calls to identify an appropriate community referral for a student who is learning to speak English as a second language
Reviewing career assessment results and post-secondary school plans with a student in your office	Chatting with a student in the hall between classes
Conducting a parent workshop focused on study skill improvement	Eating lunch in the cafeteria surrounded by singing third-graders
Performing a puppet show to newly arrived first-graders to help them transfer to your school	Facilitating a group for eight students whose parents recently divorced
Accompanying a student and his/her parents to a nearby college to discuss scholarship offers	Composing thank-you letters to parents who shared information about their careers with the fifth-grade classes
Assessing the academic performance of seventh-graders across subjects for the previous year	Conducting a faculty meeting to share the results from a parent/student survey
Meeting with your principal to evaluate your performance	Conducting a suicide assessment with a distraught ninth-grade boy
Formulating a Program Focus Statement	Making copies of flyers for an upcoming new student orientation
Monitoring detention hall while assisting students with homework	Calling a student's guardian grandparents to inform them that their granddaughter missed school again
Entering grades into the database and analyzing results to determine player eligibility for athletic competition	Reviewing the school policy manual to determine if a moment of silence due to the death of a student is permissible

What is it that makes some activities clear and others more ambiguous? Which of these activities do you feel are congruent with a CSC program?

You are not entering these experiences by yourself. During the practicum and internship, you will be receiving supervision from both your program and school counselor supervisors at the school setting where you have been placed for the clinical experiences. These individuals will provide you with direction, assist in identifying tasks to accomplish, and offer feedback and suggestions.

What Is Meant by Supervision?

According to the CACREP standards of 2016, the supervisor at the school site must have at least two years of experience as a professional school counselor, with training in supervision. This person is often referred to as a *site supervisor*. You will also have a supervisor who is a faculty member, often referred to as a *program faculty supervisor*, or in some cases you may be supervised by a doctoral-level counseling student who is also receiving supervision on his/her supervision with you by a counselor education faculty member. In this book, the students with whom you will be working will be referred to as *counselees* to avoid confusion between the SCIT and the pre-K–12 student.

Box 1.1

On-site supervision is crucial in the growth and development of school counseling students (Swank & Tyson, 2012).

The supervisors are experienced members of the counseling profession, and their main priority is to create a trustful environment for you to learn the profession of school counseling while providing feedback. The supervisor is a there to support you as the SCIT, as well as the students you will be counseling. This relationship requires the supervisor to be attentive to your needs and the needs of your counselees. As an example, one of my SCIT was assigned to a site supervisor who was well known for implementing many counseling groups and creating numerous activities and programs to address the identified competencies of the school. My graduate student was placed with this experienced professional during the internship, but after several weeks she expressed frustration at not being able to work with counselees on her own. She explained that whenever a counselee came to see her, she was not allowed to work individually with this person, but instead had to notify her site supervisor, who in turn would counsel the counselee while the SCIT observed. When we spoke with the supervisor, she explained that she was concerned about the type of care the counselee was receiving and thought the counselee was not getting the same quality of care when she was not involved. The supervisor had difficulty allowing the supervisee to work independently, and even though she was an excellent counselor, our graduate student was not provided with the opportunity to work independently. Under the supervision of your site supervisor, you will be moving from a stance in which you will need and desire more direction to one in which you will be more autonomous. These changes are part of the supervisory developmental process that you will learn more about in Chapter 5.

During your practicum, you will meet with the program faculty supervisor or doctoral-level supervisor for an average of 1 hour each week, either individually or in triadic supervision, and an additional 1.5 hours each week in which all the school counselors-in-training enrolled in the practicum will meet for group supervision. *Triadic supervision* is that in which two SCIT meet with their supervisor. You will not have more than 12 students in your group practicum class if your program follows CACREP standards.

Box 1.2

You will receive individual, triadic, and/or group supervision during your clinical experiences. Each of these types of supervision brings benefits. Supervisees stated that greater self-awareness and confidence and a focus on self were some of the advantages of individual supervision. In triadic supervision, greater knowledge about peers' supervisees, opportunities to learn from peers, and vicarious learning were the benefits of this type of supervision. However, group supervision provided greater educational opportunities and normalized experiences (Borders et al., 2012).

In internship, if CACREP standards are followed, there will be no more than 12 individuals in your class. Each SCIT will meet for an average of 1 hour each week for individual or triadic supervision with the on-site supervisor. The purpose of this supervisory experience is to discuss concerns, the school counselor's role, the counseling process, accomplishments, theoretical approach, and so forth. In addition, you will meet for an average of 1½ hours each week of group supervision, usually with the faculty supervisor. The SCIT often wonders how supervision works. The questions in Conceptual Application Activity 1.2 are designed for you to ask your site supervisor in order to get a better understanding of the expectations.

Conceptual Application Activity 1.2

When you meet with your site supervisor, ask the following questions and write down the information for future reference.

1. When will we meet?

   _____

2. How often will we meet?

   _____

3. How long will we meet?

   _____

4. Where will we meet?

   _____

5. How will the meetings be structured and what do I need to bring?

   _____

6. Who else will be present when we meet?

   _____

7. What are some of the issues that we will discuss?

   _____

8. What are the procedures I need to follow when you are absent?

   _____

9. What is the dress code?

   _____

10. What is the school schedule?

    _____

11. What are the school policies and rules?

    _____

12. Who do I contact when I am ill?

    _____

13. Who do I contact if I am going to be late?

    _____

14. What contact information do I need?

   _____

15. What contact information do you need?

   _____

16. Is there a copy of the faculty handbook that I could have?

   _____

17. Is there a crisis plan that I can study?

   _____

During the clinical experiences, you will be asked to create a contract that outlines your personal and professional goals. This contract will be based on the course objectives, the site and program supervisors' requirements, and your own needs. A sample contract and guidelines for creating a contract can be found in Chapter 4.

Too often, students training for the school counseling profession treat the clinical courses as if they were voluntary experiences. You are not a volunteer, because you have specific learning goals and objectives, receive supervision from both an on-site supervisor and a faculty supervisor, and are evaluated formally and regularly. Unfortunately, there are some occasions when SCIT believe that since they are not being paid to work in the schools, they can attend the school site whenever they feel like it if they have other competing responsibilities. *You need to be aware that the practicum and internship experiences are not only a course requirement, but are also professional responsibilities, and are to be treated as if you were working in a professional career.* It is not only the site supervisor who relies on your attendance: students, teachers, administrators, and parents also depend upon you. Imagine what it would be like for a fifth-grader who is anxiously waiting to continue counseling sessions with you, and you do not take the time to notify anyone at the school that you will be absent. Or think about the teacher who is planning to team-teach a school counseling lesson with you and you do not put in an appearance. Your decision disappoints the fifth-grader, disrupts the teacher's plans, and leaves an entire class let down.

Your attitude, motivation, and willingness to learn at these sites can make a huge difference when you are seeking employment as a school counselor. It is not uncommon for employers to contact your supervisors, principals, and any other references at the schools in which you have trained. In fact, you may be applying for full-time employment at the school where you were placed in practicum or internship.

In some cases, SCIT receive payment for their services before matriculating from their school counseling program. For instance, when schools face a shortage of school counselors, or a school counselor needs to take a leave of absence, it is sometimes necessary to hire an individual who has not yet finished with his/her school counseling program. In this situation, each state has certain criteria for working under these circumstances. Each state uses a different term, such as *alternative, transitional,* or *interim school counselor license,* for this arrangement, with various stipulations under which the school system is able to hire this individual. If you are interested in learning more about this type of license, check the Department of Education in the state in which you are interested.

What Materials Are Needed?

Since audio and/or video recordings are requirements in most school counseling programs, you will need access to taping equipment. If you do not have this equipment, first check with your college or university, or ask at the school where you are conducting practicum or internship whether the required equipment is available. Some schools will allow you to sign out this equipment during the academic term, but other sites may not have these devices readily available. Most students record sessions by using an iPad, tablet, or lap top computer. Some of these recording devices can be erased and reused, whereas others cannot. Some supervisors require audio recording, while others mandate video recording, and still others require both. Be sure to check with all parties before choosing recording equipment, size, and format. The format depends on the equipment your supervisor uses to listen to or view the recordings.

It is also possible that technology-mediated supervision may be conducted. This type of technology may take place in real time, also called *synchronous supervision,* and could include Skype, Google Voice and Video, or FaceTime. Some computers already have a built-in camera for communication ease, whereas others require a separate camera that is attached to the computer. Or instant messaging, wikis, YouTube, or email may also be a type of technology-mediated supervision, also known as *asynchronous supervision,* and occurs without the constraints of time. Asynchronous supervision allows feedback without the supervisor having to be in the room, increased availability of supervisors, and more flexibility in supervising. Some of the disadvantages of technology-mediated supervision include security and confidentiality concerns (regardless of the type of equipment needed for supervision), equipment malfunction, and limited sharing due to questionable skill regarding technology.

Because you will be recording counseling sessions, a private room will be needed to provide a quiet environment and ensure student confidentiality. In schools where space is a problem, the SCIT is sometimes placed in a classroom that is vacant when the teacher is not teaching a class or in other spaces that are less private. Using a teacher's classroom can jeopardize confidentiality, especially if the teacher needs access to the room while you are counseling students. If you have difficulty finding a secluded place for counseling, discuss this issue with your on-site supervisor.

Issues with Taping Counseling Sessions

During the clinical experiences and the practicum class, assessing your counseling skills is a primary focus, with traditional methods such as video and audio recording. Yet, with increased concern for privacy and individual rights, these as well as more sophisticated technological methods are becoming more problematic due to regulations under the Federal Education Rights and Privacy Act (FERPA) and the Health Insurance Portability and Accountability Act (HIPAA).

FERPA, also known as the Buckley Amendment, protects the privacy of student records and limits parental/guardian access to all student records, files, and documents maintained by school personnel. Record keeping permits school counselors to refresh their memory and to increase counseling effectiveness by keeping personal notes about individual counseling sessions. Many school counselors believe that they are FERPA compliant if the notes they take are sole possession notes and remain confidential. However, the US Department of Education maintained that these notes are to be considered a part of the educational record. Yet, according to the US Family Policy Compliance Office, various notes that serve as memory aids are exempt (Wheeler & Bertram, 2015). These contradictory opinions create confusion, and at some point, a final decision will be needed for clarification. However, any time notes are shared, they are no longer considered confidential. This is where confidentiality regarding taping and note-taking becomes an issue; individual sessions are shared during supervision.

Box 1.3

Are case notes truly my own, or do I have to share them if lawyers get involved? Do I have to testify? According to the ASCA, state statutes influence the sharing of notes. Privileged communication is recognized in some states, but in the majority of states, school counselors are mandated to testify in court. Discuss your concerns about testifying with the attorney if you believe that your information will not be helpful, and explain your responsibilities to students, including the importance of confidentiality and ethical standards. If the student does not have privileged communication, then you are compelled to testify (Stone, Herman, & Williams, 2012).

Although not every counseling setting is HIPAA related, HIPAA (Pub. L. 104–191) protects health information (including mental health) held by an educational institute from becoming education records unless a state law mandates differently. Counseling notes, also known as process notes, are used to help counselors recall information, and are protected by HIPAA as long as they are kept in a separate file.

Parents/guardians need to be informed about the purpose of the counseling sessions and the importance of this activity for your education. Some institutions will only allow digital recording if the counselee's identity remains unknown, such as focusing the camera on the counselee's back. Erasing tapes on a regular schedule, such as at the end of the semester, can also maintain program integrity and assist with student anonymity. Check with your program supervisor regarding tape erasure protocol.

Some training institutions respond to the taping issue by providing on-site observation in which the program or site supervisor observes a live counseling session and provides feedback immediately following the session. However, this strategy may create other concerns, such as the counselee's discomfort with the presence of another individual, the amount of time that is required, and the trainee feeling not completely autonomous in conducting the counseling session. An informed consent form and professional disclosure statement facilitate communication with parents, teachers, and administrators regarding your work with students.

Informed Consent Form and Professional Disclosure Statement

As a new, yet temporary, member of your educational community, it is often difficult to get permission to work with school-aged youth. Because you will be taping your counseling sessions with children and adolescents, written permission from parents or guardians to tape their child during counseling sessions is necessary. Not surprisingly, this could create a problem since parents/guardians may have difficulty with their child working with someone they do not know. An *informed consent form* is an ethical, legal, and clinical document

---

RELEASE FORM/PERMISSION TO TAPE

   Hello. My name is_____, and I am a graduate student in the school counseling program at _____. Your son/daughter is participating in counseling interviews with me as
I train to be a school counselor under the direction of the Counseling Department faculty at
_____. These interviews will either be videotaped or audiotaped, and portions of the
interview will be used for evaluation and/or supervision purposes only.

- Precautions will be taken to protect your child's identity.
- The taping will be used for supervision purposes only.
- After the student trainee and supervisor have met to critique the trainee's counseling skills,
  the tape will be erased.
- The tape/video recorder will be turned off at any time and/or any portion of the tape
  will be erased if requested.

   If you are willing to give permission for your child to assist with this training, please sign below.
If you have additional questions, you can contact my site supervisor at _____.

_____   _____
Parent/Guardian Signature   Date

_____   _____
Student Signature   Date

Figure 1.2 Release form/permission to tape.

that is used to explain the counseling relationship (Wheeler & Bertram, 2015) and the purpose of the counseling session, including expectations during the clinical experiences.
A *professional disclosure statement* describes who you are, your education, training qualifications, and how you will be supervised. When this information is provided to parents/guard-
ians, they are usually more willing to provide consent. An example of a consent form is
shown in Figure 1.2, and an example of a professional disclosure statement can be found in
Chapter 4.

How Do I Choose a School Site for Supervision?

Location and proximity to home, the college or university, and school site are the most
common motives for selecting a placement for the clinical experiences. Although these
reasons are practical and understandable, they are not always the best considerations in
making this choice. For instance, the potential supervisor may not have had training in
supervision, may have a different philosophy regarding the school counselor's role, may
operate under a program that does not support a CSC program, or may not have time to
provide a quality supervisory experience. Furthermore, the school may have a homogeneous
population of students and may not provide an opportunity to work with a diverse student
body. You want to work with a supervisor in a school that will give you the best experience
possible. To assist you with this decision, Conceptual Application Activity 1.3 is designed to
help you think about this process.

Conceptual Application Activity 1.3

1. With which age or group of students would you be most interested in working? Explain.

    _____

    _____

    _____

2. With what age or group of students would you feel most uncomfortable working? Write down those things that make you uncomfortable.

    _____

    _____

    _____

3. School counselors have the responsibility to work with all students, including those in special education and those who have been identified as "gifted." Identify the students with whom you feel you need additional knowledge and experiences.

    _____

    _____

    _____

How Do I Choose a Site Supervisor?

There are several methods of matching a supervisor with a SCIT. Some institutions provide flexibility in allowing their students to select a supervisor based on reputation, school system, or other special characteristics. In these cases, the program placement coordinator will probably determine if this selection is appropriate before the assignment is made. It could be that the placement coordinator is aware of the strengths and weaknesses of area supervisors and may believe that a certain placement you desire may not be the best match for various reasons. For instance, I was serving as a faculty supervisor for the practicum class, and when making a visit with a middle school site supervisor, the supervisor stated, "We teach what school counselors really need to know—not the stuff they teach at the university." This remark indicated that there was an absence of similar program goals as well as a lack of communication regarding site and academic program expectations. At the university, the benefits of a comprehensive approach to school counseling are taught, as opposed to the reactive, traditional model under which some school counselors still operate. The latter was the type of program in which this particular supervisor was working. In another situation, a motivated practicum student who was excited about the opportunity to work with school-aged youth was placed with a site supervisor who showed little interest in her middle school students. The site supervisor would flippantly dismiss the practicum student's concerns about students by stating, "That's just the way they are, and we really don't have the time to help them." As a result of this experience, this practicum SCIT left the experience disappointed and disillusioned with the profession.

In post-graduation surveys conducted by training institutions for the purpose of evaluating program needs, many graduates of school counselor programs indicate that supervision was the most important aspect of their clinical experiences. Therefore, it is important that supervisors are chosen carefully.

Regardless of whether you are placed in a setting by your placement coordinator or you choose a supervisor, be certain that you have thought in terms of the specific supervisor characteristics that you feel may best meet your needs. Consider the list of questions in Conceptual Application Activity 1.4.

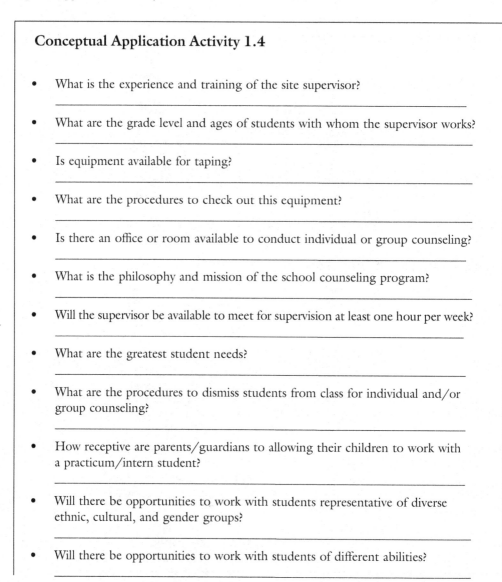

Conceptual Application Activity 1.4

- What is the experience and training of the site supervisor?

- What are the grade level and ages of students with whom the supervisor works?

- Is equipment available for taping?

- What are the procedures to check out this equipment?

- Is there an office or room available to conduct individual or group counseling?

- What is the philosophy and mission of the school counseling program?

- Will the supervisor be available to meet for supervision at least one hour per week?

- What are the greatest student needs?

- What are the procedures to dismiss students from class for individual and/or group counseling?

- How receptive are parents/guardians to allowing their children to work with a practicum/intern student?

- Will there be opportunities to work with students representative of diverse ethnic, cultural, and gender groups?

- Will there be opportunities to work with students of different abilities?

- What is the administrator's view of counseling students in the schools?

  _____

- Does this individual have the time to supervise me?

  _____

- When does the supervisor expect me to be at the school?

  _____

- Will I have the opportunity to attend such events as in-service meetings or parent conferences?

  _____

- Will I need to make a safety plan?

  _____

- Will I be expected to stay after the school day is over?

  _____

The presence of *nonprofessional interactions or relationships* (formerly known as dual relationships) is a fundamental consideration in selecting a supervisor (Note: The ACA uses the term "nonprofessional interactions or relationships" in reference to what were formerly known as dual relationships. However, the ASCA continues to use the term "dual relationships," and for this reason this term will be used in this text.). These interactions emerge as a result of family, social, community, school, or work exchanges (Wheeler & Bertram, 2015). They often occur through unanticipated circumstances such as attending a community meeting, exercising at the same gym, meeting at a book club, and so on. This type of conflicting relationship is often more common than many practicum and internship students realize.

Box 1.4

If a dual relationship is unavoidable, and the benefits outweigh the risks, consider the following steps:

- Discuss the benefits and risks with your supervisors.
- Engage in ongoing communication with your supervisors to ensure that the relationship is being managed appropriately.
- Self-monitor.

Source: Adapted from Wheeler and Bertram (2015)

In the case of supervision, a dual relationship may be a supervisor whom you know in a different context, such as a friend, relative, or even a parent of your child's friend. Dual relationships could also be in relation to teachers, parents, administrators, or even the spouse of a SCIT employed in that school setting. In one situation, a difficult SCIT was placed in an internship site without the placement coordinator knowing that this individual's spouse worked in the superintendent's office. The site supervisor was also unaware of this situation until the superintendent questioned the SCIT's poor evaluation completed by the supervisor. The school site supervisor felt personally offended that her judgment was being questioned when the superintendent asked about the negative evaluation. There are numerous considerations in beginning the supervisory journey, and it is up to you to learn as much as you can about the expectations for this experience and to take opportunities that are available so that you can feel competent and successful when you are a fully licensed member of the profession.

Conclusion

You are starting your professional journey by working in a school as a counselor during your clinical experiences, often known as the practicum and internship. These experiences are not to be taken lightly, as they are superb opportunities to get "hands-on" experience in a school counseling setting. Practicum and internship may also be the last time you will receive formal feedback on your counseling skills, because the building administrator is generally the person who supervises school counselors, and frequently this individual has no training in counseling skills and process. Therefore, it is important that your school and site supervisor are chosen wisely. This choice requires self-reflection and an understanding of both the potential supervisor's philosophy and the types of experiences that you desire for a comprehensive foundation of the school counseling profession.

Websites

- American Counseling Association (ACA): www.counseling.org/

This website provides resources for counseling practitioners and students in addition to giving recent legislative information concerning the counseling profession. The salary calculator resource available from this organization provides a tool for determining salaries in various parts of the United States.

- American School Counselor Association (ASCA): www.schoolcounselor.org/

This division of the ACA focuses on the counseling specialty of school counseling. Numerous resources are available, as well as position papers and documents that provide timely information on numerous topics commonly impacting the profession and the stakeholders.

- Council for Accreditation of Counseling and Related Educational Programs (CACREP): www.cacrep.org/template/index.cfm

This accreditation body sets standards for master's and doctoral degree programs in counseling.

- National Center for Transforming School Counseling (NCTSC): www.edtrust.org/dc/tsc

The NCTSC is dedicated to training school counselors to focus on academics and to raise achievement among all students.

References

American Counseling Association. (n.d.). *20/20: Consensus definition of counseling*. Retrieved from www. counseling.org/knowledge-center/20-20-a-vision-for-the-future-of-counseling/consensus-definition-of-counseling

ASCA. (2019a). *The ASCA National Model: A framework for school counseling programs* (4th ed.). Alexandria, VA: ASCA.

ASCA. (2019b). *The essential role of middle school counselors*. Retrieved from www.schoolcounselor.org/asca/media/asca/Careers-Roles/WhyMiddle.pdf

Bernard, J. M., & Goodyear, R. K. (2019). *Fundamentals of clinical supervision* (6th ed.). New York, NY: Pearson.

Borders, L. D., Welfare, L. E., Greason, P. B., Paladino, D. A., Mobley, A. K., Villalba, J. A., & Wester, K. L. (2012). Individual and triadic and group: Supervisee and supervisor perceptions of each modality. *Counselor Education and Supervision, 51*, 281–295. doi:10.1002/j.1556-6978.2012.00021.x

CACREP. (2019). *Directory of accredited programs*. Retrieved from www.cacrep.org/directory/?state=&dl=M&pt_id=27&keywords=&submitthis=

Stone, C., Herman, M., & Williams, R. (2012, May). Asked and answered. *ASCA School Counselor*.

Swank, J. M., & Tyson, L. (2012). School counseling site supervisor training: A web-based approach. *Professional School Counseling, 16*, 40–48. doi:10.5330/PSC.n.2012-16.40

Wheeler, M., & Bertram, B. (2015). *The counselor and the law: A guide to legal and ethical practice* (7th ed.). Alexandria, VA: American Counseling Association.

Zyromski, B., Hudson, T. D., Baker, E., & Granello, D. H. (2019). Guidance counselors or school counselors: How the name of the profession influences perceptions of competence. *Professional School Counseling, 22*. doi:10.1177/2156759X19855654

2 Understanding the School Culture

Jeannine R. Studer and Aaron H. Oberman

CACREP Entry-Level Specialty Area Standards

Foundations

b. models of school counseling programs

Contextual Dimensions

a. school counselor roles as leaders, advocates, and systems change agents in P-12 schools
d. school counselor roles in school leadership and multidisciplinary teams
m. legislation and government policy relevant to school counseling

Practice

d. interventions to promote academic development
l. techniques to foster collaboration and teamwork within schools

Chapter Objectives:

*   discuss school culture and climate and differences among settings
*   identify types of schools and opportunities for school counselors in different settings
*   provide information regarding federal and state initiatives such as School-Wide Positive Interventions and Behavioral Supports, Response to Intervention, and Every Child Succeeds Act, and the Safe Schools Improvement Act of 2017
*   identify the role of the school counselor in developing a positive school culture
*   identify various professionals within and outside the educational setting with whom school counselors will work

Introduction

As a SCIT, it is sometimes difficult to grasp the importance of understanding the school environment, protocol, school policies, and the reasons why certain procedures are in place. Although every school has some similarities, each school also has different approaches for solving problems, communicating with the community, and methods of getting things accomplished. Even seasoned educational personnel who have had experience at one setting often have difficulty comprehending the new structure and organization of schools of which they are unfamiliar. It takes time to become accustomed to the new environment and culture, and as a counseling student, it is essential for you to become involved, take initiatives that are offered to you, and enter the school with an open mind to aide in your learning experience.

The School Culture and Climate

When you think about a school culture, what comes to mind? What about the school climate? Although these terms are often interchangeable, there are distinct differences. The culture generally refers to such things as unwritten rules, traditions, language, diversity, and school vision. Climate, on the other hand, represents the attitude of the institution, or the morale of the individuals within the organization, and is often considered as the personality of the school (Gruenert, 2008).

Each school culture is multifaceted, unique, and influenced by the socioeconomic status of the community, cultural groups, and school size. Whenever we enter a school, the climate is often readily apparent from the way we are greeted when we report into the school office, the treatment of students as they change classes, to the general attitude that is expressed by the school personnel. School counselors are key personnel to create a positive school culture and climate, and are particularly influential due to the multiple individuals with whom they have interactions.

The focus of this chapter is to assist you in understanding the school counselor's role as this position influences and is influenced by the school culture. Federal and state initiatives include Every Student Succeeds Act (ESSA), that replaced the No Child Left Behind law in 2015, the Safe School Improvement Act, School Wide Positive Interventions and Behavioral Supports (SWPIBS), Response to Intervention (RtI), and the Common Core. All of these initiatives impact the school culture and climate. In addition, understanding and negotiating responsibilities such as discipline, testing, special education, and the never-ending debate regarding whether school counselors should have an education background with teaching experience are discussed. Finally, collaboration with stakeholders including Professional Learning Communities, is highlighted.

The School Counselor's Office

The location of the school counselor's office and the office space arrangement may determine how often people come to see you and contribute to making people feel comfortable when they come to your office. At times, school counselors-in-training complain that other educational resource personnel (e.g., school psychologist, speech therapist) share the space they were given for counseling purposes. Obviously, these shared space arrangements make scheduling individual counseling sessions challenging. In one case, a student SCIT was frustrated when no office space was available, and only after her site supervisor helped her reframe her predicament was this situation viewed as an opportunity to be creative. She adapted by conducting counseling sessions while walking around the school track with some of her counselees. In another instance she went to an empty gym and shot hoops with her counselee—with a twist. They would take turns shooting the basketball, and with each shot each person would make a statement about him/herself. The SCIT shared information about herself, and in turn the counselee revealed a fact about himself without the pressure of making eye contact or being compelled to talk in an office setting.

Conceptual Application Activity 2.1

Tour the school building to which you are assigned, and pay attention to space arrangements such as the administrator's office location in relation to the school counselors' offices. Consider the following questions: Where are the school counseling offices located? Are they labeled "School Counseling" or something else (e.g., guidance counselor)? Is there enough room to conduct individual and group counseling? Is the office decor and furniture arrangement inviting? Is the office in a private place for counseling to occur? Do the walls and space allow for voices to be overheard? Is there an appropriate place for students and others to wait outside the office? Will students be greeted by someone at a front desk or a sign directing them to the location of a school counselor? Is clerical assistance available and accessible to the school counselors? Are there adequate spaces for books and other materials? Is there ample storage for materials and electronic equipment? Is computer space available that can be accessed privately? Is a printer/fax machine located in an area where the printed material can remain confidential? Does the equipment need to be shared with other personnel? Is there a common area with bulletin board space available for advertising counseling events or college or career information? What suggestions for improvements would you make?

Sometimes the school counselor's office is located in close proximity to the administrator's office, causing students to associate visiting the school counselor with discipline. Even though your role is to assist students to accept personal responsibility associated with their behaviors, you are not the school disciplinarian. As stated by the ASCA position statement *The School Counselor and Discipline*, "School counselors have specialized training and skills in promoting appropriate student behavior and preventing disruptive student behavior. School counselors are not disciplinarians but should be a resource for school personnel in developing individual and schoolwide discipline procedures" (ASCA, 2019 para. 1). School counseling offices located in a thoroughfare area open to visitors, administration, staff, and students may be easily accessible, but may not provide the privacy counseling students requires. In other schools, the school counselors' offices are located in settings that are difficult to find and could significantly diminish the number and frequency of students seeking school counselor assistance.

Conceptual Application Activity 2.2

Observe the location of the school counselor offices. Are they in a suite, or are they located in different parts of the building? Look specifically at the arrangement of your site supervisor's office. Is the counselor's desk situated in a position that serves as a barrier between the counselor and counselee? Is there open space between the counselor and those seeing the counselor that creates an inviting impression for those who visit? Are papers stacked up on the desk and on shelves?

Other considerations for an inviting office may include decor placed on walls, the furniture style, desk decorations, paint color, and so forth. For instance, if the counselor has religious/spiritual artifacts in the office, these could make students uncomfortable or comfortable depending on whether they think their beliefs would or would not be accepted. Your first impressions may be similar to others' first impressions. Compare your impressions with those of your peers.

Conceptual Application Activity 2.3

In the space next to each of the items listed, place an *I* next to the items that would make the counseling office inviting, and place a *U* next to the items that would make the counseling office uninviting for students and other visitors. Add items of your own to the list and compare with lists by your peers.

_____ Family pictures	_____ Posters of athletics
_____ Confederate flag	_____ College/university diploma
_____ Rainbow symbol	_____ Candy jar
_____ Symbolic jewelry	_____ National Rifle Association Certificate
_____ Bible	_____ Candles or scents
_____ College diplomas	_____ School mascot memorabilia
_____ Counselor wearing jeans	_____ Kleenex
_____ "Right to Life" poster	_____ Pictures of pets
_____ College posters	_____ Motivational quotes
_____ Professional licenses	_____ Family planning poster
_____ Aquarium	_____ Music playing

Federal and State Initiatives and the Role of the Professional School Counselor

Every Child Succeeds Act (ESSA) and Implications for School Counselors

The Every Student Succeeds Act is a federal law that replaced the No Child Left Behind Act (NCLB) with the provisions that each state has more authority to implement the law, implement standards that would challenge students, create new assessment and accountability systems, and annually test students while measuring student progress. In addition, states are required to identify schools that are consistently underperforming and to provide support to improve these low-functioning schools (Jennings, 2018). States also make their own decisions about schools, such as what is to be measured, how the schools are doing within these identified areas, and the action that is to be taken when groups of students do not make progress.

The law requires that states choose five indicators to measure school performance which include four academic measures of achievement and a choice of a fifth indicator of school quality or success, such as school culture or climate. Schools are required to report such data as the numbers of students who are chronically absent, graduation rate, proficiency in advanced courses, and college and career transition (Chang, Bauer, & Byrnes, 2018) as long as this measure is equally applied for all students. Chronic absence contributes to adverse academic achievement when valuable academic lessons are missed. Poverty contributes to higher levels of absenteeism, but when schools adopt effective programming as outlined by the ESSA that encourages daily attendance, students are more likely to achieve (Chang et al., 2018). Furthermore, data provided on the state report cards reveal the amount of money the state provides to each district for the purpose of identifying where districts are funded inadequately (Amerikaner, 2018).

Under this law, schools which are low-performing have the opportunity to identify and address resource inequalities in the school. For example, homelessness is one area schools find challenging to address, and the McKinney-Vento Act, a central federal initiative reauthorized by the ESSA, mandates that policies and procedures are in place to assist homeless youth and their education (Center for Education Equity, 2018).

School counselors are key individuals in ensuring students are receiving the benefits of the law, recognizing warning signs of homelessness, and connecting these individuals with needed supports such as funding, transportation, and other resources (Center for Education Equity, 2018).

Safe Schools Improvement Act of 2017

The Elementary and Secondary Education Act (ESEA) of 1965 has evolved through the decades as our schools and society have changed. The Safe Schools Improvement Act was an amended section of the ESEA that required Local Educational Agencies (LEAs) to create policies that would create a nurturing, caring school environment. In addition, schools are required to notify the community of behaviors that are unacceptable and the procedures that are followed when inappropriate behaviors are displayed (Congress.gov, 2017–2018).

School counselors want to create an environment in which all students feel safe and emotionally secure. Bullying, harassment, and intimidation typically include verbal, physical, relational, and cyberattacks that take place on school property, at school-sponsored functions, and on school buses. Bullying policies frequently require that schools implement specific practices to achieve safer, less violent schools, with ongoing professional education for school employees to learn about methods to prevent harassment, intimidation, and bullying. When planning classroom school counseling lessons, consider multicultural and non-stereotypical curricula. Social-emotional learning programs that help youth become self-aware, manage emotions, build social skills, develop alternative perspectives, and learn problem-solving skills are introduced in schools with positive results. The Second Step: Student Success Through Prevention Program is one such curricular program. In one study seventh- and eighth-graders who participated in this program were given lessons on bullying, coping with stress, problem-solving, substance abuse, empathy, communication, and sexual harassment, and as a result of their involvement, significant reductions in delinquent behavior were observed (Espelage, Low, Van Ryzin, & Polanin, 2015).

Box 2.1

A Phi Delta Kappa/Gallup poll was conducted to determine adults' attitudes toward public schools. The results included the following:

- Parents and adults (77% and 75% respectively) stated that student improvement over time is a better method of assessing school quality than standardized testing.
- Approximately 75% of parents, teachers, and other adults viewed mediation and counseling as more effective than detention or suspension for curtailing student misbehavior.

Source: PDK Poll. Retrieved from https://pdkpoll.org/assets/downloads/2019pdkpoll51.pdf.

Conceptual Application Activity 2.4

Ask your site supervisor to show you how services and activities that are integral to the ESSA are documented and how the school counseling program standards are aligned with those of academic course objectives, then list them below. You can use information highlighted in Chapter 9 that outlines study skills strategies to assist in promoting achievement among students struggling academically.

_____

_____

School-Wide Positive Behavior Intervention and Supports

When students display emotional and behavioral disorders, they are at risk of peer rejection, negative teacher interactions, isolation from their peers, and poor school performance (Wagner & Cameto, 2004, as cited in George, Cox, Minch, & Sandomierski, 2018). School-Wide Positive Behavior Intervention Supports (SWPBIS; sometimes known as PBIS) is a multilevel framework with a focus on data-based interventions for creating and maintaining a positive school culture while monitoring an array of behavioral aids (Mitchell, Hatton, & Lewis, 2018). This approach is positive, data-driven, and evidence-based, and is associated with improved behavior and achievement. School-wide positive behavior supports consist of agreed-upon school rules that are stated positively, reinforced, and understood by all, based on the premise that when acceptable behavior is followed, improved academic achievement is a result.

SWPBIS consists of a continuum of three tiers of prevention. Tier 1 is a universal school-wide intervention based on reinforcing positive behaviors for all students. Tier 2 is a more intense intervention for approximately 15–10% of the students who continually fail to meet the behavioral expectations targeted in Tier 1. If students in Tier 2 continue to display patterns of severe, chronic misconduct, Tier 3, an individualized, focused intervention, is executed (Mitchell et al., 2018) (see Figure 2.2) which involves less than 5% of the students. School counselors may be involved at each of the tiers through such activities as training school personnel in crisis management, teaching behavioral modification strategies, assisting with transitions, engaging in parent collaboration, or serving as behavioral consults.

Figure 2.1 School counselors are instrumental in enhancing students' academic, career, and social/emotional growth. High school graduation as an outcome for all students is a goal of all educators.

Source: Steve Martin Photography.

As in all educational initiatives, SWPIBS is evaluated for effectiveness. Florida school districts that implemented SWPBIS evaluated their programs, and eight components were identified as contributing to program success, including: (a) a positive relationship among stakeholders such as administrators, teachers, and so forth; (b) the importance of committed coaches or trainers to ensure task completion and technical support; (c) the significance of district teaming for integrated planning and data-based decisions; (d) the emphasis on securing funding, and recognition for individual contributions, and evaluations; (e) the support of leadership by recognizing that acceptable behavior was as important as academics; (f) the use of user-friendly reports that revealed the unique needs of students' behavior; (g) the use of training in a comfortable environment with access to parking and attention to participants needs; and (h) the use of a common language with an understood connection to other educational interventions.

In a study of a PBIS counselor-led program (Sherrod, Getch, & Ziomek-Daigle (2009), the counselors implemented school-wide incentives to reward students through the use of

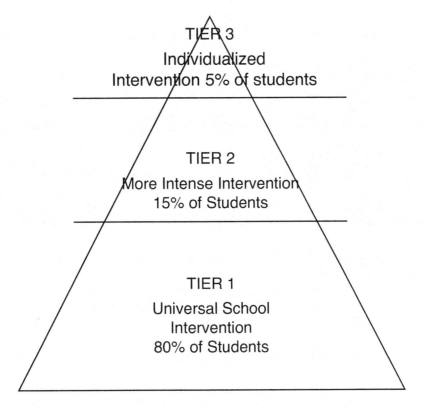

Figure 2.2 Students supported by PBIS.

"pride cards" on which students were "caught" doing identified positive behaviors. This program was associated with decreased student referrals. In another study of school-wide bullying prevention and intervention programs led by school counselors in Tier 1, results revealed an improved school culture and behavior (Goodman-Scott & Grothaus, 2018). Counselors also inspired teachers by tracking specific interventions to reveal how academic progress increased as a result of interventions in Tier 3.

Conceptual Application Activity 2.5

Discuss the School-Wide Positive Intervention Prevention Support format that has been adapted by the school site in which you are training. Share the interventions in which your supervisor is involved with those of your peers. Are there similarities? Are there differences? List them below.

_____

_____

Response to Intervention (RtI)

As you have learned, several federal and state initiatives, including the Every Student Succeeds Act of 2015, have called on schools to evaluate their accountability systems and use data-based decision-making procedures that use evidence-based strategies. The RtI is one of these models (Grapin, Waldron, & Joyce-Beaulieu, 2019), in which all educational personnel implement a multi-tiered framework to meet the needs of *all* students to improve student outcomes. Because the main goal of this system is to increase academic achievement, like SWPIBS, students are monitored through three tiers, although schools may adopt any number of tiers with identified interventions at each tier. However, the traditional RtI model uses three tiers:

- Tier 1: Tier 1 interventions are preventive and proactive actions that support the majority of the students in a school who meet grade-level expectations. Universal screening is conducted for all students with careful monitoring and documentation. The school counselor may provide classroom lessons for all students to address identified goals.
- Tier 2: Students who are not making progress in Tier 1 are given additional support in Tier 2, usually in the form of small group counseling, and continue to receive instruction in Tier 1. Students are identified for additional interventions at this level. If the student is still not making adequate progress, he/she will move to Tier 3.
- Tier 3: Students are provided with intense individual, long-term interventions with specific individuals. The school counselor may provide individual counseling as a type of intervention, or make referrals to community personnel if the student has more serious concerns. If adequate progress is still not achieved, the student may be eligible for special education services.

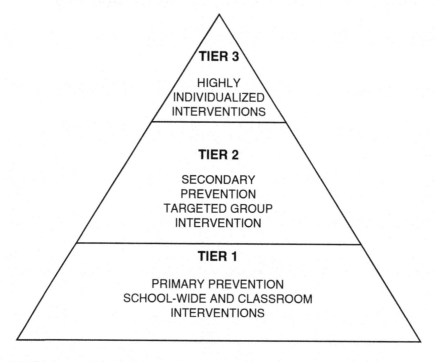

Figure 2.3 Illustration of the RtI tiers.

Conceptual Application Activity 2.6

With your school counselor supervisor, discuss his/her role with RtI. Share your supervisor's responses with your peers. Are there similarities or differences? List them below.

_____

_____

The Common Core State Standards Initiative

There is much discussion and debate regarding the Common Core standards that were developed in 2009. Today, 41 states and the District of Columbia have adapted these standards (Common Core State Standards Initiative, 2020). This set of standards was developed to correct educational inconsistencies among states, with an emphasis on increasing higher-level cognitive skills through educational rigor. For instance, without consistent educational standards, a student successfully passing algebra in Ohio could move to Pennsylvania and fail the same course due to the differences in state benchmarks. Despite the advantages of these standards, not everyone is convinced this initiative is the answer to academic proficiency.

For example, as a result of the implementation of the Common Core, many outstanding teachers left the profession due to the stress associated with being unprepared to teach the standards and the implementation of new teaching strategies (ThoughtCo, 2019). Furthermore, the cost of the technology and the purchase of new textbooks that correspond to these standards were prohibitive for many school systems, and parents expressed frustration with unfamiliar terms and their inability to assist their child with homework.

Box 2.2

With the Common Core standards, the demonstration of an understanding of the concepts is as important as getting the correct answer. This view has been labeled "fuzzy math," and parents report being frustrated and unable to help their child with math. For example, one problem students are to solve is: "Use number bonds to help you skip-count by seven by making ten or adding to the ones (i.e., $7 + 7 = 10 + 4 = ?$)."

Source: "The Core's 'fuzzy math,'" *The Week* (2014, June 6), p. 13

Conceptual Application Activity 2.7

Interview your school counselor supervisor, English or language arts teacher, and mathematics teacher. Ask them about their impression of the Common Core and their role in this initiative. Share their responses with your peers. What are some of the common themes? List them below.

_____

_____

The next section provides information about the various schools in America, how these initiatives are implemented in various schools, and how school counselors influence and are impacted by these different schools.

Types of Schools

In early America, children were taught at home, or sent to private schools if their family could afford it. Eventually, many individuals called for public, free, compulsory education for all children. As society changed, so did ideas regarding the educational system, and debates occurred regarding the advantages and shortcomings of school choice and school governance (Fiske & Ladd, 2017). Various types of school such as private, charters, magnet, and online schools are available today and are discussed below.

Private Schools and Vouchers

School vouchers are one approach to private school choice. Traditional vouchers are state-supported monies created by state legislatures for students to use at private schools rather than the public schools. Private schools which accept voucher students must meet minimum standards established by the legislatures (National Conference of State Legislatures, 2019). As with any educational system, debates regarding the effectiveness of private versus public schools ensue. With vouchers, families pay partial or full tuition for either a religious or non-religious school using funds provided by a school district (The ABCS of School Choice, 2018). Others complain that vouchers take monies away from public schools.

Research on the effectiveness of private versus public schools reveals that significant differences in performance between these two types of institutions are negligible. However, there are modest gains in graduation rates and four-year college attendance for students who attend private schools (Carnoy, 2017).

Charter Schools

Charter schools are also schools of choice (Rollins, 2006) that are tax-funded, privately managed, and required to provide transparency and accountability, yet they are exempt from some of the regulations that apply to other tax-funded schools (Charter Schools 101, 2002–2019). Over the past few decades, charter schools have emerged as one of the most popular forms of school choice, comprising approximately 8% of all public schools (Ozek, Carruthers, & Holden, 2018).

Some school counselors are employed by charter schools, yet because these schools are often exempt from hiring credentialed professionals as are employed by public schools, there is some concern about the education and training of these professionals (Rollins, 2006).

Magnet Schools

Magnet schools are public schools, and another form of school choice. Due to the specialized curricula, students with similar interests apply for admittance (The ABCs of School Choice, 2018) for curricular areas such as: (a) Science, Technology, Engineering, and Mathematics (STEM); (b) Fine and Performing Arts; (c) International Studies; (d) Career and Technical Education (CTE), and (e) World Languages.

Table 2.1 Comparison of magnet and charter schools.

	Magnet schools	*Charter schools*
Association with the public schools	Yes	Yes
Responsibility	District school and school board members	Fluctuates between state or local school, or private body
Educational standards	Must follow state standards	Charter schools are often exempt
For-profit	No	Yes
School tuition	None	None

Source: "What are magnet schools," Magnet Schools of America, http://magnet.edu/about/what-are-magnet-schools

Table 2.1 illustrates the differences between magnet and charter schools.

Online Schools

Online charter schools, also known as virtual or E-schools, can either be public or private, and parents may use vouchers to pay for this educational alternative. This school format allows students to work on a curriculum with teachers using either a format entirely online, or a hybrid program that is a combination of online and time in a traditional classroom (The ABCs of School Choice, 2018). Students are provided with computers, software, network resources, and access to teachers through the use of email, telephone, the web, or teleconferencing (Gill et al., 2015). These schools vary in size, and although the majority serve high school, others serve middle and elementary school-aged students. The vast majority of these schools serve a general population, but approximately 10% serve a specific population of students. Although these schools provide an alternative method of receiving instruction, opponents of this type of schooling argue that they may not be the most effective method of learning (Gill et al., 2015).

Communicating Responsibilities, Duties, and Tasks to Stakeholders

Through your graduate program, you will have learned about the responsibilities of a school counselor according to national, state, and local standards. The challenge is to integrate these guidelines with the culture and expectations of your school, particularly when principals, teachers, parents, other counselors, and various staff have expectations of your role that often differ greatly from your training and education. When this occurs, others define your identity for you. Find a professional method for communicating your role and revealing where you spend your time and how you contribute to the academic educational mission through concrete data. This conversation may assist in changes to your job description.

At all levels, communication is crucial. Returning phone calls and emails promptly will help promote a positive image for your position, and a solid reputation will be built through your ability to provide answers or solutions in a timely manner. As a SCIT, start this communication process now so that it becomes a regular part of your role, and continue this practice during your professional career. Leaving a lasting impression on the personnel at your clinical site will be helpful when you pursue a position as a credentialed school counselor. For example, suppose you decide to start a study skills group to enhance academic achievement and your data analysis of the group intervention reveals that the grades of student participants have improved. This leaves a lasting legacy for the school, and evidence that school counseling strategies contribute to the school mission.

Next, we turn to additional issues that impact school counselors, such as how students are assigned to counselors, the school counselor's role in discipline, testing, and how special education assignments are determined.

School Counselors' Division of Responsibilities

Factors such as the school system's budget, the school's enrollment, the needs of the particular school, and the priorities of the school district all contribute to the number of school counselors that are placed in each school. As you begin your clinical experiences, you may find counselors assigned to more than one school and some who split time between schools. Other schools may have one full-time counselor, and still others may have two or more. If you are working in a program with more than one counselor, you will need to blend your philosophies, work styles, and personalities, which requires compromise, communication, and cooperation to effectively address the needs of *all* students. Learning collaborative strategies while you are a supervisee will assist you when you begin your first school counseling position.

Often, schools with more than one counselor have different methods of assigning responsibility. Some of the more common methods of dividing responsibilities include: (a) grade-level classification, in which each counselor is assigned to a particular grade level year after year, with students having a different counselor each year; (b) alphabetically, in which students have the same counselor for all four years; (c) by specialty area such as college and career, special education, or mental health; or (d) by academies. Some schools have academy structures in which a counselor is assigned to a different career academy, such as health and sciences, or technology, and all students in this academy have the same counselor every year. In other academies, school counselors may rotate to various grade levels. Each configuration has advantages as well as drawbacks.

Conceptual Application Activity 2.8

Make a note of the division of responsibility at the school to which you are assigned, and discuss the advantages and disadvantages of this arrangement with your site supervisor. Discuss your perceptions with your classmates, then enter your observations below.

_____

_____

The School Counselor's Role in Discipline

A counselor's role with regard to discipline is, for the most part, unlike any other person's in the school. Teachers will write up students for misconduct and either discipline the students themselves, or for serious matters, send the students to a principal or assistant principal. The school counselor's role should not involve meting out discipline, due to the potential for jeopardizing the counseling relationship. Instead, the counselor can help the counselee recognize the consequences of behaviors and provide support for the counselee to remediate his/her behavior. Each school will have its own set of expectations for student conduct based on the ages of the student body as well as the school culture.

As a SCIT, be sure to implement a classroom management plan when you teach lessons. Or it may be that a teacher prefers that you use his or her own management plan when you are in a particular class. In either case, have an effective plan ready. Take advantage of your supervisor's assistance and expertise in classroom management, and take every opportunity to practice teaching school counseling lessons before you have a job of your own. Principals and other educators will want to know that a potential school counselor can teach and manage a class with confidence and skill after graduate training has ended. Refer to Chapter 9 for behavior management techniques in conducting small groups or providing classroom lessons.

Peer mediation is one effective technique that may help improve the school culture and contribute to student decision-making. Peer mediation can be used to resolve small issues between two students that, if left alone, might snowball into much bigger issues. The counselor often takes a leadership role in this program, including selecting and training peer mediators, identifying situations where mediation could be used effectively, and scheduling mediations. If the school to which you are assigned has already implemented a peer mediation program, become involved with this plan. If not, talk with your site supervisor about instituting one as part of your clinical experiences.

Conceptual Application Activity 2.9

Read and respond to the following scenario, and compare your responses with those of your peers.

It is your first day as an elementary school counseling intern. Your site supervisor has informed you that you are to share your office with the speech therapist and are to counsel students in the hallway. You have been taught about confidentiality and privacy, yet you are also keenly aware that school space is very limited. Keeping in mind your values, professional ethics, and responsibilities, in addition to the school's inadequate space, how would you respond to your site supervisor?

_____

_____

Testing

With accountability and evidence-based interventions as a central issue in today's educational environment, schools have become centers for continual testing and assessment. Unfortunately, many school districts simply name one of the counselors to assume a position as a testing coordinator and rely on that counselor to make all the testing arrangements. The ESSA requires an annual assessment in which every child from third to eighth grade is tested in math and language arts, one time in high school, with science assessed three times. With testing a norm in our schools, we have a responsibility to communicate how we support and boost student achievement, but we should not be in the role of a test facilitator. This is a time-consuming task that takes counselors away from direct student service. Due to the enormous responsibility that accompanies assessments, some systems hire a test coordinator whose sole responsibility is to be accountable for the testing program.

Some of the tests of which you should be familiar are ACT, SAT, PLAN, PSAT, and AP exams, as well as local and state end-of-course exams. Once the school receives the test results, a plan is necessary to disseminate and explain the results to parents/guardians and students. This is an opportunity for you to utilize the knowledge you have acquired in your courses that addressed testing and measurement. Test orientation and interpretation are activities you may consider including in your clinical contract, and are instrumental for individual planning and goal-setting.

Conceptual Application Activity 2.10

Read and respond to the following scenario, and compare your responses with those of your peers.

All teachers in your school are scheduled for bus duty throughout the year. When you began your internship as a SCIT, you were asked and agreed to help with lunch duty 2 days a week even though you are aware that you are required to complete at least 240 direct hours. Today, your site supervisor asked you to perform bus duty. How do you reconcile these multiple non-counseling-related requests with your university program requirements? What factors will influence your decision, and how will you proceed?

Special Education

Chapter 12 contains a more comprehensive discussion concerning the role of the counselor with students with disabilities, a population that school counselors often overlook. Assisting these students and their families may be more difficult for individuals who do not have a background in education or have not taken coursework that addresses some of the legislative issues and concerns that accompany these individuals. As stated by the American School Counselor Association (2016):

> Professional school counselors encourage and support the academic, career and social/ emotional development for all students through comprehensive school counseling programs. School counselors are committed to helping all students realize their potential and meet or exceed academic standards with consideration for both the strengths and challenges resulting from disabilities and other special needs.
>
> (para. 1)

The elementary school counselor may include counselees with special needs in such areas as conducting group lessons, leading small groups, providing individual counseling, assisting with peer relationships, mediating problems among students, and improving self-confidence. Middle and high school counselors work closely with the resource teachers as students approach high school registration, to assist in developing a transition plan for the students as they matriculate to high school and beyond.

Other Considerations

Clerical duties, testing responsibilities, and administrative tasks are often some of the biggest obstacles to overcome as you establish your role in the school. Sometimes there is a fine line between the education and training and the school counselor's job. For example, as we move into the age of electronic transcripts, high school counselors in particular have a responsibility to maintain and ensure accuracy of student records. If you are lucky enough to have a secretary, this individual will be able to handle this task, but may need to be educated about confidential materials and information that may and may not be released. For instance, if a concerned aunt called about her niece's grades, and an uninformed secretary gave this information to her, this would be a violation of the Family Educational Rights and Privacy Act (FERPA).

Building Relationships for Enhancing Student Growth

The following section provides information regarding Professional Learning Communities (PLCs), the school board, school administrators, teachers, students, parents/guardians, other counseling professionals, and other school-related personnel. As a SCIT, it is essential to understand how you can collaborate effectively with these individuals in the school milieu.

The Professional Learning Community (PLC)

The PLC is a systematic method in which educational personnel partner to share expertise to improve the academic achievement of students through research-based practices. PLCs are an

Figure 2.4 Students benefit when teachers collaborate with counselors to improve achievement.
Source: Shutterstock.

intentional school improvement strategy to reduce professional isolation by encouraging the insights and ideas of all involved with shared goals or responsibilities. For instance, fifth-grade teachers or teachers of a certain subject may meet on a regular basis to address learning best practices and commit to engaging and analyzing effective research practices. Likewise, school counselors within the district may meet to discuss such topics as new counseling strategies to identify student standards that address district competencies from pre-K–12. PLCs are most effective when four questions are addressed: (a) What areas do students need to be more aware of? (b) How will this knowledge be evaluated? (c) How do we remediate students who have not mastered concepts? and (d) In what ways can we attend to students who have already mastered these concepts (Brown, Horn, & King, 2018)? As a SCIT, look at the school counselor model that is based on the ASCA Mindsets and Behaviors for Student Success, and determine whether the questions above can be answered according to this plan.

Some individuals question whether one particular initiative can be linked to student progress due to the difficulty in attributing student performance improvements. Proponents, however, emphasize that as teachers develop more professional relationships, more effective, evidence-based practices will ensue.

Box 2.3

Advantages to school counselors participating in PLCs include:

1. collaboration with teachers and others to identify student needs
2. suggestions for quality solutions to problems
3. provision of resources for referrals to appropriate interventions for students
4. suggestions to improve student behavior and attendance
5. gathering information about social/emotional or developmental needs of students
6. sharing information about activities and programs within the school counseling program that are available to address student needs
7. facilitation of communication between PLC members.

The School Board

School systems are governed by a group of individuals who form a school board, and as a SCIT, there is an educational opportunity to study your school system's website to view the structure of the school board, the members composing this board, responsibilities of the members, and when and where meetings are held. Board members are typically elected to terms consisting of a predetermined number of years, although some school districts may have board members who are appointed to the position. School boards set policies under which school systems operate, and either appoint a superintendent or hold an election for the community to determine the leader of the school. In turn, with the approval of the school board members, superintendents hire other school personnel, including building-level administrators, and depending on the size of the school system, assistant and/or deputy assistant superintendents may be hired. The responsibilities of the school district are divided among a variety of department directors, supervisors, and specialists.

School board policies affect all school staff, faculty, and the community. Some districts hire a director of counseling who is exclusively responsible for the school counselors in the district and often works closely with school counselor training programs in placing students in the clinical sites. Or this person may be assigned duties that encompass supervising school counselors in addition to a broader array of responsibilities. It is also possible that since this person serves as a supervisor of school counselors, an administration degree will be required for this responsibility. This person may be given a title such as "School Counseling Coach" or "Dean of Students," which do not adequately reflect this individual's role or authority. Smaller systems may not have a person specifically identified to supervise counselors, and in these instances this task would probably belong to the building administrator, who may or may not have an understanding of the school counselor's scope of training.

Getting to know the school board members who represent your school or district helps build a relationship and allows the counselor to educate board members about the importance of school counseling, advocate for counseling needs in areas such as staffing, money, and materials, and communicate the counselor's education and training. In fact, once you are hired as a school counselor, consider speaking to the school board at least once a year so that the activities of the school counseling program are better understood. This occasion also provides an opportunity to show appreciation to board members who advocate for the school counseling program.

Conceptual Application Activity 2.11

Attend a school board meeting and take notes on the topics that were discussed. Share your impressions and notes with your peers. What were your impressions of this meeting? What group dynamics did you observe?

_____

_____

School Administrators

Part of a positive work culture and climate involves administrators and counselors working closely together with mutual trust, therefore it is essential that you inform your site supervisor and principal of your activities without burdening him or her with minor details. You will be receiving supervision in which you will share your concerns with your site supervisor on a regular basis, and you may want to consider getting principal approval for topics you plan on discussing in class or small groups. It is easy to venture into controversial territory with young adolescents, and it is possible that you will need the principal's support if a parent/guardian disapproves of a topic that is discussed. If there is any possibility that a discussion area might generate controversy in the community, talk to your supervisor about sending a message home prior to the discussion explaining what you plan to do, and offer parents/guardians the option of alternative activities if they do not want their child to participate in the activity. Any time you have a discussion with a parent that is not resolved in the way the parent/guardian hoped, inform your supervisor and principal of what transpired so that he/she has advance knowledge of the problem and is better able to assist with the issue.

Box 2.4

As stated by an elementary school counselor:

> I am so frustrated! I work in a very poor county school district and am assigned to two elementary schools. Neither school has art or music classes. The principal views my job as that of conducting classroom lessons while teachers are on their planning period. I teach seven 45-minute classes 2 days each week, and six 45-minute classes 3 days each week. With this schedule, I only have 40 minutes at one school each week to meet with students and parents/guardians, and 60 minutes each week at the second school I am assigned. Yet, the administrators still expect me to see students and families as well as handle typical school counselor duties. I try to meet with as many students and parents/guardians as possible but am doing so during my lunch time and before and after school. I have a long waiting list of students who would like to meet with me. This isn't what I thought this job would be like!

Conceptual Application Activity 2.12

Read and respond to the following scenario, and discuss your observations with your peers.

A father of one of your students makes an appointment to see you about his son's grades. He indicates that he is divorced from the child's mother (the custodial parent), and he does not approve of the mother's style of disciplining. He is planning on going to court to get custody, and he wants you to testify to the child's lack of progress academically. He feels that the teachers as well as your site supervisor do not keep him as informed as they should. As he talks, he gets visibly more upset. How do you handle this?

_____

_____

Conceptual Application Activity 2.13

You are leading a lesson on suicide that is integral to your internship contract and the expectations of your school counseling training program. Your principal receives an emotional call from a parent. There has been a recent suicide in the family, and the discussion in class has opened some deep wounds. As a result, the parent is angry that this topic is being discussed in school. How would you handle this situation?

_____

_____

Teachers

A school counselor's relationship with faculty and staff is vital to the success of the school counseling program, and through good communication teachers are kept informed of the work you do in your school. Posting your schedule outside your door in addition to displaying information on the school staff bulletin board, PTA newsletter, and school website are helpful methods to communicate the types of activities in which you are engaged in the school.

It may also be beneficial to present a short orientation for teachers about your role as a SCIT and provide them with a professional disclosure statement that outlines your contact information, education, training, philosophy, and so forth. Furthermore, when meeting with teachers, they can give you an idea of student concerns that need to be addressed, such as bullying, divorce, child or sexual abuse, substance abuse, basic friendship skills, self-esteem, study skills, and peer pressure. Or these educators may suggest a particular school or community problem on which to focus your attention. Be certain that you set up a schedule of dates and times in advance so that teachers know when you are coming to their classrooms for any reason.

Collaborating with teachers on ASCA Mindsets and Behaviors for Student Success that coordinate with Common Core standards is an additional strategy for revealing your contributions to student achievement. Furthermore, career readiness is an essential concept that ideally begins in elementary school, and school counselors are trained to address career and college readiness for all students as well as the skills and knowledge that are needed to address career goals.

You need to make an effort to be seen around the school. At times, school counselors are involved in myriad activities in their offices, and teachers may be uncertain who you are and how you are involved in the school. Therefore, whenever possible, try to eat lunch with different groups of teachers to build rapport with the faculty, or visit teachers during their planning time just to say hello, ask how they are doing, and ask whether you are able to give them any assistance. This attention will help tremendously in getting referrals and support for calling students from classes when you need to see them.

When you need to meet with students, stop by the teachers' classrooms to briefly speak with the teachers regarding individual students you plan to meet with that day. Early morning or teacher planning times are good opportunities to do this. Exchange any relevant information, staying within the bounds of confidentiality, and ask whether the teacher has any specific incidents that need to be addressed with the student when scheduling your day.

School counselors and teachers often compete for time with students, and scheduling times to see counselees is challenging. You may alleviate this problem by calling students to your office before or after school, during their elective classes, class change time, homeroom periods, study halls, lunch, or at other times that do not interfere with academics. However, if the situation is an emergency, teachers are usually understanding about interruptions; you will just need to talk with the teacher about the importance of seeing the student at that time.

It is not uncommon for a student to see you to avoid going to a class, and a common mistake of many SCIT is to allow students to see them without checking whether he or she has permission to be out of class. You will create resentment if teachers think you are allowing students to cut classes to see you even though this situation could happen inadvertently. If it does happen, be sure to see the teacher as soon as possible to explain or apologize.

When a teacher refers a student to you, acknowledge this referral and follow up with the teacher. If you will be seeing the student regularly, discuss this with the teacher and be sure to let him/her know that you will be checking to see whether the student has made any attitudinal or behavioral changes. Even though you cannot ethically share confidential information about a student, providing general information or suggestions for how the teacher may facilitate counseling goals will be appreciated, and teachers will be more likely to make accommodations for students.

Conceptual Application Activity 2.14

Read and respond to the following situation, and discuss your response with your peers.

A critical incident happened in a classroom in which a student seriously harmed another, and you were involved with counseling the victim. Staff and parents are concerned about the actions taken regarding this incident and ask you to tell them specifics about the incident and how it is being handled. How do you respond?

_____

_____

Students

A student is the most important resource in the school. Being responsible for numerous students can seem overwhelming at times, especially given the high student to low counselor ratio in many schools. Remember that you cannot be all things to all people, but you can be an effective presence and participant in the lives of your students. Try to get to each classroom within the first 2 weeks of school, either for a brief visit or for a regular classroom lesson to introduce yourself and tell the students why you are there and how they can contact you.

Discuss with your supervisor how students can make an appointment to see you. Having students place a note on your desk, email you, or putting a mailbox outside your counseling office are typical strategies. In addition, try to familiarize yourself with a variety of individual counseling techniques. In an elementary setting, these strategies might include bibliotherapy, puppetry, writing stories, playing games, art activities, and the use of props and charts.

Be a visible presence around the school whenever possible. If you have a few extra minutes, visit the lunchroom or playground, simply walk the halls, or attend students' musicals, plays, sporting events, and school festivals. However, there are certain limits that should be placed on interaction with students. As professional adults, counselors should never be involved with students inappropriately or in ways that would disrupt integrity. Counselors and the SCIT alike should not be "friends" with students on social networks such as Facebook, Instagram, or Twitter. There have been some incidents where the SCIT was unable to maintain appropriate boundaries with students due to unethical fraternization, which resulted in dismissal from the school counseling program.

Parents/Guardians

As a supervisee, learn how to collaborate with parents/guardians by holding informational meetings or workshops on relevant issues. Teaching parenting classes, providing information on bullying, discussing the effects of divorce, helping children with study skills, conducting workshops on financial aid, or discussing your role as a school counselor trainee are all topics that will help you get experience in working with parents/guardians while under supervision. Supplying handouts or informative technology links may also help the learning process, and offering snacks can create a relaxed atmosphere.

When holding parent/guardian conferences, be very careful with words and try to start and end every conference with something positive about the child. Keep the following suggestions in mind:

- When problem areas are being discussed, link any words of criticism to the fact that the goal is to get the student back on track so that he or she can be happy and successful.
- Be respectful and tactful about giving advice, especially if you are not a parent yourself.
- Never give the impression that you know more about the child than the parent/ guardian does. Allow caregivers to share valuable information that can help you better understand their son or daughter. They should be considered experts about their own children.
- Affirm the fact that parenting is an important and difficult job and that you want to do your part to help with any concerns.
- Use the technique of *joining*, which means establishing rapport by making small talk with the parents/guardians, matching your communication style with theirs, and using appropriate self-disclosure to relate to their experiences. If the conference concerns grades in a particular subject, the teacher of that class should be involved.
- Stay with the facts and observations that you have gathered in your interaction with the student, and look for ways to incorporate the child's strengths into the discussion with his or her parents/guardians.

Other suggestions for working with parents/guardians include normalizing children's problems through *reframing*, which means changing the negative label attributed to the child. For instance, if a young boy is described as being "bossy," you could refer to this behavior as "likes to express himself." Or you could consider establishing a library of helpful information for caregivers, such as handouts, pamphlets, books, audiovisual materials, or links to informative websites. This effort is something you can begin as a SCIT and continue throughout the entire span of your career.

Conceptual Application Activity 2.15

Read and respond to the following scenario, and discuss your responses with your peers.

Parents have called you to request a conference regarding their son. According to his parents, his grades are dropping, he seems unfocused, and his behavior in the classroom and with his peers is becoming a concern. They are adamant that you are aware of how much he disrupts their family life and that you "fix" him. How would you prepare for this conference?

_____

_____

Conceptual Application Activity 2.16

Read and respond to the following scenario, and discuss your responses with your peers.

It is Monday morning, and you are speaking with a student's mother who is requesting that you see her child for school anxiety issues. You continue to explore with the mother what her specific concerns are about the student, and what she would like to see happen as you agree to work with the student. At the end of the conversation, the student's mother adds, "I would like you to call me each week to let me know what she is talking about with you." What do you do?

_____

_____

One challenging issue, particularly for the SCIT, is how to preserve the student's right to confidentiality without alienating the parent or guardian, who has a legitimate interest in the well-being of his or her child. Minors' ethical rights to confidentiality in the counseling relationship are often misunderstood or ignored altogether, and the demands of parents to be informed of the specific content of counseling sessions sometimes overshadow the child's right to privacy. School counselors who develop a reputation for arbitrarily sharing students' information with others may find students reluctant to seek counseling. Communicating the value of confidentiality as a cornerstone of the counseling relationship to parents/guardians is a major consideration in collaborating with these stakeholders.

Technology has improved methods of communicating with parents/guardians. Counselor websites can be updated regularly with information parents/guardians need to know. For example, parent/teacher conferences, ACT and SAT dates, college admission deadlines, scholarships, year-end exams, and other student events allow parents to be aware of special dates that impact their child.

Conceptual Application Activity 2.17

Read and respond to the following scenario, and discuss your responses with those of your peers.

You are part of a parent conference in which the language arts teacher mentions that the student has written something in a journal that alludes to the fact that the student seems to be afraid of someone at home. The parent gets very angry and leans across the table in a threatening manner when the journal entry is mentioned, and menacingly states that you are no longer allowed to work with the child. You, your site supervisor, and the teacher are the only ones in the room with this parent. How do you handle this situation?

_____

_____

Interactions with Other Professionals

Maintaining positive relationships with counselors at neighboring schools or communities has obvious benefits. For instance, when students transfer schools, counselors need to communicate with one another about transfer students' academic records, guardianship issues, grades, special placements, behavior, and so forth. In other cases, when registering eighth-grade students for high school, it is helpful for counselors from all feeder schools to meet, plan, and prepare for the occasion. Talk with your site supervisor about the opportunity to observe and assist with registration so that you can learn about this responsibility firsthand. It is also an opportune time to provide career counseling by discussing how certain classes provide a foundation for identified career plans. Furthermore, although time for collaboration or idea exchanges among school counselors is scarce, counselors from the neighboring communities may want to make an effort to meet together, and it may be helpful to you as a SCIT to talk to and observe counselors in neighboring systems to learn how they conduct their program.

In addition, students may require more intense counseling than you are able to provide. In these cases, a referral to a community counselor with the appropriate skill and expertise may be in the best interests of the student. In these circumstances, a network of resources is desirable. Providing at least three experts in a particular area allows parents/guardians to make their own decision about the professional they feel is best equipped to work with their child. At times, it is frustrating when a referred student is receiving counseling from an outside professional and the school counselor would like to support the counseling plan, but is unable to receive information due to confidentiality. A signed parent/guardian consent form allows all parties to communicate about the student's progress, and a knowledge of terminology and diagnoses, collaborative plans for working with the student, and services to facilitate academic achievement aids in a smooth transition.

Box 2.5

According to ASCA (2016), comprehensive school counseling programs include state-credentialed school counselors and incorporate data-based decision-making to ensure equitable access to high-quality education to all students in a systemic fashion. With intentional program training, school counselors and administrators will likely be positioned to effectively collaborate to achieve these goals.

Source: Lowery, Quick, Boyland, Geesa, & Mayes, 2018

Other School-Related Personnel

The role of the school counselor also intersects with the duties of other school personnel such as administrative assistants, social workers, nurses, school psychologists, custodians, bookkeepers, and school resource officers. Each of these individuals is a valuable resource for learning about collaborative relationships that impact the school culture and students. The following sections summarize the roles these personnel play in the school.

Administrative Assistants

Administrative assistants are critical in establishing a welcoming climate, as they are often the first person people encounter when they enter the building or make calls to the school. The role of administrative assistants can be very stressful as these individuals are extremely busy and are constantly being interrupted. There are some school counseling departments that are fortunate to have a clerical assistant assigned exclusively to the school counselors, whereas other schools do not have this privilege and the clerical help is restricted to one or two individuals for the entire school. As a person new to the school, you will have lots of questions, and these individuals often are a great source of information, but be careful about interrupting these secretaries, and do not ask them to do small things for you that you can do yourself.

School Social Workers

Social workers are a liaison between home and school, and make home visits to social assist with school issues such as advocacy, attendance, bullying, and other areas in which a student's academic success is impeded. Furthermore, they are instrumental resources in connecting families with community agencies that provide such needs as clothing, food, shelter, community mental health counseling, and medical assistance.

School Nurses

School nurses assist in the physical health, and academic achievement of P-12 students. Nurses range from being at a school on a full-time basis to traveling from school to school throughout the school day or week. If a student requires immediate medications or procedures that are complicated, a nurse will likely be assigned to administer the necessary treatment. As a SCIT, make a point to talk with the school nurse about any concerns you have about counselees with whom you are working.

School Psychologists

There is often some confusion between the role of the school psychologist and that of the school counselor. For example, in some schools, counselors process student referrals, help with testing, and attend all or most Individualized Education Plan (IEP) meetings. In other schools, this is the role of the school psychologist. In some schools, both the school counselor and psychologist address traumatic symptoms displayed by school-aged youth. Generally, school psychologists work with a distinct population of students such as those with special needs, and in some cases exceptional students, whereas school counselors work with the entire student body. The school psychologist and school counselor can form a collaborative relationship in which each clearly understands the training and education of the other so that duties are not duplicated and a wider array of services can be offered. As a SCIT, take time to meet the school psychologist to obtain a better understanding of his or her responsibilities and how the two of you are able to assist one another.

Custodians

Custodians work long, hard hours for relatively low pay, and many are quite dedicated to the school staff and students. As a new person in the school, introduce yourself and show your appreciation for their assistance. As with the office staff, do not ask them to do minor things for you that you could do yourself. However, when you need to arrange a room or transport large materials, they can be a great help. Also, remember that custodians get to know the students on a regular basis and can be helpful resources in understanding your students better.

Bookkeeper/Treasurer

Not all school counseling programs are provided with funds to assist with purchases for counseling-related needs. Talk with your supervisor about the monies that are provided to the school counseling department and how these funds are budgeted. Hopefully, you will be given some funds to spend on your school counseling program once you are a fully credentialed member of the profession, but if not, organizations such as the Parent-Teacher Association (PTA) may provide needed funds, or you could also apply for grants. These funding opportunities will not only give you needed materials or assets they will also generate publicity for your program. As a supervisee, you may want to investigate various types of grants and complete a grant application for essentials that your school site can use. In some school systems, your expenditures will be processed through the school bookkeeper. These individuals have critically important jobs that require compliance with both state and district guidelines for spending and collecting money. As a SCIT, familiarize yourself with the particular bookkeeping procedures in your school and ask questions regarding funding, expenditures, and procuring funds so that you can have a better idea of how monies may be obtained for your program.

Security/School Resource Officer (SRO)

The school environment should be a safe haven for students. However, following recent school shootings, school personnel have the task of creating a safe environment; part of this response is to employ law enforcement. Most schools today have a school resource officer in the building on a full-time basis or on call when needed. These individuals are often members of local law enforcement agencies with specialty training to work in schools. The security officer's role is to protect students and school personnel from harm, prevent dangerous situations from occurring, and de-escalate situations that have the potential to become violent. A security officer on the premises also acts as a deterrent to anyone seeking to inflict harm on school grounds, and as a confidant to students. You may be aware of a volatile situation that should be reported as outlined in school policy, or the school security office may provide support with runaway students, contentious custody issues, or topics such as bullying and harassment. Be sure to learn about this individual's role in the school, particularly as the job relates to working with the school counselors.

Conceptual Application Activity 2.18

Interview the SRO assigned to your building. What are some of his/her responsibilities? List them below and share your findings with your classmates.

_____

_____

Community Agencies

Community agencies are instrumental in providing services to students that the school is unable to offer. Examples of referral sources used by school counselors include services for the homeless, extra clothing, investigation into suspected child abuse, mentoring relationships for children in single-parent homes, and assistance with medical or physical needs such as eye-glasses and dental care.

In addition, agencies can assist counselors by working with students who have special counseling needs. Mental health agencies facilitate groups for at-risk students, or health personnel may talk to students about issues such as pregnancy prevention or other health-related issues like anorexia and bulimia, weight problems, and handling diabetes.

Conceptual Application Activity 2.19

Learn about the various agencies in your community, and make a list of these resources for referral sources below. If you decide to stay in the community after graduation, you can expand this list of helpful community services.

_____

_____

Conclusion

This chapter provides information to help you understand the school culture and climate and how the school counselor is a contributor to the school milieu. In learning about the role of the school counselor, it is essential that you be knowledgeable of the various school-based initiatives and projects that contribute to the school atmosphere. For instance, the Every Child Succeeds Act, Safe Schools Improvement Act, Positive Interventions and Behavioral Supports, Response to Intervention, and the Common Core are discussed in this chapter. In addition, from reading this chapter, you will have a deeper appreciation for the educational personnel as you familiarize yourself with the roles of these integral school and community members.

Websites

- Common Core information: www.thoughtco.com/understanding-the-contentious-common-core-state-standards-3194614
- Every Student Succeeds Act (ESSA): www.ed.gov/ESSA

This website also provides more information on school culture and its impact on the students, community, and personnel.

- Safe Schools Improvement Act: www.congress.gov/bill/115th-congress/house-bill/1957

References

Amerikaner, A. (2018). Making ESSA's resource equity provisions meaningful. *State Education Standard, 18*, 14–17. Retrieved from www.nasbe.org/wp-content/uploads/2018/09/Amerikaner_September-2018-Standard.pdf

ASCA. (2016). *The school counselor and students with disabilities.* Retrieved from www.schoolcounselor.org/asca/media/asca/PositionStatements/PS_Disabilities.pdf

ASCA. (2019). *The school counselor and discipline*. Retrieved from www.schoolcounselor.org/asca/media/asca/PositionStatements/PS_Discipline.pdf

Brown, B. D., Horn, R. S., & King, G. (2018). The effective implementation of professional learning communities. *Alabama Journal of Educational Leadership, 5*, 53–59. Retrieved from https://files.eric.ed.gov/fulltext/EJ1194725.pdf

Carnoy, M. (2017). School vouchers are not a proven strategy for improving student achievement: Studies of U.S. and international voucher programs show that the risks to school systems outweigh insignificant gains in test scores and limited gains in graduation rates. *ERIC Digest*. Retrieved from ERIC database (ED579337).

Center for Education Equity, Mid-Atlantic Equity Consortium. (2018). *ERIC Digest*. Retrieved from ERIC database (ED585542).

Chang, H. N., Bauer, L., & Byrnes, V. (2018). Data matters: Using chronic absence to accelerate action for student success. *Attendance Works*. Retrieved from www.attendanceworks.org/wp-content/uploads/2018/09/Data-Matters_090618_FINAL.pdf

Charter Schools, 101. (2002–2019). National Education Association. Retrieved from www.nea.org/home/60831.htm

Common Core State Standards Initiative. (2020). Retrieved from www.corestandards.org

Congress.gov. (2017–2018). H. R. 1957—Safe Schools Improvement Act of 2017. Retrieved from www.congress.gov/bill/115th-congress/house-bill/1957

Espelage, D. L., Low, S., Van Ryzin, M. J., & Polanin, J. R. (2015). Clinical trial of second step middle school program: Impact on bullying, cyberbullying, homophobic teasing, and sexual harassment perpetration. *School Psychology Review, 44*, 464–479.

Fiske, E. B., & Ladd, H. F. (2017). Self-governing schools, parental choice, and the need to protect the public interest. *Phi Delta Kappan, 99*, 31–36. doi:10.1177/0031721717728276

George, H. P., Cox, K. E., Minch, D., & Sandomierski, T. (2018). District practices associated with successful SWPBIS implementation. *Behavioral Disorders, 43*, 393–406. doi:10.1177/0198742917753612

Gill, B., Walsh, L., Wulsin, C. S., Matulewic, H., Severn, V., Grau, E., ... Kerwin, T. (2015). Inside online charter schools: A report of the national study of online charter schools. *ERIC Digest*. Retrieved from ERIC database (ED560967).

Goodman-Scott, E., & Grothaus, T. (2018). School counselors' roles in RAMP and PBIS: A phenomenological investigation (Part Two). *Professional School Counseling, 21*, 130–141. doi:10.5330/1096-2409-21.1.130

Grapin, S. L., Waldron, N., & Joyce-Beaulieu, D. (2019). Longitudinal effects of RtI implementation on reading achievement outcomes. *Psychology in the Schools, 56*, 242–254. doi:10.1002/pits.22222

Gruenert, S. (2008, March/April). School culture, school climate: They are not the same. *Principal*. Retrieved from www.naesp.org/sites/default/files/resources/2/Principal/2008/M-Ap56.pdf

Jennings, J. (2018). It's time to redefine the federal role in K-12 education. *Phi Delta Kappan, 100*, page numbers not provided.

Lowery, K., Quick, M., Boyland, L., Geesa, R. L., & Mayes, R. D. (2018). "It wasn't mentioned and should have been": Principals' preparation to support comprehensive school counseling. *ERIC Digest*. Retrieved from ERIC database (EJ1180120).

Mitchell, B. S., Hatton, H., & Lewis, T. J. (2018). An examination of the evidence-base of school-wide positive behavior interventions and supports through two quality appraisal processes. *Journal of Positive Behavior Interventions, 20*, 239–250. doi:10.1177/1098300718768217

National Conference of State Legislatures. (2019). School choice: Vouchers. Retrieved from www.ncsl.org/research/education/school-choice-vouchers.aspx

Ozek, U., Carruthers, C., & Holden, K. (2018). *Teacher value-added in charter schools and traditional public schools. Working paper 183*. Manhattan Institute for Policy Research. *ERIC Digest*. Retrieved from ERIC database. (ED583625).

Rollins, J. (2006, August 10). Charter schools: Treat or opportunity? *Counseling Today*. Retrieved from https://ct.counseling.org/2006/08/charter-schools-threat-or-opportunity/#

Sherrod, M. D., Getch, Y. Q., & Ziomek-Daigle, J. (2009). The impact of positive behavior support to decrease discipline referrals with elementary students. *Professional School Counseling, 12,* 421–427. doi:10.5330/PSC.n.2010-12.421

The ABCs of School Choice: The comprehensive guide to every private school choice program in America. (2018 edition). *ERIC Digest.* Retrieved from ERIC database (ED581413).

ThoughtCo. (2019, January 17). What are some pros and cons of the Common Core State Standards? Retrieved from www.thoughtco.com/common-core-state-standards-3194603

3 Applying Counseling Theories during Your Clinical Experience

Jeannine R. Studer and Aaron H. Oberman

CACREP Standards

Foundations

a. models of P-12 comprehensive career development

Contextual Dimensions

e. school counselor roles and responsibilities in relation to the school emergency management plans, and crises, disasters, and trauma

Chapter Objectives:

*   summarize the most commonly used counseling theories used in schools
*   reflect on one's personal theory of counseling as a SCIT
*   apply theory to school-related case studies

Introduction

The school counselor's approach to counseling is influenced by the counselor's philosophical views from affective, cognitive, behavioral and relational perspectives of one or more theoretical orientations. There are myriad theoretical approaches within the counseling field, some representing an extension of preexisting theories of personality development, and others expressing a reaction against earlier systems of thought. Regardless of one's theoretical orientation, knowledge of counseling theory is critical in accurately assessing and conceptualizing a counselee's case.

Both the counselee and counselor come to the counseling situation with a unique background of cultural experiences that influence the relationship. Because no one particular theory is best suited for all counselees, it is incumbent upon the counselor to choose a theoretical approach that best fits the needs of the counselee in terms of personality factors, background experiences, available time, presenting issues, and cultural milieu.

Since you undoubtedly have a separate counseling theories class within your training program curriculum, this chapter is not intended to replace the information you will receive within that class. Instead, the contextual aspects of schools that often influence theoretical counseling orientation are provided. In addition, we introduce motivational interviewing: a "front-loaded" approach that is used with all counseling theories and summarize the more commonly used counseling theories, including person-centered counseling, reality therapy, cognitive behavioral approaches, solution-focused brief counseling, and narrative therapy. Finally, the creative counseling approaches such as the visual arts, play, and music are discussed.

Contextual Aspects of Schools

Schools provide a unique environment in which to provide counseling. Although some of the aspects unique to schools are more thoroughly discussed in Chapter 2, it is important to consider the distinct aspects of the school environment that impact school counselors' choice of theoretical orientation. Some of these aspects include the developmental age of children and adolescents as counselees, the scope of school counselor responsibilities, students' time availability, and the school mission and philosophy. First, the primary goal of school personnel is to educate children, and because school counselors focus their counseling energies primarily on children and adolescents, developmental issues influence choice of theoretical orientation. Second, school counselors are responsible for many tasks and activities which often limit the amount of energy and time the school counselor has available for counseling. As a result, school counselors may not have the resources or time to adequately counsel students who present significant mental health issues, those who require resources that are not available in the school, or students who require intensive ongoing counseling. The third aspect is the student's time availability. Students are in school to be educated, and excessive time spent in the school counseling office can take away from time spent in the classroom. Furthermore, based on the mission and vision statement of the school, certain topics may not be addressed in counseling. For example, various state legislative bodies have held debates regarding issues such as the legislation of sexuality issues and the counselor's response to students with these concerns. For example, at one time the state of Tennessee considered legislation known as the "Don't Say Gay Bill" that would have prohibited talk about sexual orientation in public schools (Barbeauld, 2014). In the state of Ohio, HB 658 was introduced to require teachers and health providers to "out" transgender students to their parents or guardians, and authorized felony charges for those who did not comply with this mandate (Ohio Legislature, 2019). In other schools, school counselors are forbidden from discussing controversial issues such as birth control or abortion.

These short-sighted approaches prevent school-aged youth from discussing concerns regarding their sexual orientation or other apprehensions. Awareness of the school policies and state legal and ethical issues may prevent costly mistakes that you could inadvertently cause. Furthermore, awareness of your personal beliefs and philosophical counseling approach assists in establishing a foundation for directing the counseling relationship.

Box 3.1

Youth needing mental health services are more likely to access those services in a school setting than in a community-based mental health environment. With 1 in 6 children aged 2–8 years of age diagnosed with a mental, behavioral, or developmental disorder (approximately 17.4%), school counselors are well positioned to assist these students and their families. Understanding the numerous mental disorders and being able to understand the *Diagnostic and Statistical Manual of Mental Disorders* is a helpful aid for working with students with diagnoses and communicating with their clinical mental health therapists.

The following theoretical counseling descriptions are not intended to exhaustively explain the tenets of any one particular theory, but are designed to serve as references when counseling with school-aged youth. Regardless of the theoretical approach you choose, motivational interviewing (MI) serves as a prelude for determining a theoretical approach and clarifying a counselee's desire for change.

Motivational Interviewing

Motivational interviewing is a dialogue that centers on strengthening a counselee's motivation and commitment to make personal changes (Kolbert, Happe, Hyatt-Burkhart, Crothers, & Capuzzi, 2017). As an initial component of the counseling process, the counselor and student are able to build rapport that facilitates change and is ideal for the school setting in that it can be implemented in one to three sessions. The interview consists of four stages: (a) engaging, or forming a partnership between the counselee and counselor in which the counselor promotes "change talk"; (b) focusing, in which the student identifies a goal he/she wishes to achieve; (c) evoking, in which the student identifies the reasons for personal behavioral change based on the premise that motivation is more likely when a counselee discusses change (Frey et al., 2011); and (4) planning, in which the counselor and student determine strategies for change to occur (Kolbert, Happe, Hyatt-Burkhart, Crothers, & Capuzzi, 2017).

The counselor's role is to use basic counseling skills to determine the counselee's motivation to change and to establish the importance of change. Questions you can use to explore the student's reasons for behavioral change are identified in Table 3.1. Central beliefs behind motivational interviewing include avoiding getting stuck on issues while keeping a positive momentum (Sheldon, 2010), and constructing a setting in which the student feels in control of the session. Measurable, achievable, specific goals are established using the acronym FRAMES, as identified in Table 3.2, that can be implemented to increase the probability of change.

A scale is used to monitor the student's motivation and confidence to change to reach an identifiable goal. For instance, as the counselor, you can ask, "On a scale of 1–10, with 1 meaning little motivation and 10 meaning high motivation, how enthusiastic are you to make your goal happen?" or "On a scale of 1–10, how confident are you that you can reach your goal?" If the student answers with a 6, the counselor then asks the student what he/she needs to do to move up to a 7. The response serves as a basis for assigning homework as a step toward change. From here, the counselor is able to select a counseling theory in work with the counselee.

As discussed earlier, motivational interviewing is a preliminary strategy most counselors find helpful to determine the student's willingness to create change. This initial interview

Table 3.1 Questions to explore change.

Why do you want to make this change now?
What are your plans for being successful with your goal?
What are three reasons why this change will help you?
On a scale of 1–10, with 10 meaning "most important," how essential is it to make this change? Why?

Source: Revised from Kolbert et al. (2017).

Table 3.2 FRAMES acronym to determine change.

Acronym	Explanation	Example
Feedback	Providing nonjudgmental feedback as facts to articulate discrepancies in what was said or done	"You are saying you want to get better grades, yet you are also telling me you don't have time to study."
Responsibility	Accepting personal accountability for actions	"What was your role in the class disruption?"
Advice	Providing information that can be used to solve a problem	"I am wondering if you have tried to speak in an assertive manner?"
Menus	Presenting a list of options as solutions to a problem	"You have tried talking, emailing, and texting your friend to explain the situation. Is there anything else to consider?"
Empathy	Building rapport by acknowledging that change is difficult	"I can imagine how uncomfortable it will be to take this first step."
Self-efficacy	Promoting autonomy and a belief in the ability to change	"This is a plan that I think makes sense, and I have confidence in your ability to carry these plans out."

aids the counselor because students are often referred to the counselor by an adult such as a parent or guardian, teacher, principal, etc., and when this occurs, the student doesn't often "own" the issue, resulting in little enthusiasm for resolving the issue. From here, individual counseling theories commonly utilized by school counselors are summarized below.

Individual Counseling Theories

Person-Centered Counseling

Dr. Carl Rogers, the founder of person-centered counseling, developed his nondirective approach in reaction to the prevailing direct method of counseling. Rogers' approach challenged the assumption that "the counselor knows best" and the prevailing belief that counselees are unable to understand and resolve their problems without direct help on the part of a counselor. Instead, he believed that all individuals have the ability to solve their own personal problems (Seligman & Reichenberg, 2014).

Rogers believed the focus of counseling should be on the person rather than the problem, and that the ultimate goal of counseling was to achieve congruence between the person's true inner self and his or her perceived self. On the part of the counselor, Rogers advocated for unconditional positive regard or nonjudgmental acceptance of the counselee, a genuine, unpretentious presentation of congruence, and accurate, empathic understanding. When the counselee experiences these conditions, he/she is able to work toward meaningful goals leading to personal change (Corey, 2017).

Person-centered counseling has been applied in a number of countries and in numerous multicultural settings. The role a counselor takes in setting aside personal values, thus completely identifying with those of the counselee, enhances the applicability of the approach with diverse populations (Sharf, 2016). This approach is also applicable and has been used with individuals, groups, and families and employed in educational settings from elementary to graduate school. Although person-centered counseling is considered a "way of being" in the counseling relationship, techniques are generally not associated with this theory.

However, experiential learning facilitates self-esteem development, with success and achievement used as stepping-stones to develop a greater sense of self-worth (Seligman & Reichenberg, 2014). Student Activity 3.1 can be adapted to promote self-esteem with students.

Student Activity 3.1

I Can, Can

Directions: Cut paper into strips. Brainstorm with the student about his/her successes, positive traits, and accomplishments, and write these down on the strips of paper. Place the completed strips of paper into a can, and whenever the student is feeling anxious or upset about him/herself, instruct the student to pull a strip of paper out of the can to read, reflect, and remind him/herself of successes.

Conceptual Application Activity 3.1

Conduct a role-play using the following scenario with a partner. One person will play the role of a person-centered counselor using the philosophical approach described earlier, and the other person will role-play the counselee described in the vignette below.

Ella is a fourth-grade student in a rural school that has few resources, poorly paid personnel, and no community mental health agencies. The closest facility that provides counseling is in a city located nearly 1 hour away. Ella arrives in the counselor's office upset, crying, and incapable of talking about the issue that brought her to see the counselor. It seems that her mother, her primary caregiver, was arrested the night before on charges of drug use and abuse. Ella was sent to live with her grandparents, a few blocks away, until her mother is arraigned. Ella's grandparents care about Ella, but have physical difficulties that prevent them from caring for her appropriately.

a. Discuss what it was like to role-play the counselor and some of the challenges in using this approach. What aspects of this theory seemed to facilitate the counseling relationship?
b. Discuss what it was like to role-play Ella. What were some of the aspects of this counseling approach that you think assisted the counseling process? What aspects detracted from the counseling process?

Reality Therapy or Choice Theory

William Glasser developed reality therapy (also called choice theory) in the early 1960s as a result of his work with institutionalized delinquent adolescent girls. Glasser emphasized the importance of taking responsibility for oneself, and similar to person-centered counseling, this theory supports and facilitates personal growth (Wubbolding, Casstevens, & Fulkerson, 2017).

Table 3.3 A summarization of the Reality Therapy WDEP system.

W	=	Wants: What do you want to be and do? Your mental picture of yourself.
D	=	Doing and direction: What are you doing? Where do you want to go?
E	=	Evaluation: Is what you are doing now working for you? Is it getting you what you want?
P	=	Planning: A plan to get you where you want to be, often represented by the acronym SAMI^{2}C^3
S	=	Simple, specific, and understandable
A	=	Attainable by the student
M	=	Measurable through the use of recording methods
I	=	Implemented immediately—with the counselor involved in providing feedback
C	=	Controlled by the student—the counselee is committed to change with consistent behavior modifications

Glasser identified five interrelated and mutually dependent needs of survival, belonging, power, freedom, and fun that all individuals attempt to accomplish (Wubbolding et al., 2017). Reality therapy suggests that the underlying issue for a troubled counselee is an absence of or lack of satisfaction with a significant interpersonal relationship. Therefore, as a counselor, you can facilitate a significant relationship with your student counselee, and in some cases *you* may be the only reliable person the student is able to trust.

In treating counselees for emotional disturbance, Glasser stated that psychiatric symptoms emerge in an attempt to meet needs stemming from an ineffective relationship. Glasser frequently converts diagnostic descriptors such as depression, anxiety, and phobia into verb forms, expressed as *depressing, anxietizing,* and *phobicing,* thus implying that the individual chooses the behavioral symptom and enacts it within his or her life (Sharf, 2016). In assessing the counselee's status in meeting his or her needs in a realistic manner, the reality counselor may use the WDEP system (Wubbolding et al., 2017) (see Table 3.3).

Glasser believed that reality therapy is successful with individuals from all cultural groups due to the universal nature of the five basic needs; however, there is little empirical evidence that it is effective with different cultural groups. For instance, the excessive use of questions may be considered offensive by some Asian cultures, and individuals who are disenfranchised may genuinely face negative social barriers. Therefore, counselors have a responsibility to communicate that each person is responsible for his/her reactions and the consequences of these behaviors.

Reality therapy is quite popular in middle and high school settings, but may be used across all grade levels by teachers, administrators, and school counselors. Questioning, optimism, humor, confrontation, and paradoxical techniques are a few of the strategies that reality therapists use to bring about change. Student Activity 3.2 may prove useful.

Student Activity 3.2

My Basic Needs

Glasser identified the basic needs of survival, belonging, power, freedom, and fun as catalysts for behavior. For each of the cues below, ask the student to draw, write, or cut out and paste pictures from magazines to represent how each of his/her basic needs is met.

Survival	Belonging	Power	Freedom	Fun

Conceptual Application Activity 3.2

With a partner, use the WDEP system and conduct a role-play with one person taking the role of a counselor and another a counselee role using the following scenarios.

- a twelfth-grade student who is having difficulty with career plans
- a seventh-grade male who is being bullied by his peers
- a third-grade female who is having problems getting along with her sister

Discuss what it was like to role-play the counselor and some of the challenges in using this approach. What aspects of this theory seemed to facilitate the counseling relationship?

a. What were your feelings about this theory as a counselee?
b. Discuss what it was like to role-play the student counselee. What were some of the aspects of this counseling approach that assisted the counseling process? What aspects detracted from the counseling process?

Rational Emotive Behavior Therapy

Albert Ellis (2004a, 2004b) developed rational emotive behavior therapy (REBT), in which principles from cognitive and behavioral theories are integrated into short-term counseling approaches. This approach is popular among counselors in all settings (Corey, 2017). REBT is based on the concept that individuals are naturally predisposed to think in inflexible and irrational manners which influence behavior and emotions (Ellis, 1962, as cited in Warren & Hale, 2016). Therefore, by changing how we interpret life situations, we also change how we feel and what we do in response to this thinking. Common cognitive distortions include all-or-nothing cognition typically represented by the words *must*, *ought*, and *should*. In addition, individuals create anxiety for themselves through such irrational beliefs such as mind reading, catastrophizing, overgeneralization, labeling and mislabeling, magnification and minimization, and personalization (Ellis, 1996). He contended that emotional problems are largely a result of mistaken beliefs, and may be rectified by recognizing the irrational nature of one's thinking, disputing such irrational cognitions, and replacing these thoughts with more rational and effective thinking.

REBT is directive and educational in nature, with an emphasis on thinking, judging, deciding, analyzing, and doing (Corey, 2017). The counselor's role in REBT is to help the counselee replace irrational with rational reasoning using the acronym ABCDE (Seligman & Reichenberg, 2014) (see Table 3.4).

Table 3.4 Ellis' Disputation Model for rational and irrational beliefs.

A	=	*A*ctivating event, or the source that initiated the irrational thinking
B	=	*B*elief and evaluation of the event, whether it is viewed as positive, negative, or neutral
C	=	*C*onsequences of the belief that may be helpful or harmful. Rational beliefs usually lead to healthier outcomes, whereas irrational beliefs often lead to destructive outcomes.
D	=	*D*ispute (or debate) of beliefs and whether they are rational or irrational
E	=	*E*ffect of new belief, and hopefully a new perspective

Once cognitive distortions are recognized, students are able to continue collaborative work with their counselor to restructure their thinking and improve their problem-solving and coping skills (Corey, 2017). Treatment strategies include behavioral rehearsal, role-play, and homework assignments for continued practice of positive cognitions and behaviors (Wedding & Corsini, 2019).

Several reviews of studies with students from diverse backgrounds who were counseled using REBT revealed its effectiveness, particularly when implemented in tandem with tiered behavioral and academic models to meet the needs of students (Banks, 2012).

Student Activity 3.3

Using REBT to Recognize Irrational Thoughts

Use the REBT approach with a student who is expressing irrational beliefs. Use the following worksheet to identify irrational thoughts and to help the student to dispute the statements.

A	B	C	D	E
Identify an event that you found upsetting.	What was your belief?	What were the consequences of the belief?	What is the evidence for this belief?	What is the consequence of this new belief?

Conceptual Application Activity 3.3

With a partner, conduct a role-play of the following situation using REBT.

A parent of one of your fifth graders comes to see you because she is concerned that her son, Kyle, is gay. According to Kyle's mom, he is not interested in sports or any type of physical activity typical for boys his age, is quiet, and prefers to play with dolls with his sister. Kyle's mom further states that it is her fault because she divorced his father when he was baby, and as a result of not having a male figure in the home, Kyle is suffering the consequences.

a. Discuss what it was like to role-play the counselor and some of the challenges in using this approach. What aspects of this theory seemed to facilitate the counseling relationship?
b. Discuss what it was like to role-play Kyle's mom. What were some of the aspects of this counseling approach that assisted the counseling process? What aspects detracted from the counseling process?

Solution-Focused Brief Counseling

Solution-focused brief counseling (SFBC) was initially influenced by the work of Milton Erickson (deShazer, 1985). SFBC posits that change always occurs and is similar to person-centered counseling (Guterman, 2006) due to the belief that each individual has strengths and resiliencies (Trepper, Dolan, McCollum, & Nelson, 2006) that drive problem-solving.

SFBC is collaborative, with a focus is on what the counselee would like to see happen rather than on talk that is problem-saturated. According to counselors who adhere to this approach, primary principles include the following: (a) the basic task of the counselor is to help the counselee do something different; (b) a shift should occur when there is a focus on a solution that may already be present within the counselee's life; (c) change, even in small increments, is productive in creating the path for further change; and (d) goals stated in positive terms create expectations for change (Seligman & Reichenberg, 2014).

In SFBC, problems are viewed as being maintained by the counselee's belief that the problem is always happening as a result of the individual repeatedly and ineffectively applying the same solutions to the problem. From here, the counselor explores times or *exceptions* when the problem doesn't occur. For instance, the counselor may ask the question, "Is there a time when you didn't have the problem?" or "Has there been a time when you were able to cope with the problem?"

When the counselee is unable to recognize a time when the problem has not occurred, the counselor then asks what is known as the *miracle question*. This question serves to help the counselee imagine the future without the trouble that brought him/her into counseling. The miracle question is generally stated as, "Suppose you went to bed this evening and while you were sleeping a miracle occurred, and when you woke up in the morning all your problems were gone. What would be different?" and "What would you be doing, thinking, feeling to let you know that your goal was reached?" (Corey, 2017). For younger counselees, another version of the miracle question could be, "Suppose I had a magic wand, and when I wave it all your problems will be gone. How would you know that the magic worked?"

During subsequent sessions, homework is provided to reinforce behaviors that result in positive change for the counselee. For instance, students may be encouraged to do more of the exceptions that were identified when the problem was not occurring. Scaling techniques are also used to help counselees recognize progress. For example, counselees are asked to rate the problem on a scale of 1–10, with 10 meaning the problem is completely solved, and 1 denoting the problem is the worst it could be. The student may rate the problem as a 5. The counselor will then ask the counselee to identify steps that could be taken to move the problem to a 6, and the responses serve as homework assignments to facilitate activities that encourage goal-setting.

Solution-focused brief counseling techniques are applicable with students of all ages, and may be applied in individual as well as group counseling settings. Furthermore, SFBC has been used successfully with various cultural groups due to the emphasis on personal strengths and the establishment of goals that are personally meaningful. However, some Asian cultures may prefer a more pragmatic approach to resolving situations, and the egalitarian relationship that is assumed in this model may be disconcerting to those who prefer a more hierarchical structure.

Conceptual Application Activity 3.4

With a partner, conduct a role-play of a school counselor and a counselee using the solution-focused brief counseling approach. Use one or more of the following scenarios to assist you with this process.

- A second-grader is upset because one of her friends will not play with her or be her learning partner in class.
- A sophomore did not get a scholarship to attend an academic camp and believes that she will never get into a good college because of this rejection.
- A parent is concerned about her 17-year-old daughter, who seems belligerent and will not listen to anything she has to say.

a.   Discuss what it was like to role-play the counselor and some of the challenges in using this approach. What aspects of this theory seemed to facilitate the counseling relationship?
b.   Discuss what it was like to role-play the counselees. What were some of the aspects of this counseling approach that assisted the counseling process? What aspects detracted from the counseling process?

_____

_____

Narrative Therapy

Michael White and David Epston are considered the primary contributors to narrative therapy. These theorists opine that an individual's reality is constructed through the expectations and messages provided by society and influential individuals (e.g. teacher, parent, mentor), and personal beliefs about self. As a result, people live according to their life stories which are based on past experiences and their perceptions of these life events (Seligman & Reichenberg, 2014), known as *dominant* plots.

Narrative therapy involves the counselor and counselee working collaboratively to: (a) co-construct the counselee's story; (b) deconstruct burdensome life stories by externalizing problems as separate from the individual; (c) identify unique outcomes or times when the counselee was able to detach him/herself from the influence of the problem; and (d) reconstruct a preferred, alternative story, thus enhancing coping and problem-solving skills, initiating goal-setting, and improving self-image (White, 1993, 1995).

The counselor listens carefully to the stories to identify themes, the influence the stories have had on different aspects of the counselee's life, and *sparkling moments*, or the times in which the problem does not occur. A primary principle of narrative counseling is to communicate the idea that the *problem* is the problem; the *person* is not the problem. To promote this belief, the concept of *externalization*, or naming the problem, gives the counselee an opportunity to perceive the problem as something external to him/herself. The counselor and counselee co-construct a "counterplot" that challenges the existing dominant plot, while re-authoring new stories (Seligman & Reichenberg, 2014). Other techniques for re-authoring the story include:

- Relative Influence Questions: Questions are used to "map" the influence of the problem on the student. Questions are asked about how the problem has influenced school, peers, family, and so on.
- Unique Outcomes: Also known as sparkling moments, these are used to emphasize exceptional conclusions, focus on the new life story without the problem, and ask how the unique outcomes can occur outside of the counseling office.

Narrative therapy may be implemented during individual or group counseling in school and in clinical settings. Researchers have integrated this approach with creative counseling strategies such as literature and visual arts in that the use of creative arts links "talk" with children's natural tendencies (Leggett, 2009). Narrative therapy may also be applied in career counseling settings to address developmental tasks such as understanding self-identity, building autonomy, decision-making and goal-setting (Finlay, 2011).

From a multicultural perspective, counselors are able to listen to a student's story through the student's cultural lens. Since the goal of narrative therapy is to bring awareness of the dominant cultural stereotypes, students may feel empowered to question these stories that they took for granted.

Student Activity 3.4

A New Story of Me

Ask a student to tell you a story in which he/she has a problem in the area of school, friends, or family. While the story is being relayed, listen for "sparkling moments" that occur, the student's successes or strengths, and themes. Ask the student to describe the story in as much detail as possible. The following questions may facilitate preferred stories, or narratives that describe how the student would like life to be.

1. How is this a problem for you? (Is it evident in relationships, behaviors, feelings, or in other ways?)
2. How is it influencing your life? (Evaluate how it is influencing school, friends, work, activities, family, etc.)
3. When do you have control over the problem?
4. When is the problem easier to handle?
5. What strengths or skills do you have that can be used to solve the problem?
6. Describe how you can use these skills to conquer the problem.

Conceptual Application Activity 3.5

With a partner, conduct a role-play of a counselor and counselee using a narrative approach. The following scenario may be used to assist with this activity.

JoAnna is very unhappy. No matter what she tries, nothing seems to turn out the way she would like. For instance, just this morning, she took a quiz in her algebra class, and even though she spent hours studying for it, she received a C. Furthermore, according to Joanna, her boyfriend recently broke up with her because she tended to "drag him down." She comes to see you because she doesn't feel as if she has many friends and is lonely.

a. Discuss what it was like to role-play the counselor and some of the challenges in using this approach. What aspects of this theory seemed to facilitate the counseling relationship?
b. Discuss what it was like to role-play JoAnna. What were some of the aspects of this counseling approach that assisted the counseling process? What aspects detracted from the counseling process?

Creative Counseling Approaches

Creative counseling approaches, also known as expressive therapies, are therapeutic interventions in which the counselee uses creative energies to enhance self-awareness or self-expression. Three creative counseling approaches frequently employed in school counseling settings are visual art therapy, play therapy, and music therapy, all of which have the potential of improving emotional growth and physical health by helping counselees become more understanding of themselves and others (Bray, 2017).

Visual Arts in Counseling

For many years, art has been used as an interpretative tool to better understand thoughts, memories, and feelings of individuals who may be unable or unwilling to express themselves verbally, and as a less threatening mode of communication with individuals who present emotional or behavioral difficulties. In this chapter, visual art therapy will be defined as a form of expressive communication in which the counselee expresses thoughts and feelings through the creation of art products using one or more media.

Ethically, school counselors who do not have the training to use art therapy as a projective personality assessment should refrain from interpreting materials without the appropriate supervision and preparation. However, art can be incorporated into counseling as a means to create a comfortable relationship, as a form of self-expression, and as a source of information.

Art therapy is easily integrated into the typical school counseling office through such media as multicolored paper, pencils, crayons, markers, paints, glue, magazine cutouts for a collage, modeling clay, pipe cleaners, and papier-mâché. If the school counselor is

Table 3.5 Media for expressive arts in counseling.

Art	Song	Images	Movement	Theater
Drawing	Songs with lyrics	Print	Bounce, skip sway	Family sculpting
Sketching	Music without lyrics	Digital	Drum circle	Role-playing
Painting	Beats	Video	Shadow movement	Puppet creation
Sculpting	Rhythms	Documentary	Body sculpting	Marionettes
Collages	Song creation	Real or created	Mind maps	Drama

Figure 3.1 Art in counseling provides a creative means for expressing oneself.
Source: Steve Martin Photography.

fortunate enough to have a private office and responsibilities in a single building, materials may be stored in cabinets or file drawers until ready for use. However, many school counselors are placed in more than one school, share an office with another educational professional, or travel from classroom to classroom. In these cases, a tote bag loaded with art supplies may be one solution, or requisitioning a cart with wheels to transport the materials may also be an answer.

Art therapy is suitable for counselees of all ages and areas of need, including developmental, academic, social, and emotional. For example, art has been helpful in reducing stress (Montgomery, 2018) by projecting images in drawings, paintings, and sculptures, and also enhancing coping in times of stress and separation anxiety precipitated by illness or injury. In addition, children and adolescents diagnosed with autism spectrum disorders (ASD) are often referred for art therapy to aid their communication and behavioral problems due to its non-verbal approach (Schweizer, Spreen, & Knorth, 2017). Furthermore, when immigrant students who were experiencing difficulty due to language differences and psychological instability created collages, there was a noted growth among these students (Wang & Kim, 2019). Finally, art therapy is also recommended as a means to promote self-acceptance and developmental growth (Goldner, Sachar, & Abir, 2018).

Figure 3.2 Angry monster, drawn by a third-grade boy who was discussing his anger issues with his school counselor.

Box 3.2

Questions to Ask About Artwork

When working with students regarding their artwork, the following questions can guide the discussion:

- What do you see (not what does it mean)?
- What is missing from the drawing?
- If you could go anywhere in that picture, where would you go?
- What title would you put on the picture?
- What feelings does this picture have?
- Can you relate this drawing to anything in your life?
- If you could change something about you, how would this picture be different?

Student Activity 3.5

Draw Your Feelings

Ask a student to explore a troubling time by expressing it through drawing. After the student has completed the drawing, explore the picture for deeper meaning and/or associations with other problematic areas in his/her life. Next, have the student draw a picture of what life would be like without the problem.

Conceptual Application Activity 3.6

Take a blank sheet of paper and colored markers. Think about either your practicum or internship experience, and draw your feelings that represent this experience. Let your mind wander while you think in terms of how you would like to represent your feelings and thoughts about this clinical experience. Do not evaluate your work, and do not worry if you are unable to represent these feelings and thoughts accurately. After you are finished, put this picture away, and then carry out this same activity at the end of your program. Compare the two pictures to see how your feelings and thoughts may have changed based on your artwork. Identify one way you might use a similar art activity with one of the students in your school.

Play in Counseling

Child-centered, nondirective play therapy is a popular treatment for children and adolescents in both school and clinical settings, and is based on the claim that the child processes experiences and communicates his/her perceptions of reality through the natural means of play. According to Swank, Cheung, and Williams (2018), children develop empathy, interpersonal relationships, and self-regulation when they relate to and interact with their peers and adults—skills that are associated with a decline in behavioral problems and academic progress (Girard & Girolametto, 2013, as cited in Swank et al., 2018).

Box 3.3

The use of play therapy is congruent with the American School Counselor Association National Model. School counselors meet the needs of all students through counseling and instruction. Expressive arts can be integrated with various theoretical models and infused across the delivery component (Trice-Black, Bailey, & Riechel, 2013).

Although school counselors work with students on myriad issues, aggressive students often create anxiety among these professionals. The release of aggressive behaviors in the counseling setting is often seen as helpful, yet counselors are often bewildered as to the best methods of addressing these behaviors (Davis, Flick, Mendez, & Urbina, 2018). Using

Table 3.6 Toys for play in counseling.

Nurturing	Expressive	Cultural considerations	Representations of nature	Toys that represent aggression
Stuffed animals	Pipe cleaners	Dolls with various skin tones	Shells	Representations of scary reptiles or animals
Dolls	Crayons	Utensils from other cultural groups	Rocks or stones	Toy guns
Families	Paints	Jewelry from other cultures	Leaves	Rubber knife
Furniture	Play-Doh	Artifacts from cultural groups	Sand	Aggressive hand puppets
Play dishes and utensils	Magazine pictures	Dolls representing ethnic groups	Twigs	Burglar mask
Nursing bottle, bib, diaper	Scissors and glue	Cultural toys	Flowers	Handcuffs

a Gestalt therapy approach, clay has been used to address aggressive behaviors, as students have an opportunity to mold, shape, pound, and twist the clay as a tactile outlet to deal with anger (Davis et al., 2018).

Through the use of Adlerian counseling, students are able to identify their mistaken beliefs and goals which may contribute to their aggressive tendencies, and are able to expressive themselves in a way that words are unable to express (Froeschle & Riney, 2008, as cited in Davis et al., 2018). Additionally, play may be incorporated with cognitive behavior therapy (CBT) to teach children and adolescents coping skills. For instance, teaching students to take deep breaths while concentrating on blowing out the breaths provides an opportunity for thought processing and calming and relaxing self.

Play therapy materials should include only toys or objects conducive to self-expression. A wide variety of materials, including toys for aggressive or violent expression such as punching bags, plastic knives, plastic hammers, or blocks that may be thrown, facilitate expressiveness. However, when using aggressive types of toys, be sure to communicate the value of these toys with administrators who enforce zero-tolerance policies. A list of toys that may be included in initiating play in counseling is shown in Table 3.6.

The use of play is effective in individual as well as group counseling interventions, and play may bridge cultural differences that exist between the counselor and counselee, relieve stress among students as they transition to new academic settings, and improve self-esteem. These outcomes are associated with academic gains among students from diverse backgrounds.

Student Activity 3.6

Expressing Self through Games

Using Legos, blocks, or the Jenga game, the counselor and student take turns to make a tower. As each person places a block on the tower, a feeling statement is made, for instance: "I was upset when I got a D on my Language Arts quiz," or "I was frustrated when I wasn't able to understand the teacher's instructions." The game continues until the tower falls over.

Conceptual Application Activity 3.7

Observe a child playing. Make note of this child's developmental and chronological age. Note some of the actions exhibited by this child, and compare your observations with a partner's observations and notes. Discuss how you might use play in a counseling session with one of your students.

_____

_____

Music in a Counseling Setting

Music has been referred to as the "universal language" and is capable of producing a wide range of mental, emotional, physical, and/or spiritual responses (Gladding, 2016). Children are naturally active, and music provides an outlet for expressing themselves intuitively, yet with an emphasis on academics, the educational setting does not always emphasize music as a learning strategy.

Although school counselors are not able to use music as a counseling strategy without obtaining proper certification or licensure, counselors are able to use music as a method to

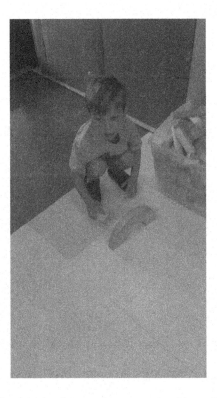

Figure 3.3 Some states credential school counselors to work with pre-K students. A variety of creative strategies are used to engage these young children.

engage students in the counseling process. Early childhood teachers have incorporated music activities into their programs to stimulate children's motor coordination and self-regulation, which are related to academic achievement and lifelong success (Blair and Raver, 2015, as cited in Williams, 2018).

School counselors are able to incorporate music in individual or group counseling as a means for listening and sharing feelings and thoughts about a piece of music in the form of writing lyrics, playing an instrument, singing, or sharing thoughts about the lyrics. In addition, music and song may be incorporated into elementary school counseling activities to enhance attentiveness, strengthen the social bond between the counselor and a group of children, and serve as a teaching aid to enhance coping during difficult life transitions such as parental divorce and relocation (Williams, 2018). At the middle and high school levels, music may be employed during classroom and group counseling programs to build rapport between peers, teachers, and the school counselor and student counselees.

Music has also been effective in treating conditions such as epilepsy (Brackney & Brooks, 2018), and to promote effective communication and social interactions (Eren, 2018), intellectual development, including literacy and mathematics, self-confidence, emotional sensitivity, and relaxation (Hallam, 2015, as cited in Lee, Krause, & Davidson, 2017).

Figure 3.4 Music in counseling may be utilized to create music, sing, move and listen. It is also a therapeutic means for facilitating communication without the use of words.

Source: Steve Martin Photography.

Student Activity 3.7

Expressing Myself through Music

Have students bring in a piece of music that "speaks to them." Play the music in a counseling group or in a group lesson. Ask students to listen to excerpts of the music and discuss the meaning behind the lyrics. If the music is instrumental with no lyrics, ask students what the music represents for them.

Conceptual Application Activity 3.8

Bring in music that has special meaning for you. Play the music in class, and talk about why the music you brought to class is meaningful to you. Describe how this music or song selection relates to your SCIT experience. How might you use a similar activity with students in your school?

_____

_____

Box 3.4

Additional Expressive Arts Techniques

Additional examples of using expressive arts in counseling include:

Drama—Create the family with handmade puppets and then act out a scene or issue to which the student relates.

Words—Take a meaningful quote and rewrite it, or write a short story and explore its personal meaning for the student.

Photography—Over the period of a week, ask the student to take digital snapshots of his/her environment or items/people of importance. Ask the student to bring the photos to a session to discuss.

Movement—Ask your student to show you how he/she feels with movement instead of words.

Conclusion

School counselors, faced with overwhelming responsibilities and demands, rarely have the luxury of 50-minute sessions considered routine by professionals in community and private settings. In addition, student counselees are often resistant to counseling because they are generally referred by parents or teachers rather than seeking assistance through self-referrals. In view of such conditions, the need arises for counseling methods that are time-effective, engaging, and effectual with school-aged youth. This chapter includes a brief overview of several counseling theories frequently employed in school settings which are generally time-limited, collaborative, and empowering. Furthermore, research suggests that these approaches lead to enhanced academic achievement and improved learning outcomes.

This chapter also contains information on expressive counseling techniques such as art, play, and music which are successful strategies used with students of all ages. School counselors are encouraged to develop an in-depth knowledge base of different counseling approaches, to select ideologies that appeal to themselves as practitioners within the schools, and to address the developmental and emotional needs of their counselees.

Websites

Cognitive Behavioral Approaches

- This link will provide you with information about Albert Ellis and his REBT approach: https://albertellis.org/about-albert-ellis-phd/
- This YouTube video will give you a glimpse of Albert Ellis providing "Gloria" with counseling using REBT: www.youtube.com/watch?v=tcq4RMzSyng
- Compare Ellis' counseling approach with that of Carl Rogers: www.youtube.com/watch?v=ee1bU4XuUyg

Music Therapy

- This website from the American Music Therapy Association provides answers to frequently asked questions about music therapy: www.musictherapy.org/faq/
- This YouTube shows music therapy in action: www.youtube.com/watch?v=ciubgEkE1i4

Narrative Therapy

- For more information on Narrative Therapy, including techniques, interventions, and worksheets, go to: https://positivepsychology.com/narrative-therapy/
- To watch an excerpt of Narrative Therapy, view this short YouTube clip: www.youtube.com/watch?v=gYaDrVp_DyI

Person-Centered Counseling

- This link is a classic case of a client "Gloria" who was counseled by Carl Rogers: www.youtube.com/watch?v=vG9zIHqJpB0
- A brief biography of Dr. Carl Rogers and his beliefs on the "Fully Functional Individual" can be found in this 2014 article by Saul McLeod: www.simplypsychology.org/carl-rogers.html

Play Therapy

- This link will take you to the homepage of the Association for Play Therapy. An overview of play therapy, and links to play therapy organizations can be found on this site: www.a4pt.org/page/PTMakesADifference/Play-Therapy-Makes-a-Difference.htm
- This link provides an explanation of Person-Centered Play Therapy and an explanation of techniques: www.youtube.com/watch?v=ZeLL6u4RGhc

Reality Therapy or Choice Theory

- This YouTube video portrays a description of Reality Therapy based on the philosophy of Dr. William Glasser: www.youtube.com/watch?v=OOo75EyKUC4
- For more information on the William Glasser International Organization, this website will provide you with resources and training institutes, as well as membership information: www.wglasserinternational.org

Solution-Focused Brief Therapy

- This link will take you to the Institute for Solution-Focused Therapy: https://solution focused.net/what-is-solution-focused-therapy/
- This short YouTube video shows Insoo Kim Berg providing counseling: www.youtube.com/watch?v=6Fe8D0hAQh0

Using Visual Arts in Counseling

- This link provides a scholarly article on the benefits of visual arts in the counseling setting: www.ncbi.nlm.nih.gov/pmc/articles/PMC5798551/

This link will take you to art therapy activities that you can adapt with school-aged youth: www.arttherapyblog.com/c/art-therapy-activities/#.U3UptS-F2v1

References

Banks, T. (2012). Rational emotive behavior therapy with diverse student populations: Meeting the mental health needs of all students. Retrieved from www.researchgate.net/publication/267777784_Rational_Emotive_Behavior_Therapy_with_Diverse_Student_Populations_Meeting_the_Mental_Health_Needs_of_All_Students

Barbeauld, P. H. (2014). "Don't say gay" bills and the movement to keep discussion of LBGT issues out of schools. *Journal of Law and Education, 43*, 137–146. Retrieved from www.questia.com/library/journal/1P3-3190445031/don-t-say-gay-bills-and-the-movement-to-keep-discussion

Brackney, D. E., & Brooks, J. L. (2018). Complementary and alternative medicine: The Mozart effect on childhood epilepsy—a systematic review. *Journal of School Nursing, 34*, 28–37. doi:10.1177/1059840517740940

Bray, B. (2017). Behind the book: The creative arts in counseling. *Counseling Today.* Retrieved from https://ct.counseling.org/2017/04/behind-book-creative-arts-counseling/#

Corey, G. (2017). *Theory and practice of counseling and psychotherapy* (10th ed.). Belmont, CA: Thomson Higher Education.

Davis, E. S., Flick, S., Mendez, P., & Urbina, B. (2018).Aggression in sessions: Strategies and interventions for school counselors. *Journal of School Counseling, 16.* EJ1185891.

deShazer, S. (1985). *Keys to solutions in brief therapy.* New York, NY: Norton.

Ellis, A. (1996). The humanism of rational emotive behavior therapy and other cognitive behavior therapies. *Journal of Humanistic Education and Development, 35*(69–88). EJ548738.

Ellis, A. (2004a). *Rational emotive behavior therapy: It works for me—it can work for you.* Amherst, NY: Prometheus.

Ellis, A. (2004b). *The road to tolerance: The philosophy of rational emotive behavior therapy.* Amherst, NY: Prometheus.

Eren, B. (2018). Teaching the skill of reading facial expressions to a child with autism using musical activities: A case study. *Journal of Education and Learning, 7*, 156–164. EJ1192371.

Finlay, G. (2011). Let's talk about solutions! *The Irish Journal of Adult and Community Education*, 99–109. EJ954306.

Frey, A. J., Cloud, R. N., Lee, J., Small, J. W., Seeley, J. R., Feil, E. G., … Golly, A. (2011). The promise of motivational interviewing in school mental health. *School Mental Health*, 3, 1–12. doi:10.1007/s12310–010–9048

Gladding, S. (2016). *The creative arts in counseling* (5th ed.). Alexandria, VA: American Counseling Association.

Goldner, L., Sachar, S., & Abir, A. (2018). Adolescents' rejection sensitivity as manifested in their self-drawings. *Art Therapy Journal of the American Art Therapy Association*, 35, 25–34.

Guterman, J. T. (2006). *Mastering the art of solution-focused counseling*. Alexandria, VA: American Counseling Association.

Kolbert, J. B., Happe, B. L., Hyatt-Burkhart, D., Crothers, L. M., & Capuzzi, M. (2017). Motivational interviewing, the transtheoretical model of change, and academic development. *Journal of School Counseling*, 15, 1–30.

Lee, J., Krause, A. E., & Davidson, J. W. (2017). The PERMA well-being model and music facilitation practice: Preliminary documentation for well-being through music provision in Australian schools. *Research Studies in Music Education*, 39, 73–89. doi:10.1177/1321103X17703131

Leggett, E. S. (2009). A creative application of solution-focused counseling: An integration with children's literature and visual arts. *Journal of Creativity in Mental Health*, 4, 191–200. doi:10.1080/15401380902945269

Montgomery, A. (2018). Anxiety reduction drawing activities in secondary education. ED585255. Retrieved from https://files.eric.ed.gov/fulltext/ED585255.pdf

Ohio Legislature. (2019). House Bill 658. Retrieved from www.legislature.ohio.gov/legislation/legislation-summary?id=GA132-HB-658

Schweizer, C., Spreen, M., & Knorth, E. J. (2017). Exploring what works in art therapy with children with autism: Tacit knowledge of art therapists. *Art Therapy: Journal of the American Art Therapy Association*, 34, 183–191. EJ1169555.

Seligman, L., & Reichenberg, L. W. (2014). *Theories of counseling and psychotherapy* (4th ed.). Upper Saddle River, NJ: Pearson.

Sharf, R. (2016). *Theories of psychotherapy and counseling: Concepts and cases*. Boston, MA: Cengage.

Sheldon, L. A. (2010, Fall). Using motivational interviewing to help your students. *Thought & Action*, 153–158.

Swank, J. M., Cheung, C., & Williams, S. A. (2018). Play therapy and psychoeducational school-based group interventions: A comparison of treatment effectiveness. *The Journal for Specialists in Group Work*, 43, 230–249. doi:10.1080/01933922.2018.1485801

Trepper, T. S., Dolan, Y., McCollum, E. E., & Nelson, T. (2006). Steve deShazer and the future of solution-focused therapy. *Journal of Marital and Family Therapy*, 32, 133–139. doi:10.1111/j.1752-0606.2006.tb01595.x

Trice-Black, S., Bailey, C. L., & Riechel, M. E. K. (2013). Play therapy in school counseling. *Professional School Counseling*, 16, 303–312. doi:10.5330/PSC.n.2013-16.303

Wang, G., & Kim, Y. (2019). A case study on the collage art therapy for immigrant youths. *Education and Information Technologies*, 24, 1115–1129.

Warren, J. M., & Hale, R. W. (2016). Underrepresented students through rational emotive behavior therapy: Recommendations for school counselor practice. *The Professional Counselor*, 6, 89–106. doi:10.15241/jw.6.1.89

Wedding, D., Corsini, R. J., & Wedding, D. (2019). *Current psychotherapies* (11th ed.). Belmont, CA: Brooks/Cole.

White, M. (1993). Deconstruction and therapy. In S. Gilligan & R. Price (Eds.), *Therapeutic conversations* (pp. 23–51). New York, NY: Norton.

White, M. (1995). *Re-authoring lives: Interviews and essays*. Adelaide, South Australia: Dulwich Center.

Williams, K. E. (2018). Moving to the beat: Using music, rhythm, and movement to enhance self-regulation in early childhood classrooms. *International Journal of Early Childhood, 36*, 85–100. EJ1174147.

Wubbolding, R. E., Casstevens, W. J., & Fulkerson, M. H. (2017). Using the WDEP system of reality therapy to support person-centered treatment planning. *Journal of Counseling & Development, 95*, 472–477. doi:10.1002/jcad.12162

4 An Overview of Supervisory Practices

Aaron H. Oberman and Jeannine R. Studer

CACREP Standards

2. Contextual Dimensions

a. school counselor roles as leaders, advocates, and systems change agents in P-12 schools

3. Practice

h. skills to critically examine the connections between social, familial, emotional, and behavior problems and academic achievement

Chapter Objectives:

* assess personal readiness for supervision
* assist in setting supervision goals
* provide strategies for personal wellness
* discuss technology in counseling and supervision

Introduction

Supervision is considered a vital key to successful practicum and internship experiences, and provides an opportunity for the SCIT to connect counseling skills learned in the classroom to authentically address K–12 student needs (Swank & Tyson, 2012). Furthermore, SCIT state that their clinical experiences are the most influential and beneficial aspect of their academic training. Therefore, practicum and internship supervision conducted by a professional school counselor who has had training in supervision and experience as a school counselor is critically important. As mentioned in Chapter 1, you may have the opportunity to choose your own supervisor, or the program placement coordinator may select a site supervisor for you. This placement will be based on the coordinator's knowledge of the school site counseling program, and the supervisor's ability to supervise, philosophy of school counseling, and willingness to meet with you on a regular basis. In either case, you need to discuss your personal and professional goals with your placement coordinator to address any needs you may have. For example, there are some students who had transportation difficulties, and finding a quality school site which trainees were able to access via public transport helped address their needs. Once a supervisor is identified, meeting with this individual and learning about the school is an essential first step. The information and activities in this chapter are designed to assist you in thinking about the process of supervision under the watchful eyes of an experienced professional. Making an initial contact with your supervisor, appropriate dress, understanding school policies and procedures, and methods for introducing yourself to the individuals with whom you will work are included in this chapter.

Making the Initial Contact

Remember that you are a guest in the school. Once you have been assigned to a supervisor, making a contact is an essential first step. This contact can be conducted through a phone call or email exchange with the supervisor, and because it makes a lasting impression, you want it to be a good one. If you make a phone call, be certain that you speak slowly and clearly. There is nothing more frustrating than receiving contact information that is given so quickly that a message needs to be replayed several times before accurate information can be understood. Keep in mind that many school counselors are difficult to reach due to their varied schedules and the number of schools to which many are assigned. Therefore, sending a clear, well-crafted, and error-free email may be a better option (refer to Figure 4.1). When you have scheduled an appointment time, be sure to dress professionally and arrive on time. Be aware that with school safety policies in place, many schools have only one entrance, which is often locked. Entry is often gained after ringing a bell and speaking into an intercom to announce the purpose of your visit. Once you gain entry, reporting to the main office, signing in, and receiving a name badge are common procedures. In addition, stopping by the main office once you have completed your visit to sign out is also common procedure.

Subject: Practicum/Internship Meeting:

Dear (Ms./Mrs./Mr./Dr. Last Name of Supervisor):

I am writing to schedule an appointment with you to discuss and plan my practicum (or internship) experience with you this coming semester at (name of school). I am a master's degree school counseling student enrolled at (name of school/institution). My faculty supervisor's contact information is

Name
Title
Telephone numbers
Email

I am available to meet you at your school, in your office at the following dates and times: (Provide at least three different dates and times).

I will bring my resume, proof of liability insurance, my professional disclosure statement, and the program practicum/internship handbook for your records. Please contact me if there is anything else I should bring to our initial meeting. I look forward to meeting you and conducting my practicum (or internship) under your direct supervision.

Sincerely,

(Your full name)
(Phone number and email)

Figure 4.1 Sample initial email to site supervisor.

Dress

The school is a professional setting, and the attire you are accustomed to wearing in the classroom as a graduate student may not be acceptable in a pre-K–12 school environment. If you are unsure how to dress, it is better to dress up rather than face embarrassment if you are sent home to change clothes due to your inappropriate attire. Unfortunately, there have been incidents when supervisees who were inappropriately dressed in revealing clothing were sent home by the school principal to change into more modest and professional attire. A nonprofessional look may include such things as visible tattoos and body piercings, open-toed sandals, flip-flops, shorts, jeans, revealing blouses, T-shirts, shirts with slogans, and short skirts. In fact, one principal told a trainee that he was expected to cover up all of his tattoos if he wanted to work in the school. Workplace dress and hygiene policies have been established to promote a productive work environment and enhance the institutional image (Brannen, 2014). You are an adult role model to pre-K–12 students, and your appearance and behavior influence the lives of school-aged youth more than you may realize.

Each practicum and internship school is unique, and the dress code reflects the mission of each school. Some schools have a uniform policy, and educational personnel are required to dress according to this procedure. Discuss the dress requirements with your site supervisor during your initial meeting.

Absences, Tardiness, and Attendance

Even though you are not being paid during your practicum and internship, you still need to act as if you were an employee of the school. When you leave the confines of the academic institution and enter the school setting, you are in direct contact with your future colleagues and potential employers. In fact, you may desire a job in the school in which you conduct your practicum or internship experience.

Ask your supervisor about the procedures for reporting absences or tardiness. Anytime you suspect that you may be tardy or absent, immediately contact your site supervisor and inform him or her of your circumstances (this is especially easy if you have stored your supervisor's telephone number on your cell phone). However, occasionally mishaps occur. When you communicate with your site supervisor, do not make excuses. Briefly inform him or her of the facts, own your responsibility in causing the tardiness or absenteeism, state that it will not happen again, and move on.

Attendance is another professional responsibility. Keep in mind that the school calendar is often different than the academic calendar where you are enrolled as a school counseling student. For liability reasons, many programs are reluctant to allow their students to start or end their clinical experiences in a K–12 school building when their own training institution is not in session. Other programs recognize the importance of being in the school when the school year begins or ends, and as a result allow supervisees to observe in their assigned school and accumulate indirect hours until their university/college program begins. Check with your faculty supervisor as to when you are able to begin this experience.

School Policies and Procedures

Before beginning your practicum or internship, familiarize yourself with the school policies and procedures. Ask for a faculty handbook that outlines such things as the dress code, the schedule, the policy for excusing students from class, the academic calendar, grading policy, and a listing of the resources and personnel in the school. In addition, some schools also require personnel to wear identification in the form of a lanyard. Check with your site supervisor to see whether this is something you will need and how to obtain one. In addition, most school systems are requiring individuals to have a background check and drug screen tests before they are able to enter the schools. Verify whether you will need to have these tests. Furthermore, with increased pressure for students to demonstrate academic achievement, and educators held accountable for their growth, teachers are often reluctant to release students from their classes to meet with you. To create and maintain a positive working relationship with each teacher, be sure to confirm the best times to release students, the procedures for excusing them, and the policy for returning students to class. Also, communicate to the teacher and students that missing classroom time to meet with you does not excuse the student from missed work or information.

Introducing Yourself to the Students, Staff, and Parents

The various stakeholders with whom you will be working are often hesitant to release a child or adolescent to someone who is unknown to them. Arrange for a time to meet and introduce yourself to each of these constituents. Faculty meetings provide an opportune time to meet with the faculty and staff and to provide your credentials and information about yourself and how you may be reached. In addition, Parent Teacher Student Association (PTSA) meetings are an excellent opportunity to introduce yourself to parents/guardians. Bringing a professional disclosure statement to be distributed to faculty and parents/guardians is one strategy to help them get to know you better. This document should include a description of the clinical course in which you are enrolled, your education, your experiences related to counseling, the names of your supervisors (both site and program), your professional membership, the nature of your counseling or philosophy, and a statement regarding confidentiality. An example is shown in Figure 4.2.

Erin Mavredakis
8534 College Avenue
City, State, Zip
Cell Phone
Email

Education

MS in School Counseling—anticipated date of graduation 2020
The University of the Smokies

BA Psychology 2016
The College of the Pines

Clinical Experiences

James Anderson Elementary—Practicum
    Supervisor—Ellen Woods

Holston Middle School—Internship
   Supervisor—Nancy Keller
Bloom High School—Internship
   Supervisor—Jeff Steckel

Work Experience

Waitress at Kitchen Chef Restaurant, Winnebago, Illinois 2012–present

Philosophy of Counseling

I adhere to a cognitive-behavioral approach to counseling, and I believe that all individuals have the ability to set goals and make decisions that positively impact their lives. I also believe that school counselors enhance education of all students in academics, career decisions, and social/emotional growth.

Professional Memberships

American School Counselor Association (ASCA)
State School Counseling Association

Professional Code of Ethics

I abide by the American School Counselor Association Code of Ethics and the guidelines that are established by the school board of education.

Contact Information

I will be available during my internship on Monday, Wednesday, and Friday from 8:00–3:30 throughout the semester. Please feel free to contact me if you have any questions or concerns, or my campus clinical supervisor_____, or my site supervisor

Signature_____   Date _____

Figure 4.2 Critical components of a professional disclosure statement.

Conceptual Application Activity 4.1

Develop your professional disclosure statement by following the sample below:

1. Name and contact information

2. Education and training

   _____

3. Work experiences

   _____

4. Names of supervisors

   _____

5. Nature of counseling/philosophy

   _____

6. Professional memberships

   _____

7. Professional code of ethics

   _____

8. Hours and days available

   _____

You will also need a plan for meeting with students to introduce yourself and explain your role in the school and how you can be contacted. When students know who you are, they are more willing to work with you. Your site supervisors can help make arrangements for you to meet students, which may include arranging a time with teachers to enter the classroom to introduce yourself. The introduction needs to be based on the age of the students and their level of understanding. For younger students, simple terminology and creativity help to keep their attention and assist in helping them remember you and your role. Several other strategies include:

1. Stand in the hallways when students are changing classes and introduce yourself as they pass by in the halls. Shake their hands and tell them who you are and how they can contact you.
2. Post a brightly colored paper with your photograph explaining who you are, days and times when you are available, where you are located, and how you can be contacted.
3. Make up business cards so that older students or adults can put them in their wallets or purses. Include your name, contact information, and where you can be reached. The website www.youprint.com/ allows you to create your own customized business cards.
4. Attend extracurricular activities. Students appreciate your attendance, and you will have an opportunity to understand different aspects of the school environment.
5. Eat lunch in the cafeteria, and sit with groups of students to learn their names and interests and to provide an opportunity for the students to get to know you.
6. Post your information on the school website.
7. For younger students, design a crossword puzzle that includes keywords such as your name, what you do, where you can be reached, and so forth. There are several online resources available for quickly and easily creating crossword puzzles. You simply need to identify key words, then supply a clue for each word. Computer programs can automatically create a crossword puzzle from these key words and clues. A few websites that help create crossword puzzles include: www.crosswordpuzzlegames.com, www.armoredpenguin.com/crossword/, and www.eclipsecrossword.com/.

Conceptual Application Activity 4.2

With your peers, brainstorm other ways that you could introduce yourself to parents, students, and teachers.

_____

_____

Self-reflection of Readiness for Supervision

The purpose of practicum and internship is to build your school counseling knowledge, skills, and values through application of theory in a real work setting. Too often, SCITs look at these experiences as "something that has to be done to fulfill the degree requirements." If this statement reflects your thinking, you may need to reconsider your decision to enter the school counseling profession, because this profession requires passion with the potential to positively impact the lives of numerous children. Clinical experiences are designed to help you become an excellent school counselor, and it is up to you to use these opportunities to help yourself grow personally and professionally.

Research indicates that factors such as the counselor's age, gender, education, and personality influence the counseling process (Reupert, 2006). Although these elements are important, it is the relationship between the counselor and counselee that is considered the most essential factor (Reupert, 2006) impacting counselee growth. This leads to the questions, "What are other factors that promote an effective counseling session?" and "What are the qualities that are essential to be an effective counselor?" As stated by Jeffrey Kottler, "The process is far too mysterious and complex to ever get a handle on all the nuances of [counseling]" (Shallcross, 2012). Several expert counselors provide their view of effective counselors and counseling, with responses including those shown in Table 4.1.

Table 4.1 Attributes of effective counselors.

Understanding	Genuineness	Trustworthiness
Committed	Risk-taking	Tolerance
Flexibility	Unbiased	Congruence
Empathy	Authentic	Unconditional regard
Advocacy	Courage	Authenticity
Ability to listen	Compassion	Interpersonal skills
Patience	Creativity	Humility
Self-awareness	Sense of humor	Trust
Empathy	Willingness to learn	Compassion
Rapport	Insight	Respectful
Nonverbal skills	Trust	Collaborative
Nonverbal	Competence	Commitment
Encouragement	Appropriate	Self-confidence
Self-honesty	Motivated	Consistent
Forgiveness	Perception	

Conceptual Application Activity 4.3

Are there additional personal qualities an effective counselor should have other than those above? Write your responses below.

_____   _____   _____
_____   _____   _____
_____   _____   _____

Now compare your list with your peers. What are some of the similarities and differences?

_____
_____

Conceptual Application Activity 4.4

Counseling experts have identified qualities that they believe are essential for effective counselors. These characteristics are listed below. Circle those you believe define who you are. When you are finished, give this list to someone who knows you well, and ask that person to circle those qualities that they believe apply to you.

Understanding	Genuineness	Tolerance
Committed	Risk-taking	Congruence
Flexibility	Unbiased	Unconditional regard
Empathy	Authentic	Authenticity
Advocacy	Courage	Interpersonal skills
Ability to listen	Compassion	Humility
Patience	Creativity	Trust
Self-awareness	Sense of humor	Compassion
Empathy	Willingness to learn	Respectful
Rapport	Insight	Collaborative
Nonverbal skills	Trust	Commitment
Nonverbal	Competence	Self-confidence
Encouragement	Appropriate	Motivated
Self-honesty	Perception	Consistent
Forgiveness	Trustworthiness	

Now compare your list with the list provided by your significant other person and discuss the similarities and differences between the two lists. If there are discrepancies between your view of yourself and the perceptions of that other person, discuss the different perceptions. Recognizing your strengths and areas in which you need to improve gives you an opportunity to identify personal goals for your practicum and internship experiences. Include these goals on your practicum and/or internship contract and strategies to reach these objectives.

Goal-Setting

When you have a good understanding of the practicum and internship experiences, you are less likely to be disappointed. Likewise, the supervisor also needs a thorough understanding of the clinical experience and his or her role in supervision. Not everyone enters the clinical experiences with the same training or education. For instance, those with a background in education usually have a better knowledge of such things as the school structure, policies, educational terminology, and classroom management. Those who have a human services background may have a better understanding of the counseling process and application of theories and techniques.

After you have thought about your strengths and areas in which you need more experience, gather ideas from the counselors at your school site to determine specific projects you could accomplish to meet your goals as well as those that would address curricular school needs. Some examples include updating and formalizing the school critical incident management plan, creating a resource appendix for college scholarships, collecting community agency information for referral purposes, and implementing a group for students from divorced parental homes. A contract that outlines the expect-ations for the supervisory relationship and the activities you are to perform is essential. The contract, then, serves as a type of "job description" that outlines what you are going to do.

The American School Counselor Association promotes a comprehensive school coun-seling (CSC) program. The Mindsets and Behaviors for Student Success outline the knowledge and skills that pre-K–12 students are to know and practice in the academic, career, and social/emotional domains. The standards serve as a foundation for the ASCA National Model that was developed as a prototype for school counselors to use when developing their own programs (ASCA, 2019). However, many school counseling programs have not yet made the transformation to a comprehensive school counseling program. Even if you are assigned to a school with a traditional school counseling pro-gram, many activities the counselor/supervisor performs are still reflective of those in the ASCA National Model. It is up to you to identify the activities that support a CSC program during your clinical experiences in order to be prepared to take a leadership role in developing such a program when you transition into a position as a school counselor.

The following story illustrates one example of how a school counseling intern contributed to the school through a public relations activity that is a component of the management element of the ASCA National Model.

Elsa was in her internship experience at an inner-city middle school in which approxi-mately 58% of the students were on free and reduced lunch. There was a strong need to assist students with academics, and Elsa decided that she would conduct a weekly study skills group for seventh- and eighth-graders for the semester that she was in her school site. Figure 4.3 illustrates the gains several of the students made in their GPA from the beginning of the semester until the completion of the group. Elsa's concrete documentation revealed to teachers that she was a contributing member of the school, and they asked her site supervisor to have future interns continue this project.

An example of personal and professional goals that are included on an internship contract based on the ASCA Model is shown in Figure 4.4.

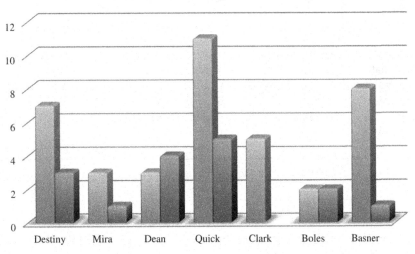

2nd to 3rd Term Changes in Student GPA

Destiny Mira Dean Quick Clark Boles Basner

▪ Number of Students with Increased GPA   ▪ Number of Students with Decreased GPA

Figure 4.3 An example of a chart that represents student growth as a result of a group intervention based on classrooms of students.

Sample Goals

Professional goal	Performance activities	Evaluation	ASCA component
The intern will develop, distribute, and analyze a needs assessment	1. Design a needs assessment for seventh-grade students 2. Administer the needs assessment 3. Analyze and design a graph to reveal results	Feedback from site supervisor	Manage
The intern will conduct a small group	1. Organize and lead a small group for eighth-grade students based on needs assessment	Results of group assessment Feedback from site supervisor	Deliver

Figure 4.4 Sample internship contract.

The school counseling faculty promote a comprehensive school counseling program as outlined by the ASCA National Model, and request that the activities provided to the school counselor intern correspond with this model. The Mindsets and Behaviors for Student Success were developed for pre-K–12 students, and school counselors perform activities that meet these standards and those identified within the school curriculum. The intern is expected to perform identified activities within the components of the ASCA National Model to learn about his/her role. Goals, activities, evaluation, and the corresponding components are outlined in the contract.

Conceptual Application Activity 4.5

Review the ASCA National Model in Chapter 6, Figure 6.1. In consultation with the program supervisor and your on-site school counseling supervisor, identify professional and personal goals you wish to accomplish during your practicum and internship experiences. When you think about the activities to include on your contract, be sure they are supported in a CSC program.

Supervisory Contract (to be completed by intern with assistance from supervisors)

Professional goal	Performance activities	Evaluation	ASCA program component/section

Personal goal	Performance activities	Evaluation	ASCA program component/section

Table 4.2 The ASCA National Model components and sections.

Define	Manage	Deliver	Assess
Student Standards ASCA Mindsets and Behaviors for Student Success	**Program Focus** Beliefs, Vision, and Mission Statements	**Direct Student Services** Instruction	**Program Assessment** School Counseling Program Assessment Template
Professional Standards ASCA Ethical Standards for School Counselors ASCA School Counselor Professional Standards Competencies	**Program Planning** Data *Participation Mindsets and Behaviors Outcome*	**Direct Student Services** Appraisal and Advisement	*Program Assessment Annual Results Reports Classroom and Group Mindsets and Behaviors Results Report Analysis Closing the Gap Results Reports Analysis*
	Program Planning Annual Data Review	**Direct Student Services** Counseling	**Program Assessment** Data Over Time
	Program Planning School Data Summary	**Indirect Student Services** Referrals, Consultation, Collaboration	**Program Assessment** Reporting Program Results

(Continued)

Table 4.2 (Cont.)

Define	Manage	Deliver	Assess
	Program Planning Annual Student Outcome Goals		**School Counselor Assessment and Appraisal** ASCA School Counselor Professional Standards Competencies Assessment
	Program Planning Action Plans *Classroom and Group Mindsets and Behaviors Action Plan* *Closing the Gap Action Plan/Results Report* **Program Planning** Lesson Plans **Program Planning** Calendars *Annual Calendar Template* *Weekly Calendar Template* **Program Planning** Annual Administrative Conference **Program Planning** Use-of-Time Calculator **Program Planning** Advisory Council		**School Counselor Assessment and Appraisal** School Counselor Performance Appraisal Template

---

Box 4.1

Practicing school counselor supervisors were surveyed to investigate the factors that exemplify effective supervision. Seven themes emerged from their responses. Good school counseling supervision: (1) facilitates the intern's professional growth and development; (2) enables a collaborative relationship between the supervisor, intern, and stakeholders; (3) establishes a learning environment that is flexible and well defined; (4) provides opportunities based on the intern's developmental level; (5) is based on the supervisor serving as a consultant, teacher, and counselor; (6) is provided by a self-aware, reflective supervisor; and (7) provides opportunities to gain a school counselor identity (Ladbury, 2012).

A personal safety plan is another preparation strategy. You may be placed in a school setting that is located in what is regarded as a high-crime area, but regardless of where your school site is located, a personal safety plan is an important consideration. Ask your supervisor to share the school crisis plan with you, and ask him/her to assist you in creating your own plan.

Personal Safety Plan

No one enters the school counseling profession thinking in terms of school violence, but the threat of violence is very real in schools today. Some school-aged youth could pose a threat to your safety as well as others. We once had a graduate student in our school counseling program who grew up in a small, upper-middle-class suburban area of Ohio that was characterized as fairly homogeneous and "safe." He attended a small liberal arts college with a student body similar to that of his high school. When he found out he was placed in an urban high school for his practicum, he was concerned about his safety and immediately sought out the program placement coordinator to request a different setting. He was instructed to talk with his site supervisor about the school safety plan and to ask for assistance in making up his own personal safety plan. Reluctantly, he agreed to do this. After only a week, he began to speak enthusiastically about his practicum school and relayed how much he was learning from this unique experience. Eventually, he actually thanked his placement coordinator for not transferring him to a different site, and after graduation he secured a position as a school counselor in an urban middle school. No school is exempt from school violence, and personal well-being is of utmost importance.

Most schools have adopted a policy that specifies procedures for alerting teachers and faculty when an emergency occurs. This plan outlines the action each person is to take, including the school counselor's crisis management responsibilities. Every person who works in the school should know how to implement the plan, and you are no exception. In fact, it is possible that you will be a key player in crisis intervention if a crisis plan needs to be activated. Consider the following:

- When you are working with a student who is angry, keep the office door open and ask your supervisor to sit in on the session.
- If your supervisor is not available, it may be best to speak with an angry student in the hall or waiting area if there is one available.
- Look for signs of mounting tension, irritability, and so forth. When potential violence is evident, ask the student to discuss his or her feelings, because verbalizations are better than violently acting out emotions.
- Speak in a calm, quiet voice to calm the student.
- Park in a well-lit area in the parking lot.
- Leave the school building with another person.
- Leave expensive jewelry and clothing at home.

Conceptual Application Activity 4.6

Read the school safety plan at your clinical site and compare this plan with those of your peers. Develop your own safety plan.

Wellness as an Integral Component of the Profession

Wellness is a foundation of the counseling profession. Helping students become healthy entails an integration of mind, body, and spirit (Meyers, 2014), yet it also requires us to be take care of ourselves if we are going to be effective as helpers. A study by Lawson and Myers (2011) examined levels of wellness among counselors who were members of ACA who reported activities that helped them sustain personal wellness. Wellness activities included:

- spending time with partner/family
- maintaining a sense of humor
- maintaining a balance between professional and personal lives
- maintaining self-awareness
- reflecting on positive experiences
- engaging in quiet leisure activities

Conceptual Application Activity 4.7

List five stressful situations you have encountered in the past year. Now list specific ways you attempted to manage each stressful situation.

Situation	Stress Management Strategies

Put a plus (+) in front of the strategies that are positive or healthy and bring about constructive results. Put a minus (–) next to those strategies that are negative or bring about unhelpful consequences. How successful are the strategies you use? If you note a number of unhelpful strategies, it is time to try some new ways of managing your stress. Be sure to share your list with your peers and listen carefully as they share their strategies that help them handle difficult situations.

Self-care

Listening to students' stories of pain from deleterious life experiences can eventually impair the ability of school counselors to provide effective care to others and to themselves (Ray, Wong, White, & Heaslip, 2013). A national survey that examined counselor wellness and results indicated that school counselors experienced more compassion fatigue and burnout compared with counselors working in private practice (Lawson, 2007, as cited in Todd & Chehaib, 2019). Compassion fatigue (CF) may result when a caregiver is preoccupied with distressed students and experiences stress and tension (Ray et al., 2013) due to a connection with the counselee's trauma. Although CF is similar to burnout, CF is related to the student's trauma, whereas burnout, considered as a risk factor for developing CF, is related to the work environment. CF leads to a sense of helplessness, isolation from others who could serve as sources of support, and an inability to empathize with others (Injeyan et al., 2011). School counselors in particular are at risk for burnout and compassion fatigue due to administrator requests that include non-counseling related duties, large caseloads, working in schools that did not meet their adequate yearly progress, a lack of adequate supervision, insufficient resources, and providing fewer direct student services. In addition to these demands, paperwork, parental conferences, and testing responsibilities contributed to their stress in the schools (Kim & Lambie, 2018).

In a study of secondary school counselors, participants reported difficulty in separating personal from professional life, difficulty sleeping, recurring dreams about work, headaches, weight gain, and fatigue—all indicators of burnout (Wall, 2004). Increased levels of stress lead to physical, emotional, and intellectual difficulties that may result in poor performance and negative feelings among school personnel (Wilkerson & Bellini, 2006). Some of the warning signs of CF or burnout include:

- isolating self from family and friends
- difficulty in being emotionally engaged in relationships
- increased absenteeism
- Decreased empathy and social skills
- increased self-obsession
- rejecting professional responsibilities to others (Williams, 2007)

In your internship, you will be performing many school counselor activities, and as in starting any new job, this requires learning and experiencing various responsibilities in short periods of time. On top of these stressors, many supervisees continue to take additional classes while in their clinical courses, and some even choose to be employed. This makes for a full and demanding schedule. Furthermore, there is the added responsibility of forming new relationships with those at the school, and with parents and community members. Taking care of yourself is vital, and devoting time to ensure physical, emotional, and psychological health is important or your performance could be negatively impaired. The following suggestions are provided to assist in alleviating burnout and compassion fatigue (Paine, 2009):

- Know what you are able to handle.
- Recognize triggers of stress.
- Recognize your own experiences with trauma and how it could interfere with your effectiveness.
- Recognize your physiological symptoms of stress.
- Connect with supportive family and friends.
- Eat healthy foods.
- Try to get restful sleep without the use of sleep aids.
- Maintain your regular routine as much as possible.
- Ask for assistance from others.
- Practice the following:
  - meditation
  - mindfulness techniques
  - exercise
  - massage
  - biofeedback
  - listening to music
  - engaging in enjoyable activities
  - journaling
  - yoga

Box 4.2

School counselors have unique roles in the school which enable them to promote wellness. Yet, school counselors experience emotional exhaustion due to feelings of detachment from other educational personnel, lack of positive feedback from administrators, and few opportunities for professional development. This dissatisfaction results in reduced productivity.

Source: (Mathews, 2013)

The Use of Technology in Counseling and Supervision

Practicing school counselors depend on computers to be more effective on the job, and awareness of the different types of technology used by school counselors will be beneficial to you as you enter your clinical experiences. However, it is wise to balance any temptation to become technology-dependent. For example, Carlson, Portman, and Bartlett (2006) warn counselors who rely on email communication that they may miss opportunities for instrumental face-to-face communication that are necessary for developing trust and rapport in counseling relationships.

Counselors use technology for such tasks as (1) creating and storing student information, (2) tracking courses, (3) developing schedules, (4) disseminating career information, (5) providing greater visibility of the school counseling program, (6) creating websites and sending/receiving email, and (7) administering tests. Internet convenience is also helpful when counselors want to assist teachers and parents to develop an awareness of cyberbullying (also known as harassment, intimidation, or threats) or sexting by providing links to credible Internet resources.

Computers can also assist in finding accessible professional development opportunities. By joining an electronic mailing list (or listserv), such as SCENE provided by the ASCA, discussion board questions can be posted to which numerous school counseling professionals can respond. This format is also useful for identifying professional concerns from archived questions and responses. However, even an electronic mailing list poses challenges. Almost anyone can join an electronic mailing list, so empirically based and accurate responses are not always provided. You are professionally responsible to take reasonable steps to ensure that the information you receive and disseminate is sound and valid.

Counselors also use computers to accommodate students with disabilities. For instance, for a student with impaired vision, software can translate written words to spoken text. For a student with a hearing loss, verbal instructions can be converted to text. And for a student with a fine motor physical disability, a touch screen may be a helpful accommodation.

School counselors were surveyed to determine the technology competencies considered most important to their job (Sabella, Poynton, & Isaacs, 2010). Ethical and legal knowledge of technology was considered most important, with data management skills considered the second most important item. With the need to prove effectiveness, it is not surprising that the use of technology to track data was ranked as important, since monitoring data on student progress, making decisions, and advocating for students and the program are essential school counselor tasks.

A study was conducted to examine the content of school counseling program website information, and based on this analysis, school counselors were not making good use of the website as a means of transmitting information. Furthermore, the researchers discovered that a majority

Figure 4.5 Using online resources. When working with students on web searches, school counselors are aware of website evaluative criteria that answer the questions, Who? (is the author or sponsor), What? (is the purpose of this site and the qualifications of the author or publisher), When? (was the website published or revised), Where? (can you find the author or publisher), Why? (was the website published), and How? (accurate or current is the information or citations).

Source: Shutterstock

of the school counselors who did have website availability still referred to themselves as "guidance counselors" rather than professional school counselors (Milsom & Bryant, 2006).

As a SCIT, you may have better technology skills than your supervisor, including the ability to build a website. Your technology skills may provide an opportunity for you to contribute to your school site by introducing current software or teaching your supervisor basic technology skills to make cumbersome tasks more manageable. For example, you could educate your supervisor about technology such as EZAnalyze, a free tool designed to analyze data and create graphs, or TimeTracker, a tool that school counselors use to show where time is spent and to generate reports (both can be found at www.ezanalyze.com/).

You may find that technology is also being used in supervision. Program supervisors may have difficulty making on-site visits to schools in rural communities or in areas located a considerable distance from the school counseling training program. Instead, synchronous supervision and consultation with the site supervisor may need to occur through a video call on Skype or FaceTime. This type of supervision challenges contemporary thought about how supervision can be conducted, particularly in regard to issues of confidentiality and the possibility of misinterpreting messages (McAdams & Wyatt, 2010).

Conceptual Application Activity 4.8

List six different forms of technology you use every day. Now identify one possible method for which this technology could be used in a school counseling program. Compare your list with your peers' lists.

Form of Technology	Skills	Use in School
_____	_____	_____
_____	_____	_____
_____	_____	_____

Although there are many advantages to technology, these are accompanied by safety and ethical concerns, such as awareness of antivirus software to prevent malicious computer viruses from infecting and damaging data files. Additionally, installing and updating security software to keep others from accessing computer-stored confidential records is a must.

Conclusion

This chapter provides essential information as you are preparing for your clinical experiences. Advance preparation assists in making these new opportunities less stressful. Identifying and starting activities such as contacting your site supervisor and learning about the school policies and procedures, attendance policy, crisis plan, and personal safety plans will provide you with an orientation to help you gain a better understanding of expectations. In addition, once you have a better understanding of the school's needs, you can develop a contract that is aligned with the ASCA National Model for a better understanding of how a school counselor assumes a leadership role in a CDSC program.

With wellness as a basic construct of the counseling profession, you have a responsibility to practice and model healthful living for the students and stakeholders with whom you work. Supervision is an ideal time to learn about your role as a professional school counselor and leader of a CDSC program. Observe, learn, practice, and self-reflect on your fit within the profession and how your skills can make a difference in the lives of others.

Website

- ASCA SCENE: https://scene.schoolcounselor.org/home

This is a professional networking site where you are able to pose questions, provide answers to questions asked by other professionals, and become part of a discussion group. In addition, you can receive forms, lesson plans, and other professional materials. You must be a member of ASCA to receive this information.

References

ASCA. (2019). *ASCA National Model: A framework for school counseling programs* (4th ed.). Alexandria, VA: ASCA.

Brannen, A. D. (2014, February 14). *United States: A few guidelines for appearance policies.* Retrieved from www.mondaq.com/unitedstates/x/293060/employee+rights+labour+relations/A+Few+Guidelines+For+Appearance+Policies

Carlson, L. A., Portman, T. A. A., & Bartlett, J. R. (2006). Professional school counselors' approaches to technology. *Professional School Counseling, 9*, 252–256.

Injeyan, M. C., Shuman, C., Shugar, A., Chitayat, D., Atenafu, E. G., & Kaiser, A. (2011). Personality traits associated with genetic counselor compassion fatigue: The roles of dispositional optimism and locus of control. *Journal of Genetic Counseling, 20*, 526–540. doi:10.1007/s10897-011-9379-4

Kim, N., & Lambie, G. W. (2018). Burnout and implications for professional school counselors. *The Professional Counselor, 8*(3), 277–294. doi:10.15241/nk.8.3.277

Ladbury, J. L. S. (2012). *School counseling supervision: A qualitative summary from the perspective of school counseling site-supervisors.* (Doctoral dissertation). Retrieved from ProQuest (UMI 3523989).

Lawson, G., & Myers, J. E. (2011). Wellness, professional quality of life, and career-sustaining behaviors: What keeps us well? *Journal of Counseling & Development, 89*, 163–171.

Mathews, T. F. (2013). *The school counselors' description of their experiences of emotional exhaustion: A phenomenological study.* (Doctoral dissertation). Available from ProQuest Dissertations and Theses database (AAI3553926).

McAdams, C. R., & Wyatt, K. L. (2010). The regulation of technology-assisted distance counseling and supervision in the United States: An analysis of current extent, trends, and implications. *Counselor Education & Supervision, 49*, 179–189.

Meyers, L. (2014, March). In search of wellness. *Counseling Today, 56*, 34–59.

Milsom, A., & Bryant, J. (2006). School counseling departmental web sites: What message do we send? *Professional School Counseling, 10*, 210–216.

Paine, C. K. (2009). School crisis aftermath: Care for the caregivers. *Principal Leadership, 10*, 12–16.

Ray, S. L., Wong, C., White, D., & Heaslip, K. (2013). Compassion satisfaction, compassion fatigue, work life conditions, and burnout among frontline mental health care professionals. *Traumatology, 19*, 255–267. doi:10.1177/1534765612471144

Reupert, A. (2006). The counsellor's self in therapy: An inevitable presence. *International Journal for the Advancement of Counselling, 28*, 95–105.

Sabella, R., Poynton, T. A., & Isaacs, M. L. (2010). School counselors perceived importance of counseling technologies. *Computers in Human Behavior, 26*, 609–617. doi:10.1016/j.chb.2009.12.014

Shallcross, L. (2012, December). The recipe for truly great counseling. *Counseling Today.* Retrieved from http://ct.counseling.org/2012/12/the-recipe-for-truly-great-counseling/

Swank, J. M., & Tyson, L. (2012). School counseling site supervisor training: A web-based approach. *Professional School Counseling, 16*, 40–48. doi:10.5330/PSC.n.2012-16.40

Todd, A., & Chehaib, H. (2019).Exploring how school counselors practice self-compassion. *Journal of School Counseling, 17.* EJ12113152.

Wall, J. E. (2004). *Enhancing assessment through technology.* ASCA School Counselor, 30–35.

Wilkerson, K., & Bellini, J. (2006). Intrapersonal and organizational factors associated with burnout among school counselors. *Journal of Counseling & Development, 84*, 440–450.

Williams, R. (2007, March/April). Superhero or super stressed? *ASCA School Counselor*, 10–12.

5 Supervision as a Developmental Passage

Jeannine R. Studer and Aaron H. Oberman

CACREP Standards

Foundations

d. models of school-based collaboration and consultation

Chapter Objectives:

- provide an overview of supervision models
- highlight challenges in supervision

Introduction

Supervision is a key element for training the next generation of school counselors to connect classroom concepts to practice. Master's-level school counseling programs do not generally include training in supervision, and without this knowledge, supervisors are uncertain as to how they can adequately provide the supervision the SCIT needs (Merlin-Knoblich, Harris, Chung, & Gareis, 2018). This lack of training in supervision is problematic as CACREP standards state that site supervisors must have at least a master's degree, preferably in counseling, appropriate certifications or licenses, a minimum of 2 years of experience in the supervisee's program, knowledge of the program's expectations, and training in counseling supervision (CACREP, 2016, p. 16). Furthermore, the ASCA Ethical Standards (ASCA, 2016, D.b.) state that school counselor supervisors must have "the education and training to provide clinical supervision. Supervisors regularly pursue continuing education activities on both counseling and supervision topics and skills." The reasons why school counselors do not provide supervision include a lack of release time (Dollarhide & Miller, 2006, as cited in Cook, Trepal, & Somody, 2012), insufficient time to provide supervision, and inadequate knowledge of supervision.

As you read this chapter, you are probably wondering why you are learning about supervision since you are still a student learning about the profession, and being a supervisor is a role you will not assume for a while. Yet knowing what to expect in supervision will alleviate some of your anxiety regarding this experience as a supervisee, and when you are in a position to supervise another SCIT, you will have a better idea of the expectations of this position. So let's get started talking a little more about supervision.

Supervision Roles

The professional literature (Bernard & Goodyear, 2018) broadly identifies three categories of supervision models: (1) developmental models, (2) Discrimination and Social Role Models, and (3) the School Counselor Supervision Model. The first two categories include models developed specifically for supervision, whereas the last category may more accurately be described as a model specifically for school counselors.

Developmental Models

Developmental models of supervision are empirically supported and focus primarily on how supervisees will grow and change over time (Carlson & Lambie, 2012). Although there are many supervisory approaches that utilize a developmental approach, they all have fundamental concepts in common (Carlson & Lambie, 2012) that include: (a) supervisees move through levels of development based on educational and situational experiences, and (b) supervisors provide experiences to supplement their SCIT's growth and development. For instance, you will be at a developmental stage at the beginning of your practicum that will be qualitatively different from the stage you will reach during the end of your internship. As a result, you may benefit from different supervisory interventions in the beginning of the supervised experience compared with those during the later stages in the internship. Furthermore, you will grow in both confidence and skill over time, which requires awareness and flexibility from your supervisor.

In this section, we will provide an overview of what Bernard and Goodyear (2018) have described as the most widely used developmental model of supervision, the Integrated Developmental Model, a model that was originally developed by Stoltenberg (1981) and expanded upon with Delworth in 1987. Stoltenberg & Delworth (1987) describe counselor development as occurring through four levels: (1) the beginning of the journey, (2) trial and tribulation, (3) challenge and growth, and (4) integrated. Additionally, the supervisee (that's you!) is described as "progressing in terms of three basic structures—self- and other-awareness, motivation, and autonomy" (Stoltenberg & Delworth, 1987, p. 35). Interactions among these three structures and the four levels of development are described.

Level One: The Beginning of the Journey

In the first level of counselor development, you enter the supervisory relationship with limited training and experience (Bernard & Goodyear, 2018). At this level, you are dependent on the supervisor, seeking to imitate skills and techniques rather than branching out and experimenting with different methods. This level is characterized by high levels of anxiety, self-perceptions of inadequacy, and hesitancy to embrace supervision (Lee, 2013). As you advance through the levels of supervision, there are times when you will feel uncertain, hesitant, with thoughts that you are not improving your skills. Yet you need to remember that even experienced school counselors have situations in which they are indecisive, and in these instances the prudent professional seeks advice from others. Use this opportunity to ask questions, brainstorm solutions, and recognize the various elements that support decisions you make. Recognizing and remembering your feelings at the beginning of the clinical experience may help you to more effectively supervise school counselors-in-training after you have gained experience and knowledge as a member of the profession. The structures and descriptions within this level are discussed below.

SELF- AND OTHER-AWARENESS

Awareness of yourself and others is typically low at this stage of development, and it is not unusual to be sensitive about any sort of evaluation. To assist you in gaining a better understanding of yourself and others, it may be beneficial to you to seek extra activities that could help you grow in these areas.

Box 5.1

"I pursued the school counseling profession because I want to help people succeed . . . . Counseling is powerful enough that the students I meet with will always carry what they gained from our therapeutic relationship within themselves."

Source: Clair Nowajchik, Winner of the Ross Trust Graduate Student Essay for Future School Counselors, *Counseling Today* (2014, July), p. 58

MOTIVATION

At the beginning, you may have high levels of motivation that is also accompanied with high levels of anxiety. It is often difficult for supervisees at this level to try different activities or interventions for fear that they are doing the "wrong" thing. Naturally, there is also a vast amount of information that needs to be learned, and coupled with a desire to perform adequately, anxiety is a natural result.

AUTONOMY

The supervisee at this level is highly dependent on the supervisor, typically expecting the supervisor to provide structure and specific instruction. You may not yet be ready to work by yourself, and as a result may benefit from regular input, encouragement, and positive feedback.

Conceptual Application Activity 5.1

Spend 10 minutes with one or two of your school counseling peers. Reflect back to when you first began your practicum or internship experience, and share with each other your thoughts and feelings regarding your self- and other-awareness, motivation, and autonomy level at that time. Consider your supervision expectations, too.

Motivation

_____

_____

Autonomy

_____

_____

Self- and Other-Awareness

Expectations of Supervisor

Level Two: Trial and Tribulation

At this level, supervisees are conflicted as they try to be more independent yet still need to seek the advice and direction of their supervisor (Stoltenberg & Delworth, 1987). According to Stoltenberg (1981), counselors at this stage are developing greater self-awareness while also striving for independence. If you are at this stage, you may begin to find yourself more independent, but this autonomy may also create anxiety during supervision. For example, you may be eager to try new strategies, but at the same time apprehensive about the supervisor's attitudes toward these new actions. To understand this level more, the structures integral to this model are discussed below.

SELF- AND OTHER-AWARENESS

You are now better able to understand the needs of the supervisee and are better able to focus on this individual rather than being more concerned about your own self and needs. You may begin to distinguish your own values and issues from those of the counselee, and you are more aware of your own less productive thoughts, habits, and values that interfere with the counseling process. This increased awareness may also create frustration for you as countertransference develops.

Box 5.2

Teaching interns new ways of seeing is an important task of supervision. Using the metaphor of a rock climber as a means of recognizing the progression of steps toward becoming a competent counselor may assist you in understanding the stages of development (Sommer, Ward, & Scofield, 2010).

MOTIVATION

Motivation and confidence are fluctuating at this level. This may be partially due to the more advanced SCIT taking on counselees who are more difficult, taking on more complex interventions, or having a greater understanding of all the forces that influence decision-making. You may feel confident one moment and confused or unsure the next, which can impact motivation, or you may feel motivated for specific tasks and at other times lack motivation for other responsibilities.

AUTONOMY

Supervisees are more assertive, choosing to implement new interventions of their own choosing. At this stage, you may not be copying your supervisor's style and theoretical approach; however, dependency on the supervisor may still occasionally be present. For example, supervisor input may be more desired when you encounter a new counseling situation, an ambiguous ethical dilemma, or responsibility for a unique school activity.

Level Three: Challenge and Growth

At the next level of development, supervisees should be coming into their own style and having a better idea of their own style of counseling. Stoltenberg and Delworth (1987) call this stage the "calm after the storm" (p. 93).

SELF- AND OTHER-AWARENESS

The supervisee is aware of self, including both strengths and weaknesses, and recognizes areas that need to be improved. To gain confidence, it is helpful to engage in tasks to strengthen areas in which you feel less self-assured. A better understanding of your counselee provides the means to be fully in the moment with the counselee, and to also pull back when appropriate.

MOTIVATION

The level three supervisee is relatively stable in terms of motivation and commitment to the profession, and although you may still have doubts about the profession, these doubts should not be immobilizing. You might begin to recognize that doubts and concerns are occasionally a natural part of the developmental process.

AUTONOMY

Although you are primarily self-directed at this level, you will also find yourself seeking assistance from the supervisor for specific things. Supervision tends to be more collegial in nature.

Level Four: Integrated

We all start out as beginning counselors in the initial stages of development, and with perseverance and supervision, many of us are privileged to practice as counselors and eventually attain this ultimate stage in counseling development. Stoltenberg and Delworth (1987) called this stage *integrated*, to signify the integration of the supervisee across all three structures: motivation, autonomy, and self-/other-awareness. These authors also assert a belief that most counselors require at least 5 or 6 years of professional experience to reach this level.

SELF- AND OTHER-AWARENESS

The supervisee is aware of self, including specific strengths and weaknesses. He or she has developed professional confidence and readily seeks input from others for self-improvement. Empathy allows the counselor to fluidly adjust to being fully in the "here and now."

MOTIVATION

The level three supervisee is motivated and committed to the counseling profession. When you reach this level, you should have few doubts about your role in the profession, but at the same time you will realize that you will have occasional doubts and concerns, which are a natural part of the developmental process.

AUTONOMY

At this stage, you should be very self-sufficient. Most decisions should be made independently, with occasional assistance from your supervisor for specific things. Supervision is collegial in nature.

Conceptual Application Activity 5.2

Identify a counselor you think personifies level three, integrated characteristics. Write down ways this counselor demonstrates integration.

Motivation

_____

_____

Autonomy

_____

_____

Self- and Other-Awareness

_____

_____

Keep in mind the four levels offered by Stoltenberg and Delworth (1987): (1) the beginning of the journey, (2) trial and tribulation, (3) challenge and growth, and (4) integrated, and being mindful of your own levels of awareness, motivation, and autonomy. Take a few minutes to reflect and think about where you are, developmentally, in your journey toward becoming a professional school counselor.

In the preceding pages, we provided an overview of Stoltenberg and Delworth's (1987) developmental model of supervision. Our focus with the developmental model was on stages of supervisee development across time.

In the discussion that follows, the focus of supervision will be on the role of the supervisor, known as the *Discrimination and Social Role Models*. Although we are aware that you are still trying to navigate your role as a supervisee, the following information will assist in your understanding of the various roles your supervisor will assume at various levels of supervision.

The Discrimination and Social Role Models

Social Role

Social role models, as described by Bernard and Goodyear (2018), delineate different roles the supervisor might employ during the course of supervision. These roles are specifically identified in the literature are teacher, counselor, and consultant (Bernard & Goodyear, 2018). However, it is important to note that although supervision has similarities within each of the roles, each uses a qualitatively different skill. Bernard and Goodyear (2009) stated that supervision is similar to teaching, similar to counseling, and similar to consulting, but different in all these areas. As we discuss, one social role model of supervision, Bernard's (1979) Discrimination Model, gives special attention to the nuances of each of the roles: supervisor, teacher, counselor, and consultant.

Areas of Focus

Three supervisor roles and three areas of focus for supervision are identified in the Discrimination Model Bernard (1979) identifies. The focus areas are *intervention skills* (overt behaviors

Table 5.1 Examples of the Discrimination Model.

Focus of supervision	Teacher	Counselor	Consultant
Process skills or intervention	Counselor would like to learn a specific skill. Supervisor teaches the skill.	Counselor rarely addresses feelings during sessions. Supervisor attempts to help counselor determine how discussing feelings impacts him or her and how this might be limiting his or her ability to focus on feelings in session.	Counselor wants to use a sand tray technique in session. Supervisor works with counselor to identify resources that provide information about the technique.
Conceptualization skills	Counselor is unable to identify themes between counseling sessions. Supervisor points out connections between sessions, helping counselor identify overarching themes.	Counselor is unable to identify appropriate goals for counselee. Supervisor helps counselor identify personal triggers that may be blocking ability to identify goals in session.	Counselor would like to conceptualize counselee from a different theoretical orientation. Supervisor discusses beliefs of that particular theory and how conceptualization might look.
Personalization skills	Counselor is unaware that his or her tendency to maintain direct eye contact makes counselee uncomfortable. Supervisor talks about multicultural diversity and the fact that making eye contact is considered disrespectful in some cultures.	Counselor becomes defensive when counselee indicates preference for a different counselor. Supervisor discusses why being liked is so important to the counselor.	Counselor would like to feel more comfortable and competent working with gay or lesbian counselees. Supervisor helps counselor to identify several things that might help to increase both his or her comfort and competence with counselees who are gay or lesbian.

of the supervisee), *conceptualization skills* (covert behaviors, including how the supervisee understands what the counselee is saying and recognizes themes), and *personalization skills* (ability of the supervisee to hear feedback from both counselee and supervisor, and ability to recognize and be comfortable with the counselor's own feelings, values, and attitudes).

According to the Discrimination Model (Bernard, 1979), the supervisor must first determine the area of focus and then choose a role from which to respond. As previously indicated, the roles include teacher, counselor, and consultant. Bernard cautions the supervisor to remember that there are nine choices for the supervisor to consider and that each circumstance should be approached as a unique situation. As shown in Table 5.1, each of the supervisor roles is identified with a particular focus for supervision.

Figure 5.1 Supervisor giving feedback to her school counselor-in-training.
Source: Shutterstock.

Conceptual Application Activity 5.3

Consider and answer the questions to the following scenario, and compare your responses with those of your peers.

Amy is a practicum student in an elementary school. Juanita, a third-grade student, comes to see Amy because she is concerned about her brother, Miguel, who is being deployed with the Army. Amy has difficulty working with Juanita because it brings up her own feelings for her father, who is also being deployed to a foreign country.

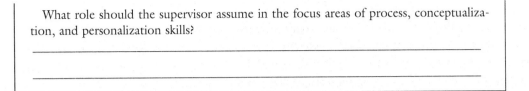

What role should the supervisor assume in the focus areas of process, conceptualization, and personalization skills?

_____

_____

Thus far, we have discussed two models of supervision: the Integrated Developmental Model (Stoltenberg & Delworth, 1987) and the Discrimination Model (Bernard, 1979). Although both were developed for the explicit purpose of supervising counselors, some (Luke & Bernard, 2006; Wood & Rayle, 2006) have wondered whether traditional models of counselor supervision are meeting the supervision needs of the SCIT given the tasks they are expected to perform as part of their comprehensive school counseling programs. To address that gap, we will provide an overview of an expanded version of the Discrimination Model that was developed specifically for school counselors (Luke & Bernard, 2006).

School Counseling Supervision Model

School counseling supervision must attend to all the various activities in which the school counselor engages which are addressed in Luke and Bernard's School Counselor Supervision Model (SCSM), which is based on Bernard's Discrimination Model (Brown, Olivárez, & DeKruyf, 2018). Although this model is dated, the SCSM still is relevant to school counselors today. The SCSM utilizes the supervisors' roles of teacher, counselor, and consultant, and the intervention, conceptualization, and personalization skills that are essential to the Discrimination Model. Gysbers and Henderson (2012) identified four sections within the components of a CSC program that should be addressed in supervision with the SCIT, including: (1) large-group interventions; (2) responsive counseling and consultation, (3) individual and group advisement, and (4) programmatic planning, coordination, and evaluation (Brown et al., 2018). Accordingly, the SCSM is conceptualized as a 3 × 3 × 4 model addressing three supervisor roles, three foci of supervision, and four points of entry:

Supervisor role: teacher, counselor, consultant
Focus of supervision: intervention, conceptualization, personalization
Point of entry: large-group interventions; responsive counseling and consultation; individual and group advisement; programmatic planning, coordination, and evaluation

Conceptual Application Activity 5.4 is designed to provide you with a better understanding of how the School Counselor Supervision Model is integrated with the Discrimination Model.

Conceptual Application Activity 5.4

School counselors engage in many tasks on any given day, but most duties will fall into one of the four categories designated as a point of entry. Therefore, the first step for a supervisor utilizing the SCSM is to identify which domain (point of entry) is being addressed in supervision (Luke & Bernard, 2006).

Once the domain is determined, the supervisor should be more readily able to identify the focus of supervision, and finally the supervisory role. However, when conceptualizing the SCSM as an extension of the Discrimination Model, it is important to remember that "the supervisor uses the same template ... but broadens the focus of supervision to include the interventions, conceptualization, and personalization that are involved in successfully implementing all aspects of a CSCP [comprehensive school counseling program]" (Luke & Bernard, 2006, p. 286).

Conceptual Application Activity 5.5

Spend 10 minutes with one or two peers. Reflect back to your last supervision session. Can you identify a supervision intervention your supervisor used that addressed one of the points of entry issues identified in the SCSM? Once you have identified a point of entry, try to determine the role in which your supervisor responded, and finally, which focus area was addressed.

Point of entry
Large-group intervention; responsive counseling and consultation; individual and group advisement; programmatic planning, coordination, and evaluation

_____

_____

Supervisor role
Teacher, counselor, consultant

_____

_____

Focus area
Intervention, conceptualization, personalization

_____

_____

Brown et al. (2018) investigated the effectiveness of the SCSM, and as a result of this study, supervisors who received training in this model revealed greater self-efficacy in supervising their school counseling trainees compared to supervisors who did not receive training. It is vital that supervisors be grounded in some theory from which to conceptualize supervision. However, it is also important to attend to the supervisory relationship and the inherent challenges presented within that dyad. Therefore, we will transition our focus to an overview of the supervisory relationship and your role in this process.

Supervisory Relationship and Supervision Challenges

Although it is essential to understand supervision models and their function in the supervision process, it is equally important for you to understand the supervisor–supervisee relationship now as well when you may become a supervisor in the future. Bernard and Goodyear (2009) describe the supervisory relationship as the feelings and perceptions individuals have in relation to one another. Some believe that the supervisor–supervisee relationship may be at the heart of a successful practicum and internship. The working alliance, individual differences, and evaluation are integral components of the supervisory relationship, and are discussed next.

Working Alliance

The development of a working alliance is perceived to be as important as the supervisory relationship (White & Queen, 2003). A supervisory relationship involves mutual agreement regarding the tasks and goals of supervision, what is to be accomplished, and the relationship between the partners. Furthermore, establishing safety, a trusting atmosphere, and reciprocal regard between supervisor and the SCIT provides an environment in which the SCIT feels comfortable asking questions and appreciates feedback from the supervisor.

Individual Differences

Individual differences add to the complexity of the relationship. According to Borders and Brown (2005), "each supervisee and supervisor brings unique personalities, life experiences, interpersonal histories, professional motivations and goals to the supervisory context" (p. 68). For example, not all supervisors and supervisees interact with others in a similar manner or react to the same situation in the same way. Each is influenced by his or her respective distinctiveness.

It may be even more problematic if there are age differences with the SCIT being much older than the supervisor, if philosophical differences between the SCIT and supervisee are evident, or if the supervisor does not supervise according to the guidelines of the school counseling program.

Evaluation

Another distinguishing feature and significant part of supervision is evaluation. Evaluation is a necessary component of supervision, and is inherent to the supervisory process. Baird (2018) defines evaluation as giving and receiving feedback about the value of one's performance. Haynes, Corey, and Moulton (2003) assert that evaluation is necessary for the accomplishment of the four goals of supervision: fostering development, ensuring counselee welfare, acting as gatekeepers for the profession, and developing autonomous professionals.

The evaluation process has the potential to cause you, as a SCIT, discomfort, stress, and anxiety, yet these are natural reactions to this experience, and it is therefore important that you and your supervisor openly discuss this process at the outset of supervision. Evaluation is a delicate balancing act: You need honest and helpful feedback in order to learn and grow, yet the supervisor must strive to maintain the bonds established in the relationship.

The evaluative component of supervision further complicates the supervisory relationship for several reasons, including, but not limited to, the following: it may be the first time you have experienced supervision, you may fear supervisor disapproval, and you may be anxious about having your performance and skills examined (Kiser, 2008). Evaluation can cause difficulties because there is an inherent power differential ever-present in the process. This unequal distribution of power can produce stress and conflicts in the relationship because "supervisees are asked to be vulnerable and self-disclose their professional inadequacies and their personal biases to the same person who will grade them, write letters of recommendation, or complete reference forms for licensure" (Borders & Brown, 2005, p. 67).

Keep in mind that evaluation is an essential component to improve your knowledge and skills to assist you to become a productive member of the school counseling profession.

Conceptual Application Activity 5.6

Spend 10 minutes with one or two peers. Reflect back to your last supervision session. Can you identify a supervision intervention your supervisor used that addressed one of the points of entry issues identified in the SCSM? Once you have identified a point of entry, try to determine which role your supervisor responded in, and finally, which focus area was addressed.

Think of a time when you received evaluative feedback from your supervisor. Was the feedback helpful? If so, why? If not, why not?

1. How might your supervisor give you feedback that would be more helpful?

    _____

    _____

2. Did you implement the feedback you received? If so, how?

    _____

    _____

Other Challenges

Several other challenges underlie the basic principles of the supervisory relationship. For example, multicultural influences, supervisee anxiety and resistance, the parallel process, and dual roles/relationships warrant discussion, and are covered in the next sections.

Multicultural Influences

The environment and community in which we develop and mature influence each of us. Additionally, we are oriented to family norms, attitudes, and family culture. These same norms and values can be expected to influence the counselee–counselor relationship as well as your relationship with your supervisors. To work successfully with individuals from diverse backgrounds, it is vital to be aware of your personal history, other individuals' personal histories, and the impact of both on the counseling and supervision relationship (Borders & Brown, 2005). As maintained by Borders and Brown (2005), some supervisees may not be able to identify problems or issues stemming from multicultural concerns; thus, "it is the supervisor's responsibility to introduce multicultural issues early in the supervision relationship, check in about them often, and invite the supervisee to discuss them at any time" (p. 70). You are likely to encounter multicultural issues you may not know how to manage. In such situations, it will be important for you to discuss them with your supervisor during group supervision. At the same time, it is an opportunity for self-discovery, self-evaluation, and for expanding your knowledge and awareness of multicultural issues.

Likewise, multicultural issues, different worldviews, and unique values will be present within the supervisor–supervisee relationship. In addition to dealing with these issues related to your counselees, it is important for you and your supervisor to discuss your own diverse life experiences, thoughts, and perspectives. This open discussion, mutual respect, and willingness to learn from one another models a healthy counselor–counselee relationship. Diversity as it relates to differences in schools is discussed in greater detail in Chapter 12.

Anxiety and Resistance

Anxiety is an expected reaction during the clinical experiences, especially as the SCIT engages in identified tasks and questions whether he/she has the necessary competencies and personality to effectively fulfill his/her expected duties (Kurtyilmaz, 2015). Furthermore, Bernard and Goodyear (2009) contend that supervisees feel apprehension not only when working with counselees, but also during supervision. Certainly, observation and evaluation are customary components of both practicum and internship, and can be very intimidating, particularly if you have never experienced supervision. Nonetheless, anxiety in and of itself can be beneficial because it encourages you to be prepared for supervision. Conversely, too much anxiety may interfere with your effectiveness and the ability to recall needed skills during sessions.

During the practicum and internship, you will be expected to present cases, video and audiotape recordings, and experience site observation that may contribute to feelings of anxiety. Performance anxiety can threaten your sense of competence and ability; it is not unusual for you to have an unrealistic view of the counseling process and set high expectations for yourself even though you lack experience. However, your anxiety will decrease over time as you understand that feelings of anxiety, concerns about counseling skills, receiving feedback, and having to self-disclose are normal and expected elements of supervision. Also, keep in mind that feelings of anxiety decrease with experience and change in any given situation.

Resistance

A consequence of anxiety is resistance, and it is a common aspect of the supervisory process that you may experience as a SCIT. Borders and Brown (2005) state that "supervisees necessarily must find ways to handle their anxiety, and sometimes their attempts are not productive …. [R]esistance may reflect the supervisees' attempt to reduce anxiety to a manageable and productive level" (p. 72). Some of the underlying factors related to supervisee resistance include rigidly holding to a specific theory, giving advice or problem-solving before the counselee has identified the problem, being confrontational about taping, and expressing vulnerability associated with the evaluation process (Borders & Brown, 2005).

Resistant activities, as with anxiety, can impede the learning process; therefore, recognizing the basis for the resistance and finding ways to diminish the supposed threat will increase your ability to deal with conflict in a positive manner. An open and honest discussion of struggle in supervision can increase awareness of these behaviors, and in the process could enhance your development. As an example, one of our SCIT was particularly antagonistic toward supervision during her internship experience. She was reluctant to discuss her feelings towards her supervisees and repeatedly refused to answer any personal questions that were posed to her during her supervisory sessions. It eventually became apparent that she was desperately afraid of revealing any aspects of herself due to her traumatic childhood experiences. Although she was not suitable at this time for the school counseling profession, a benefit of this experience was her willingness to recognize that she needed to receive personal counseling for her own personal mental health.

Parallel Process

As in the counseling relationship, transference and countertransference is an ethical issue within the supervisory relationship (Bryant-Young, Bell, & Davis, 2014). As an example, imagine a SCIT presenting a tape in which the counselee discusses a tumultuous relationship with his mother. If a supervisor who listens to this tape has had a similar relationship with her own mother and reacts with negativity to the mother expressed on the tape, this could create friction during the supervisory process.

Parallel process is similar to transference and countertransference, traditional concepts in psychoanalytic theory. Searles (1955) was the first to make use of the concept of parallel process, which he referred to as "the reflective process." He defined parallel process as "the process at work currently in the *relationship between* patient [in schools, this would be the student] and therapist ... often reflected in the *relationship between* therapist and supervisor" (p. 135). Furthermore, "When patterns between counseling and supervision occur, the role of the supervisee and supervisor duplicate the role of client and counselor" (White & Russell, 1997, as cited in Koltz, Odegard, Feit, Provost, & Smith, 2012, p. 234). In summary, exploration and reflection of the parallel process in supervision can be constructive when they enhance your ability to gain insight into the way you interact with counselees (Bernard & Goodyear, 2018; Borders & Brown, 2005).

Dual Roles

Kiser (2008) defines dual roles or relationships as follows: "Dual relationships occur when a helping professional assumes a second role with a counselee or colleague in addition to the professional role" (p. 253). For example, suppose the SCIT is having difficulties with his wife and the supervisor, rather than providing the supervision that is needed to fulfill identified tasks, instead provides counseling. The American School Counselor Association Ethical Standards for School Counselors (2016) states in section A.5, "Dual Relationships and Managing Boundaries," that the professional school counselor should "Avoid dual relationships that might impair their objectivity and increase the risk of harm to students .... Supervisors are responsible for helping you avoid, identify and correct, and learn from dual relationships."

Borders and Brown (2005) suggest two possible types of dual roles: social and sexual. Social role boundaries may be less difficult for the school counselor to maintain with students, given that their counselees are usually younger than they are. However, the possibility of social relationships increases when working with parents similar in age and interests and with whom you may develop a personal relationship. Maintaining constructive and professional boundaries may be more challenging with students' adult parents or caregivers. Be mindful that your professional obligations and responsibilities to your students supersede social relationships, and remember that you should avoid any social interaction that might cause loss of objectivity (Borders & Brown, 2005).

Conceptual Application Activity 5.7

Read and respond to the following case study. Compare your answers with those of your peers.

Caroline is in her fourth year working as an elementary school counselor when one of her former professors asks if she would be willing to supervise a school counselor intern. Not sure initially, Caroline hesitates. With encouragement from her former professor, she cautiously agrees. The following semester, James, a timid intern, shows up at Caroline's school ready to begin his internship. As expected, James is thrown right in. With Caroline's assistance, he begins leading classroom lessons, starts two groups with first- and third-grade girls, and even sees two students for individual counseling. When the university instructor goes to the school for a site visit, both James and Caroline report that everything is great.

Seven weeks into the semester, James is watching the evening news, shocked at the tragedy unfolding on the television. An automobile accident involving multiple cars has traffic backed up on the interstate as helicopters are airlifting victims to nearby hospitals. James thinks back about 10 years to a time when he first heard that his 16-year-old sister had died after a truck ran a stoplight, hitting the car she was driving. As James goes to sleep that evening, he is saddened by the possibility of fatalities connected with the car accident he had witnessed earlier in the evening. It is not until early the following morning that James begins to realize the full extent to which this event is going to affect his life. Two of the victims from the accident were an 8-year-old boy and his father. The child attended the school where James is interning, and the boy's 6-year-old sister was in one of James's groups. He had no idea where to begin as he attempted to focus on helping the students while grappling with his own reactions to the tragedy.

Fortunately, James has a supervision session scheduled for the following day. Conceptualizing supervision from the School Counseling Supervision Model, how would you proceed with James?

1. Where do you think the supervising counselor should begin in working with James?
2. What focus area would you want your supervisor to take if you had a situation similar to James—process skills, conceptualization, personalization?
3. What role would you want your supervisor to assume—teacher, counselor, consultant? Why?

Sexual involvement with a counselee is prohibited by virtually all ethical codes. Even given the legal and professional liability and consequences, sexual relationships between students and school professionals unfortunately continue to be reported in the news media. What happens to well-intentioned school professionals that leads to misconduct and poor professional judgment? Counseling, by its very nature, can be isolated and intimate. As part of the therapeutic process, counselees share private information, in confidence, with the school counselor or with you, as the SCIT. These interactions are often conducted in a private or semiprivate setting. Counseling session interactions may occur on a sporadic or regular basis over a long period of time. All of these factors are similar to more personal and intimate relationships outside of counseling, and can be confusing to the counselee and to you. Role confusion occurs and builds when the school counselor or you, as a SCIT, fail to regularly review and maintain the primary reason for or goal of the relationship, which is helping the counselee to change or adapt to environmental conditions or relationships outside the counseling setting or relationship. It is paramount that you establish, review, and maintain this therapeutic focus with your counselees. It is equally important that your supervisor do this with you.

Role confusion and dual roles are issues for you to discuss and clarify during supervision. Undoubtedly, sexual relationships confound and impede the counseling and supervision relationship and cause injury to the counselee or supervisee. Therefore, it is imperative that sexual relationships are avoided at all costs and any potential issues be brought up in supervision.

Finally, Borders and Brown (2005) suggest that the closeness of the supervisory relationship and the power differential make it difficult to avoid dual role problems. Supervisors have a responsibility to clarify their role at the beginning of supervision, and supervisors who set up appropriate professional boundaries are good role models to teach you how to develop appropriate boundaries.

Conclusion

School counseling students graduating from a school counseling program accredited by the Council for Accreditation of Counseling and Related Educational Programs typically receive an average of approximately 100-plus hours of supervision (combined site and university) over the course of a 700-hour field experience. The considerable amount of time devoted to supervision provides perspective about the importance of the supervisory relationship. Due to this essential component of your clinical experiences, it is important that you have a better understanding of the supervision process, your role as a SCIT, and the crucial role of your supervisors.

Website

- "Providing Administrative and Counseling Supervision for School Counselors": www.counseling.org/docs/default-source/vistas/providing-administrative-and-counseling-supervision-for-school-counselors.pdf

  This article describes the supervisory process that surrounds the CSC program.

References

ASCA. (2016). *Ethical standards for school counselors.* Retrieved from www.schoolcounselor.org/asca/media/asca/Ethics/EthicalStandards2016.pdf

Baird, B. N. (2018). *The internship, practicum, and field placement handbook: A guide for the helping professions* (8th ed.). Upper Saddle River, NJ: Prentice Hall.

Bernard, J. M. (1979). Supervisor training: A Discrimination Model. *Counselor Education and Supervision, 19,* 60–68.

Bernard, J. M., & Goodyear, R. K. (2009). *Fundamentals of clinical supervision* (4th ed.). Columbus, OH: Pearson.

Bernard, J. M., & Goodyear, R. K. (2018). *Fundamentals of clinical supervision* (6th ed.). Boston, MA: Allyn & Bacon.

Borders, L. D., & Brown, L. L. (2005). *The new handbook of counseling supervision.* Mahwah, NJ: Lahaska Press.

Brown, C. H., Olivárez, A., & DeKruyf, L. (2018). The impact of the School Counselor Supervision Model on the self-efficacy of school counselor site supervisors. *Professional School Counseling, 21,* 152–160. doi:10.5330/1096-2409-21.1.152

Bryant-Young, N., Bell, C. A., & Davis, K. M. (2014). A supervisory issue when utilizing the ASCA National Model framework in school counseling. *Georgia School Counselors Association Journal, 21.* EJ1084445.

CACREP. (2016). *2016 Standards.* Retrieved from www.cacrep.org/wp-content/uploads/2018/05/2016-Standards-with-Glossary-5.3.2018.pdf

Carlson, R. G., & Lambie, G. W. (2012). Systemic-developmental supervision: Clinical supervisory approach for family counseling student interns. *Family Journal: Counseling and Therapy for Couples and Families, 21,* 29–36. doi:10.1177/1066480711419809

Cook, K., Trepal, H., & Somody, C. (2012). Supervision of school counselors: The SAAFT Model. *Journal of School Counseling, 10,* 1–22.

Gysbers, N. C., & Henderson, P. (2012). *Developing and managing your school guidance and counseling program* (5th ed.). Alexandria, VA: American Counseling Association.

Haynes, R., Corey, G., & Moulton, P. (2003). *Clinical supervision in the helping professions: A practical guide.* Alexandria, VA: American Counseling Association.

Kiser, P. M. (2008). *The human services internship: Getting the most from your experience* (2nd ed.). Belmont, CA: Thompson Brooks/Cole.

Koltz, R. L., Odegard, M. A., Feit, S. S., Provost, K., & Smith, T. (2012). Parallel process and isomorphism: A model for decision making in the supervisory Triad. *The Family Journal: Counseling and Therapy for Couples and Families, 20,* 233–238.

Kurtyilmaz, Y. (2015). Counselor trainees' views on their forthcoming experiences in practicum course. *Eurasian Journal of Educational Research, 61.* doi:10.14689/ejer.2015.61.9

Lee, T. (2013) Integrating a developmental supervision model with the adaptive supervision in counselor training model. *Vistas Online.* Article 84. Retrieved from www.counseling.org/docs/default-source/vistas/integrating-a-developmental-supervision-model-with-the-adaptive-supervision-in-counselor-training-model.pdf

Luke, M., & Bernard, J. M. (2006). The School Counseling Supervision Model: An extension of the Discrimination Model. *Counselor Education and Supervision, 45,* 282–295.

Merlin-Knoblich, C., Harris, P. N., Chung, S. Y., & Gareis, C. R. (2018). Reported experiences of school counseling site supervisors in a supervision training program. *Journal of School Counseling, 16.* EJ1181069.

Searles, H. F. (1955). The informational value of the supervisor's emotional experiences. *Psychiatry, 18,* 135–146.

Sommer, C.A., Ward, J. E., & Scofield, T. (2010). Metaphoric stories in supervision of internship: A qualitative study. *Journal of Counseling & Development, 88,* 500–507.

Stoltenberg, C. D. (1981). Approaching supervision from a developmental perspective: The counselor complexity model. *Journal of Counseling Psychology, 28,* 59–65.

Stoltenberg, C. D., & Delworth, U. (1987). *Supervising counselors and therapists.* San Francisco, CA: Jossey-Bass.

White, V. E., & Queen, J. (2003). Supervisor and supervisee attachments and social provisions related to the supervisory working alliance. *Counselor Education and Supervision, 43*(3), 203–218.

Wood, C., & Rayle, A. D. (2006). A model of school counseling supervision: The goals, functions, roles, and systems model. *Counselor Education and Supervision, 45,* 253–266.

Part II

The ASCA National Model (4th ed.) as a Structure for Understanding the Role of the School Counselor

6 The ASCA National Model as a Supervisory Guide

Aaron H. Oberman and Jeannine R. Studer

CACREP Standards

a. foundation and models of P-12 comprehensive career development
c. models of school-based collaboration and consultation

Contextual Dimensions

a. school counselor roles as leaders, advocates, and systems change agents in P-12 schools
f. competencies to advocate for school counseling roles
j. qualities and styles of effective leadership in schools

Chapter Objectives:

*   review the ASCA National Model
*   introduce the ASCA National Model as a template for supervision
*   discuss time percentage recommendations as a tool to guide supervisory activities.

Introduction

In recent years, the school reform movement has served as a catalyst for all school personnel to demonstrate how their programs contribute to the growth of all their students; school counselors are no exception. Although some people believe that educational accountability is a recent focus, demonstrating effectiveness has historically been an issue. Since "guidance workers," now known as professional school counselors, first entered schools in the early part of the 20th century, people were curious as to how these professionals made a difference in the lives of students (Gysbers, 2004). As a profession, we have been remiss in demonstrating contributions to student success despite the urging of our predecessors to prove how we are significant contributors to student growth. By now, you have probably been introduced to a traditional approach to school counseling and how comprehensive school counseling programs have replaced this service-oriented approach with one that is proactive and preventive. In this chapter our intention is to assist you in understanding school counselor activities that mirror programming advocated by the American School Counselor Association.

A Summary of the Development of the ASCA National Standards (Now ASCA Mindsets and Behaviors for Student Success)

The profession of school counseling has a relatively brief history. Yet, despite societal changes and historical efforts of leaders of the American School Counselor Association to standardize our profession, counselors continued to perform numerous but different tasks. These tasks varied from school to school, grade to grade, and even among counselors within the same school setting.

The initial impetus behind our profession was the Industrial Revolution, in which there was a need to train school-aged youth for the emerging occupations that resulted from this event. Teachers were given this task with no training and no relief from their classroom responsibilities. Later, the push to compete with Russia's Sputnik in the race for space drove the first "guidance counselors" to direct or guide students into the fields of math and science. Making a difference was measured by increased student enrollment in math and science majors in colleges and universities. In the 1960s and 1970s, the proliferating free spirit movement brought about greater recognition of concerns such as civil rights, women's issues, and students with special needs. School personnel, including "guidance counselors," were confronted with increasing student diversity and legislative mandates and requirements that supplemented their already existing responsibilities. As a result, school counselors responded to these cumulative issues from a reactive stance rather than proactively engaging in prevention activities. Slowly, there was a shift in evaluating essential tasks, and with this awareness there was a change in the vocational title from "guidance counselor" to *professional school counselor*. (Unfortunately, we are aware that even today, not all school counselors embrace this title and continue to refer to themselves as guidance counselors.)

The ASCA responded to the demand for educational reform by standardizing the school counselor role and developed the ASCA National Standards (revised in 2012 to ASCA Student Standards, and later renamed Mindsets and Behaviors for Student Success). Initially implemented in 1997, these standards identify student competencies and indicators in the academic, career, and personal/social (renamed social/emotional) domains. In 2003, these standards were incorporated into the first edition of the ASCA National Model, which served as a prototype to a comprehensive school counseling program (ASCA, 2019). In 2019, the ASCA introduced the fourth edition of the National Model, in which the language was defined to more accurately reflect educational modifications. The model contributes to legitimizing the school counseling profession and assists school counselors as they reorganize and reconstruct their traditional approach to working with students and other constituents, and reflects the trends of the profession.

A fundamental philosophy underlying ASCA-supported programs is to promote student academic achievement. In addition, the ASCA National Model (ASCA, 2019):

- ensures that all students have equal access to a rigorous curriculum that is delivered systematically
- identifies the knowledge and skills all students are to acquire upon graduation from high school
- emphasizes data collection and analysis to make informed decisions

The Define, Manage, Deliver, and Assess components are the organizational structures of the ASCA National Model and provide guidelines for school counselors in leading a CSC program (ASCA, 2019). Core themes of leadership, advocacy, collaboration and teaming, and systemic change are repeated throughout the components to emphasize the vital services school counselors perform within these areas. The ASCA National Model is shown in Figure 6.1.

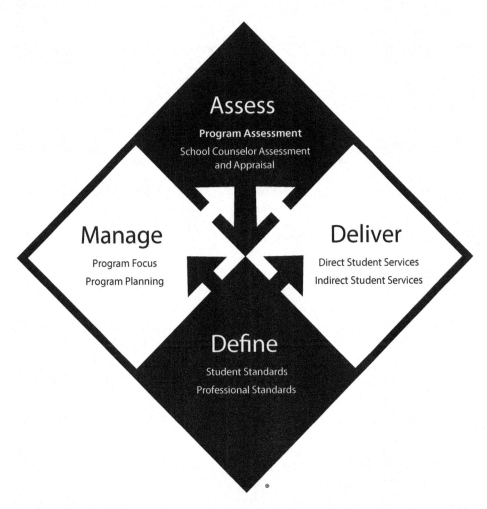

Figure 6.1 ASCA National Model.

Source: Reprinted with permission from American School Counselor Association (2019), *The ASCA National Model: A Framework for School Counseling Programs*, 4th edition.

Historically, the school counselor's role and identity changed as economic, political, and social variables influenced educational initiatives, and the ASCA continually advocated for school counselors and their contributions to the educational mission Yet there continues to be debate as to the primary role of professional school counselors. Today, with the growing numbers of students who display risky behaviors, there is a growing need for school counselors to engage in prevention and risk management (Joe & Bryant, 2007). In a study by Harris and Jeffery (2010), school counselors reported working with students in such high-risk behaviors as suicide attempts, self-mutilation, bullying, and eating disorders. Yet some participants in this study believed that despite their interactions with students' high-risk behaviors, this was not their role (Harris & Jeffery, 2010). Others (Brown & Trusty, 2005) believe that school counselors can show their contributions to student growth by "establishing the efficacy of interventions that increase academic achievement" (p. 14). Comparatively, administrators often do not have a full understanding of a school counselor's role in leading an effective school counselor program, and as a result, administrators often ask school counselors to serve in a responsive, reactive mode to a few designated students (Stone & Dahir, 2009, as cited in Dahir, Cinotti, & Feirsen, 2019). To add even more confusion, the ASCA posits that the role of the professional school counselor is to serve as a certified/licensed *educator* who is trained to address academic, career and personal/social development needs of all students (ASCA, 2019). Therefore, a fundamental professional identity question remains: "Is the school counselor a mental health expert who works in an educational setting, an educator who works with social/emotional and career concerns to increase academic growth, or a collaborator with others?"

Conceptual Application Activity 6.1

Discuss the school counselor's role with your site supervisor and learn about his/her perceptions on school counseling. In class, share what you learned from your site supervisor with your peers, and discuss your perception of the school counselor's role in the school.

Regardless of how you see yourself within the school setting, the ASCA National Model is a template for you to utilize during your clinical experiences and when you transition into a role as a professional school counselor. The Define component serves as the *what* of the program (ASCA, 2019) or a supporting program base. The Deliver component describes direct and indirect student services. The Assess component is designed for program analysis and decision-making, and the Manage component stipulates tools and assessments for addressing program needs (ASCA, 2019).

Box 6.1

School counselor interns at the high school level are more likely to receive experience in individual planning than are middle and elementary school interns, whereas elementary and middle school trainees are more likely to engage in accountability procedures than are high school counselors-in-training (Oberman & Studer, 2016).

The four themes of leadership, advocacy, collaboration and teaming, and systemic change are assimilated into the model framework. Leadership includes assisting student success through the delivery of a CSC program and performing tasks that support school counseling training and education (ASCA, 2019). Leadership is a concept that is not always attributed to school counselors, but is often viewed as an administrator role. Yet school counselors do serve as leaders of CSC programs and assume positions of authority and decision-making by building a respectful school culture to construct collaborative relationships (Wingfield, Reese, & West-Olatunji, 2010). As advocates, counselors assist all students and serve as support for students who have not had the same opportunities afforded to more advantaged students. As a collaborator, the school counselor works cooperatively with other school staff to ensure that student needs are met and additional help is provided (ASCA, 2019). Finally, as a systems change agent, the school counselor works on behalf of students and with students at the micro and macro levels. Each of the ASCA National Model components and your role as a trainee in each of these areas will be discussed in more detail in the following chapters.

As you discover the advantages of working within a CSC program, it will be stimulating and educational to put these concepts into practice during your clinical experiences. However, it may be discouraging to you when you recognize that not all school counselors have implemented a program that reflects the philosophy of the ASCA. Some programs still have a traditional focus. If this is the situation in your clinical setting, recognize that school counselors are still performing many of the tasks that reflect a CSC program. This is an opportune time to recognize and identify those tasks that reflect this philosophy and to include them in your clinical contract. If your supervisor is unfamiliar with the ASCA National Model or uncertain as to where to

Figure 6.2 Elementary students in a classroom activity.
Source: Shutterstock.

begin this type of programming, this is an opportunity for you to be the teacher and share your knowledge with him/her. Tracking activities has several benefits. First, this procedure will help you gain a better understanding of how school counselors operate in a traditional type of a program. Second, you can share the list of corresponding activities with your school counselor supervisors to inform them of the specific ways they already embrace the contemporary philosophy and National Model. Third, you can distribute the ASCA National Model guidelines to compare the corresponding components and themes with those that are not yet conducted on a routine basis. Sharing this tracked data may provide new insight and encourage system change.

It seems clear that there is much to gain from implementing a complete and effective school counseling program following the ASCA National Model, and when you are able to provide substantial research to reveal how CDSC programming enhances the growth of students, you are advocating for the profession and for the students with whom you are working. Evidence as to how this programming is critical to the growth and achievement of school-aged youth is summarized below.

Studies Supporting the Benefits of a Comprehensive School Counseling Program

A statewide study of middle schools in the state of Washington concluded no significant differences between CSC middle schools compared with non-CSC middle schools. Although this was a disappointing finding, upon further analysis, when student achievement scores were measured longitudinally, it was found that sixth- and seventh-grade students in schools in which a CSC program had been implemented for 5 or more years scored significantly better in identified academics (Sink, Akos, Turnbull, & Mvududu, 2008). Therefore, counselors who are in the process of implementing a comprehensive school counseling program are to be aware of the time it takes to implement a program, to celebrate the successful steps that are taken toward full implementation, and to embrace the positive results that are attained after a period of time. Other research has been conducted that focused on the domains inherent to the ASCA National Model; the results of these studies may be used as a foundation for possible projects you could implement as a trainee in your clinical experiences.

Academic Domain

School counselors work collaboratively with teachers to improve the achievement of under-performing students. Students who do not achieve academically are at risk for dropping out of school or not being successful in postsecondary education or in a career (Berger, 2013). An 8-week group intervention was provided to 13 high school students from three different high schools in South Florida with the intention of increasing student achievement as defined by t GPA, and decreasing absences and discipline referrals. The researcher used a version of the Achievement Orientation Model (AOM) that was designed to increase the motivation level of underachieving youth. In addition, the School Motivation and Learning Strategies Inventory (SMALSI) was used to measure motivation before and after the group intervention. Although two participants revealed significant changes in GPA, overall there were no significant differences between the pre- and post-test results. However, students reported that not only did the group help them learn something new about themselves in relation to goals and motivation, they also learned effective skills to enhance academic achievement. Furthermore, one of the school administrators requested that the school counselors continue the curriculum for future students (Berger, 2013). It is possible that more robust results may have occurred if this program had been in effect and measured over a period of time.

In another study, by Brigman, Webb, and Campbell (2007), the Student Success Skills (SSS) program designed to teach academic, social, and self-management skills was used with students in grades 5–9 in group classes and small group interventions. The final results of this intervention revealed significant gains in academic achievement and improved behavioral performance.

Career Domain

The Social Cognitive Career Theory (SCCT) was developed to explain the contextual factors and cognitive variables for career development. Through the use of this theory as a guiding model, Tang, Pan, and Newmeyer (2008) conducted a study with high school students from a Midwest high school to determine the effectiveness of this theory, how learning experiences influence career choices, and in what way gender and career choices intersect. Females expressed higher self-efficacy in careers that involve working with people and ideas, and communicated more interest in careers that led to self-satisfaction. Boys were more interested in careers that involved data and things. A significant implication for school counselors is the awareness of how self-efficacy and learning experiences shape career interests.

A total of 152 inner-city eighth- and ninth-grade students participated in a study to ascertain whether or not there were significant gender and ethnicity differences in vocational personality (Turner et al., 2008). The Self-Directed Search (SDS) was used to measure participants' interests in activities as well as their perceptions of ability and self-competence (Turner et al., 2008). Although this study did not reveal any differences in personality type among ethnic groups, there were gender differences. Boys expressed interest in realistic and investigative careers, whereas girls expressed greater interest in artistic careers. The results of this study indicate that school counselors need to assist students with careers based on personal interests, as opposed to gender-based careers.

Social/Emotional Domain

Children who have experienced the death of a parent feel emotions such as shock, guilt, and anger, and often have an impaired support system due to the grief experienced by surviving family and friends (Eppler, 2008). In many cases, it is the school counselor who has the training and available resources to facilitate the child's recovery from this devastating event. Eppler (2008) studied the resiliency factors that serve as defenses against greater traumatization and promote successful growth among children aged 9–12 who mourned the death of a parent. In order for the researcher to better understand each child's unique experiences and to serve as a guide for the child to remember the circumstances surrounding his/her parent's death, participants were given a series of questions, such as "What are some of your early family memories?" and "Who do you talk to when you are sad/happy/scared?" Each child was then asked to write a biblio-narrative to express his/her grief, which was then analyzed to identify resiliency factors. Bereaved children expressed sadness as the primary emotion, yet they also revealed the ability to thrive in the midst of challenging times. School counselors are able to use the components of the ASCA National Model to conduct support groups with these children. Furthermore, school counselors are able to integrate strength-based activities into the school setting by providing information and resources to teachers and parents to better understand the bereavement process and methods for assisting the grieving child (Eppler, 2008).

ASCA School Counselor Professional Standards and Competencies

You are entering the profession at a time of significant transition. As mentioned earlier, school counselor supervisors may lack familiarity with the new model, which may create an understandable tension. Direct service to students, as acknowledged in the Deliver component, has traditionally been one of the most challenging counseling components for school counselors. Administrators and teachers experience enormous amounts of pressure to perform and fulfill ever-growing responsibilities. Teachers are trained for their unique and specific classroom responsibilities, and principals are often experienced teachers who returned to school for administrative training. Therefore, most administrators understand the role of the teacher and their role as administrator. However, few teachers and administrators were informed as to the roles and responsibilities of the school counselor. This could be problematic when principals assign tasks to school counselors based on their personal experiences in a pre-K–12 school, which may have little resemblance to the ideal role as espoused by the ASCA.

School counselor responses to task requests by administrators must be measured carefully. Helping others often creates a natural tension for the school counselor, as he/she is a trained helper and wants to assist whenever and however he/she is able. Yet there could be legal/ethical implications when performing tasks for which we are not trained, and there is the additional risk that these tasks may define our role.

School Counselor Professional Standards and Competencies Assessment is identified within the 2019 ASCA National Model. Within this document, mindsets and behaviors are outlined that school counselors should hold to initiate and continue a comprehensive school counseling program. Mindsets are beliefs regarding student achievement and success, whereas behaviors are those that school counselors demonstrate. The behaviors include professional foundation skills, direct and indirect student services, and program planning and evaluation. You can use these competencies to self-evaluate your knowledge, abilities, skills, and attitudes that are essential to your success as a competent, effective professional.

Box 6.2

School counselors-in-training reported that individual counseling and group counseling were the tasks most frequently conducted during their internship, whereas meeting with an advisory board, program planning, and tasks associated with the management system were performed less frequently during this clinical experience (Oberman & Studer, 2016). Although the time spent on group and individual counseling activities is not surprising due to these being significant program expectations, supervisees also need experience in tasks that are more commonly performed by more experienced members of the profession.

Recommended Percentage of Time Performing School Counseling Activities

It is obvious that the school counselor performs myriad activities and has a responsibility for gaining the knowledge, skills, and behaviors needed to perform the job effectively. Yet too often the school counselor's time is disproportionately spent in some areas and not others.

The ASCA National Model recommends that 80% of time be spent in direct and indirect student services, and 20% be spent in program planning and school support (ASCA, 2019).

These percentages vary according to the school level and the developmental ages of the students, so it is possible that you or your supervisor will not necessarily meet these criteria exactly. However, keeping track of your time and analyzing where time is spent can provide information you can share with stakeholders. As a SCIT, you will probably receive requests to assist with activities that do not meet the philosophy and intent of a CSC program. In a few cases, we have had some school counseling students who openly refused to participate in an activity they felt was beyond the scope of their supervisory contract. This is not an appropriate time to decline, and may even create ill will. Instead, go ahead and participate in the experience so that you can take what you learned to advocate for yourself when you are hired as a professional school counselor.

Conclusion

The ASCA National Model (fourth edition) was revised and designed as a template for today's school counselors to use when developing a CSC program. Within this chapter, the various components and sections have been summarized along with practical strategies for you to consider as you delve into the school counselor's role during your clinical experiences. A brief overview of the development of the ASCA National Model and the research that documents how students grow in the academic, career, and social/emotional domains as a result of participation in this type of programming were discussed. As you engage in activities during your clinical experiences, note how your supervisor spends time within the ASCA National Model, and where you spend your time. Even though your clinical experiences may not be in a school setting that has transformed its school counseling program to one that reflects the philosophy and goals of a CSC program, note the myriad activities performed by the school counselor that easily fit within this model. Through observation and participation, you will have opportunities to understand how this type of empirically based programming reveals its benefits to students, parents, teachers, and the community.

Websites

- *School Counselor Professional Standards and Competencies Assessment*, which outlines school counselor mindsets and behaviors as they lead a school counseling program, can be found on this website: www.schoolcounselor.org/asca/media/asca/home/SCCompetencies.pdf
- This link provides information on how to obtain the ASCA National Model, *A Framework for School Counseling Programs* (4th ed.): www.schoolcounselor.org/school-counselors-members/asca-national-model

References

ASCA. (2019). *The ASCA national model: A framework for school counseling programs* (4th ed.). Alexandria, VA: ASCA.

Berger, C. (2013). Bring out the brilliance: A counseling intervention for underachieving students. *Professional School Counseling, 17*, 86–96. doi:10.5330/PSC.n.2013-17.80

Brigman, G. A., Webb, L. D., & Campbell, C. (2007). Building skills for school success: Improving the academic and social competence of students. *Professional School Counseling, 10*, 279–288.

Brown, D., & Trusty, J. (2005). The ASCA national model, accountability, and establishing causal links between school counselors' activities and student outcomes: A reply to Sink. *Professional School Counseling, 9*, 13–15.

Dahir, C. A., Cinotti, D. A., & Feirsen, R. (2019). Beyond compliance: Assessing administrators' commitment to comprehensive school counseling. *NASSP Bulletin, 103*, 118–138. doi:10.1177/011926365 19830769

Eppler, C. (2008). Exploring themes of resiliency in children after the death of a parent. *Professional School Counseling, 11*, 189–196.

Gysbers, N. C. (2004). Comprehensive guidance and counseling programs: The evolution of accountability. *Professional School Counseling, 8*, 1–14.

Harris, G. E., & Jeffery, G. (2010). School counsellors' perceptions on working with student high-risk behavior. *Canadian Journal of Counselling, 44*, 150–190.

Joe, S., & Bryant, H. (2007). Evidence-based suicide prevention screening in schools. *Children & Schools, 29*, 219–227.

Oberman, A. H., & Studer, J. R. (2016). An exploratory study of the tasks school counselor trainees perform in internship. *Georgia School Counseling Association Journal, 23*, 6–15.

Sink, C. A., Akos, P., Turnbull, R. J., & Mvududu, N. (2008). An investigation of comprehensive school counseling and academic achievement in Washington state middle schools. *Professional School Counseling, 1*, 43–53.

Tang, M., Pan, W., & Newmeyer, M. (2008). Factors influencing high school students' career aspirations. *Professional School Counseling, 11*, 285–295. doi:10.55330/PSC.n.2010-11.285

Turner, S. L., Conkel, J. L., Starkey, M., Landgraf, R., Lapan, R. T., Siewert, J. J., ... Huang, J. (2008). Gender differences in vocational personality types: Implications for school counselors. *Professional School Counseling, 10*, 317–326. doi:10.5330/PSC.n.2010–11:317

Wingfield, R. J., Reese, R. F., & West-Olatunji, C. A. (2010). Counselors as leaders in schools. *Florida Journal of Educational Administration & Policy, 4*, 114–128.

7 Understanding How to Define Your School Counseling Program Using the ASCA National Model

Caroline A. Baker and Sibyl Cato West

CACREP Standards

G. School Counseling

3. Practice

a. development of school counseling program mission statements and objectives
b. design and evaluation of school counseling programs
h. skills to critically examine the connections between social, familial, emotional, and behavior problems and academic achievement
l. techniques to foster collaboration and teamwork within schools

Chapter Objectives:

- apply the Define section of the American School Counselor Association National Model to clinical experiences, including:

   o a review of the ASCA School Counselor Professional Standards and Competencies
   o a review of the ASCA Mindsets and Behaviors for Student Success
   o a review of the ASCA Ethical Standards for School Counselors

Introduction

Think about the school in which you are working as an intern or practicum student. It is probably durable, serving hundreds if not thousands of students and staff every day, having done so for many years. How did the physical structure of the building come to exist? What had to take place in order for the structure to be sound and stable? It is reasonable to assume that the building follows specific codes, standards for construction, electricity, plumbing, and safety? A team of people collaborated to design the building and thought about its function, the needs of the population to be served, and the longevity of the building materials. In other words, the project of designing and building a school rested on a solid foundation of standards and expertise. Likewise, establishing your comprehensive school counseling program using the Define section of the American School Counselor Association National Model (ASCA, 2019b) allows the Manage and Deliver sections to assemble, and it is integral to Assess your school counseling program. Comprehensive school counseling programs rely upon a sturdy, professionally agreed upon, clear foundation. How do you determine what to do? How do you ensure professional competency? And how do ethical standards influence programs?

This chapter will help you understand the answers to the questions above, as well as the implementation and application of the Define section of the National Model. The Define section includes student and professional standards, specifically:

- the *ASCA Mindsets and Behavior Standards for Student Success* (ASCA, 2014)
- the *ASCA School Counselor Professional Standards and Competencies* (ASCA, 2019a)
- the *ASCA Ethical Standards for School Counselors* (ASCA, 2016)

The ultimate goal of a comprehensive school counseling program requires you to define a solid foundation to ensure that all students receive the necessary services to help them succeed, and you are instrumental in contributing to this aim.

ASCA National Model History

The ASCA National Model is currently in its fourth edition, having originated in 2003. Throughout the evolution of the framework, the three domains of academic, career, and social-emotional learning and behavior have been central. In the early versions, however, the ASCA Diamond rested on the Foundation component. The Foundation was your starting place to create a comprehensive school counseling program. At this stage, you would explore your beliefs about students, your specific, measurable, achievable, realistic, and time-bound goals for the program. From this, you can determine how to deliver your program, and how to manage and assess its efficacy to be accountable to stakeholders (ASCA, 2019b). In the current fourth edition of the ASCA National Model, program focus shifts to the Manage section, and the overall terminology reflects the active (rather than passive) voice. This change more accurately reflects the active nature of your school counseling role!

Now, school counselors are tasked with establishing a comprehensive program that serves all students, but is based in professional competencies, student standards for success, and ethical standards to guide our decision-making. We provide thoughtful, purposeful, professional services based on specific criteria. This promotes uniformity in professional identity, which is good for advocacy, yet it still allows room for interpretation based on the unique needs of your school. Let's explore the standards from which you will define your comprehensive school counseling program.

Conceptual Application Activity 7.1

How Have School Counselors Interpreted the ASCA National Model?

Talk with your site supervisor and other school counselors about the unique ways they maintain a comprehensive school counseling program while also meeting the specific needs of their school site. Write down three ideas for further reflection.

_____

_____

_____

ASCA Mindsets and Behaviors for Student Success: K–12 College- and Career-Readiness Standards for Every Student

The ASCA National Standards were first developed as a smorgasbord of competencies from which school counselors were able to choose for the purpose of addressing the knowledge, skills, and attitudes students need in order to attain academic, career, and social/emotional success. To align with current research and trends, these standards are now renamed the ASCA Mindsets and Behaviors for Student Success: K–12 College- and Career-Readiness Standards for Every Student (2014). The ASCA Mindsets and Behaviors align with grade-level competencies and Common Core state standards to facilitate school counselors' ability to support student growth through collaboration, group and individual counseling, and team teaching. These student competencies integrate the academic, career, and social/emotional domains, and are applicable across developmental levels. These standards are shown in Table 7.1 below (ASCA, 2014).

These ASCA Mindsets and Behaviors for Student Success supplement the Common Core standards and state-developed student competency standards. By crosswalking these standards with the state's standards to identify overlap and to establish program goals, more credibility is provided for their application. Furthermore, the crosswalk may serve as a checklist to show what the school counselor is doing and what activities need to be done to eliminate disparities in defining the comprehensive school counseling program.

School Counselor Professional Competencies and Standards

Not only do students have identified knowledge, skills, and behaviors to achieve as a result of participating in a school counseling program, school counselors also have a responsibility to attain identified competencies to serve as effectual leaders of a comprehensive school counseling program. The ASCA School Counselor Professional Competencies and Standards

Table 7.1 General categories and subcategories of ASCA Mindsets and Behaviors.

Category 1: Mindset Standards
Personal psycho-social attitudes and individual beliefs about his/her academic ability
School counselors encourage the following mindsets for all students:

1. self-confidence in ability to succeed
2. belief in development of the whole self, including integration of academics with activities at school, home, and in the community that enhance learning and life experiences
3. understanding that postsecondary education and lifelong learning are necessary for long-term career success
4. belief in using their abilities to their fullest to achieve high-quality results and outcomes
5. positive attitude toward work and learning

Category 2: Behavior Standards
Students will demonstrate learning strategies, self-management skills, and social skills
The Behavior category is sub-grouped into:

a. *learning strategies*: strategies used to aid in thinking, remembering, or learning
b. *self-management*: the ability to focus on a goal, avoid distractions, and prioritize
c. *social skills*: appropriate behaviors that enhance social interactions with others

(ASCA, 2019a) may be used by school counselors to assess their own competence and areas for growth on an annual basis. Furthermore, you can use this checklist to evaluate your competencies as you begin your clinical experiences and to ascertain personal goals as you progress through the profession. Combining knowledge of personal values, professional ethics, federal and state laws, ASCA Mindsets and Behaviors for Student Success, and professional competencies yields a vast body of information that aids in forming a comprehensive school counseling program definition.

Conceptual Application Activity 7.2

Professional Competencies and Goals

Review the ASCA School Counselor Professional Competencies and Standards to determine your areas of strength and areas for growth. Ask your site supervisor to complete it with you. Once you have discussed the results with your site supervisor, develop three goals for your own professional and personal development. Are the goals SMART (specific, measurable, attainable, results-oriented, and time-bound)?

_____

_____

_____

As you begin to understand the elements that support the Define section, you are also applying a code of conduct that guides our profession. The ASCA Ethical Standards for School Counselors (ASCA, 2016) support the mission of the profession and the principles that define ethical behavior and practices. Although Chapter 11 provides you with more detailed considerations regarding these practices, the following section presents a glimpse of how our values shape the professional decisions we make.

Ethical Standards and Laws

Defining a comprehensive school counseling program requires familiarity with professional ethical standards and awareness of laws and policy. Perhaps the starting place for defining a strong comprehensive school counseling program is to identify personal and professional values about education and students and to compare those values with the ASCA Ethical Standards for School Counselors (ASCA, 2016), and state and local laws. How do you define a value? Although there are numerous definitions, a definition provided by the American Psychological Association (2007) states that a value is "a moral, social, or aesthetic principle accepted by an individual or society as a guide to what is good, desirable, or important" (p. 975). Your idea of "good, desirable, or important" might mean such things as collaborating through teamwork, working hard to achieve goals, helping all students succeed, and balancing work with self-care. But what do these values actually look like in practice? How do they compare with your ethical code or established law?

Box 7.2

"Cheshire Cat," asked Alice, "would you tell me, please, which way I ought to go from here?" "That depends a good deal on where you want to go," said the Cat. "I don't much care where," said Alice. "Then it doesn't matter which way you go," said the Cat.

Source: Charles "Lewis Carroll" Dodgson,
Alice's Adventures in Wonderland

The ASCA Ethical Standards for School Counselors (ASCA, 2016) outline best practices for navigating often ambiguous situations to ensure that student and parent rights are upheld. When school counselors face sensitive or tricky situations, ethical standards provide guidance as to the collectively agreed upon standards of practice. The ethical code also outlines a decision-making model to employ in situations with which you may be confronted. Further, consultation with professional peers, while maintaining confidentiality, is considered ethical practice.

Sometimes our values align with the ethical code. Sometimes they do not. An example might be regarding cultural competence and working with diverse populations. The ASCA Ethical Standards require that school counselors "respect students' and families' values, beliefs, sexual orientation, gender identification/expression and cultural background, and exercise great care to avoid imposing personal beliefs or values rooted in one's religion, culture or ethnicity" (ASCA, 2016, p. 1). Are you able to do this for all students, regardless of their identity? How might your values impact your work with students and other stakeholders?

Conceptual Application Activity 7.3

Aligning Personal Beliefs with Ethics

Read the following case outline and respond to the questions.

A student with wrinkled, dirty clothes and unkempt hair comes to you and reports that a teacher constantly harasses her and makes rude comments about her friends. You have seen the student in the halls and at lunch, always with a group of friends. After looking up the student's file, you find that the student has been to the counseling office for several concerns throughout her high school career.

a. How did you immediately picture the student? In your mind, how did you picture the student's race, gender, age, ability level, socioeconomic status, sexual orientation, and personality? What assumptions did you have about the teacher?

b. How do you define yourself regarding the aspects of identity listed above? Are your characteristics the same as or different from the student's?

c. Review the ASCA Ethical Standards for School Counselors for guidance around working with diverse populations. How do your assumptions/beliefs match up with the ethical standards? Discuss this with your site supervisor, instructor, or peer.

Figure 7.1 School counselors have an ethical responsibility to maintain confidentiality unless the
        student indicates harm to self or others.
Source: Shutterstock.

Further, how do the state and federal laws intersect with your ethical code and your
values? The ASCA Ethical Standards (ASCA, 2016) require that confidentiality be upheld to
ensure that students feel safe in the counseling relationship. School counselors must "promote the autonomy of students to the extent possible and use the most appropriate and
least intrusive method to breach confidentiality, if such action is warranted" (p. 2). You
might be a parent or teacher, so your values might tell you that information would be helpful to share with anyone invested in the student. Law may tell you that your information is
legally required or subpoenaed in a civil or criminal case involving your students. Although
it is usually the student who has privilege, the counselor has the responsibility of maintaining
this right (Wheeler & Bertram, 2012). Check to see whether or not "privileged communication," a legal term, exists between the student and school counselor in your state. According
to the ASCA Ethical Standards (ASCA, 2016), privileged communication is "conversation
that takes place within the context of a protected relationship, such as between an attorney
and client … and in some estates, a school counselor and a student" (p. 10).

When you get into your practicum and internship field experiences, pay close attention to
how your site supervisor handles sensitive situations, and ask questions to gain an understanding of the reasons why events were handled in a certain manner. Do you feel comfortable with the way in which he or she talks to other school professionals about certain
students and certain confidential situations? If not, how would you handle it? Similarly,
school personnel may seek a counseling relationship with you; you will need to identify how
to maintain appropriate professional and role boundaries.

Conceptual Application Activity 7.4

Ethical Case Processing

Ask your site supervisor to tell you about a recent ethical decision he/she had to make. Find out what ethical codes applied to the case, the decision-making model that was used, whether your site supervisor consulted with another professional to determine the decision, and what the outcome was. On your own, reflect on this discussion and determine your own ideas about working through the ethical case.

_____

_____

Conclusion

School counselors play vital roles in the success of all students and are essential in integrating the school counseling program with the mission of the school. In order to do this, the school counselor must define the comprehensive school counseling program using standards of the profession. How do school counselors do this? They assess professional competencies guiding practice as a school counselor. They review and become familiar with professional ethics and local and federal laws. They work toward student competency in areas outlined by states and the school counseling profession. Once the program definition is initiated and maintained, delivering, managing, and assessing the program will follow, with purposeful and specific goals in mind.

References

American Psychological Association. (2007). *Dictionary of psychology*. Washington, DC: American Psychological Association.

ASCA. (2014). *ASCA mindsets and behaviors for student success: K–12 college- and career-readiness standards for every student*. Retrieved from www.schoolcounselor.org/asca/media/asca/home/MindsetsBehaviors.pdf

ASCA. (2016). *Ethical standards for school counselors*. Retrieved from www.schoolcounselor.org/asca/media/asca/Ethics/EthicalStandards2016.pdf

ASCA. (2019a). *School counselor professional standards and competencies*. Alexandria, VA: ASCA.

ASCA. (2019b). *The ASCA National Model: A framework for school counseling programs* (4th ed.). Alexandria, VA: ASCA.

Wheeler, A. M., & Bertram, B. (2012). *The counselor and the law: A guide to legal and ethical practice*. Alexandria, VA: American Counseling Association.

8 Understanding How to Manage Your School Counseling Program Using the ASCA National Model

Aaron H. Oberman and Jeannine R. Studer

CACREP Standards

Foundations

d. models of school-based collaboration and consultation
e. assessments specific to P-12 education

Contextual Dimensions

k. community resources and referral sources

Practice

o. use of data to advocate for programs and students

Chapter Objectives:

- present an overview of the Manage component in a comprehensive school counseling program
- discuss beliefs, vision, and mission statements that are integral to a program focus
- provide information on program planning, including data, student outcome goals, action plans, calendars, administrative conference, use-of-time calculator, and advisory council

Introduction

A program cannot exist without first developing a program focus that includes beliefs, vision, and mission statements. Nor can it exist without thoughtful program planning for meeting the needs of all students, without people who are responsible for certain duties, a plan for when activities will occur, or administrative support for the system structure. Not only is it important for you to be aware of all the individuals with whom you will be interacting, it is also essential for you to be aware of the hierarchy of supervision and communication patterns that exists. When you first enter the school, policies and procedures will already be in place, and it is up to you to determine how your academic training requirements can be fulfilled within the parameters of the school mission and goals.

The Manage component, like all the components in the American School Counselor Association National Model, does not stand by itself. This component can be compared to a general contractor building a house, who is responsible for balancing multiple roles that are scheduled on a master calendar. The general contractor must have oversight control and agreements among the subcontractors, all of whom need to be aware of the scheduled completion dates and how each person will work with other individuals involved with the project. Finally, consideration needs to be given to how stakeholders will view the final results (e.g., the home buyer's satisfaction with the completed home). Much like the layout of a home, the school structure will partially dictate when and where you will conduct activities, and is influenced by the physical floor plan of the school (e.g., the location of offices, classrooms, cafeteria, gymnasium, theater). Within this section, assessments and tools are created to manage the organizational structure of the school counseling program, yet space, school culture, and climate influence decisions and the school counselor's role.

Program Focus and Program Planning are the two sections within the Manage component, with various elements that better define these sections. A discussion of each of these sections and the various elements within each will now follow.

Program Focus

Beliefs, vision, and mission statements are the elements within this section. Although you may have already taken a class on the ASCA National Model and developed your beliefs, vision, and mission statements as an assignment in this class, keep in mind that as you gain more experience in understanding the school counselor's role, your beliefs surrounding the school counseling program and school counselor's role will probably change. You will develop new insights and knowledge with each person you encounter, and in turn, these opportunities will impact your thoughts about yourself and the profession. Therefore, your values are ever-evolving, and what you think is essential to the profession at this time may not be a priority in the future. As you read this chapter, the conceptual application activities are designed to help you either rethink these initial efforts or to help you begin the process of developing these fundamental affirmations if you have not had an opportunity before now.

Creating the focus of your school counseling program is one of the most important aspects of your role as a school counselor. The program focus articulates your beliefs, vision, and mission statements, and targeted goals that the school counseling program hopes to achieve regarding the academic, career, and social/emotional development of students. Without a defined program focus, school counselors have a greater chance of being assigned non-school counseling duties that detract from student needs being met.

Beliefs

A belief is defined by the *Merriam-Webster Dictionary* as the "conviction of the truth of some statement or the reality of some being or phenomenon especially when based on examination of evidence." Think about the experiences you had as a student with your pre-K–12 school counselors. Did you have good experiences and fond memories of your interactions with these individuals? Or did you have disagreeable involvements? Did these situations serve as catalysts for entering the school counseling profession? Building a belief system about school counselors and the program they lead requires you to think about your beliefs regarding education, students, and other stakeholders. As you shape your beliefs, you may find that they will be transformed through conversations with school counselors and other professions. And it is likely that the experiences you have in the school will inform how you think about school counseling. It is likely that your beliefs will change as you continue to gain experience in the schools. Conceptual Application Activity 8.1 is designed to assist with this process.

Conceptual Application Activity 8.1

The following questions are designed to help you think about your beliefs surrounding school counseling.

1.   What is the role of the school counselor? _____
     _____

2.   How is the school counselor an integral professional in the school setting? _____
     _____

3.   How are students different as a result of participating in a school counseling program?
     _____

4.   How do school counselors work with stakeholders? _____
     _____

5.   How do school counselors demonstrate their effectiveness? _____
     _____

6.   Share your beliefs statements with your peers, and as a group write a short paragraph that is a consensus of your beliefs. _____
     _____

Vision and Mission

School counselors who believe in and follow the principles behind the ASCA National Model and who effectively meet the needs of their school serve as excellent resources for describing and modeling a school counseling identity. These professionals have integrated their training, values, and beliefs with the existing school and district mission statements to form a collaborative alliance that functions as a framework to facilitate student success. If you are provided with the opportunity to create or revise a vision or mission statement for your school building or school counseling program, be aware that the task will not be simple. The task is to look ahead to the future and to incorporate personal, professional, and collective values about student success and what success will look like in five or more years. Keep in mind, however, that the reason you are creating a vision is to pave the way toward greater student and school success. The ASCA National Model (ASCA, 2019) provides excellent examples of vision statements for you to consider while you undertake this task.

According to the ASCA National Model (ASCA, 2019), an effective mission statement incorporates the mission of the school district and state regarding education and addresses the success of every student. This means that the collective belief must be that *all* students can succeed, and must be given access to equitable resources to do so. In addition, the focus of the mission statement should have each student in the forefront, with an indication of the long-range objectives for all students. Creating a mission statement from scratch is not an easy task, especially if the school counselor is new to the role or to the school building. Including key stakeholders, such as teachers, parents, and administrators, is essential for forming a vision and associated mission statement for the CSC program.

Conceptual Application Activity 8.2

Using your notes from Conceptual Application Activity 8.1, develop your own vision and mission statement for your site's school counseling program. Carefully craft your statements using data and your beliefs about students. Once you feel comfortable with your statements, compare them with the vision and mission statements endorsed by your site. How do they compare? Was there anything you left out or included that was significantly different from your site's statements? What will you take away from this activity? Discuss this with your site supervisor.

_____

_____

Box 8.1

"I don't care how much power, brilliance, or energy you have. If you don't harness it and focus it on a specific target and hold it there, you're never going to accomplish as much as your ability warrants."

Source: Zig Ziglar

Program Planning

Program Planning is the second section of the Manage component and includes data, program planning, school data summary, annual student outcome goals, action plans, lesson plans, calendars, annual administrative conference, use-of-time calculator, and the advisory council.

Data

Data help us to understand school needs, students who are not receiving vital services, and program and intervention effectiveness. Data touch on myriad National Model components and sections, and within the Manage component, the school profile is reviewed, evaluated, and decisions made based on disaggregating data to determine whether certain groups of students are not being reached. As you have learned, accountability is in the form of revealing who receives services from the members of the school counseling program, how academic, college and career readiness, and by what means social/emotional development is impacted and enhanced based on these interactions. These primary standards are based on data known as *Participation, Mindsets and Behaviors*, and *Outcome*.

Participation Data

Identifying an audience based on needs assessments or other data determined by surveys, the school profile, or action-based research creates a participation focus. For instance, suppose a needs assessment indicated that fifth-grade students needed more assistance with social skills. The school counselor might work with teachers to identify students for participation in a small friendship group or provide classroom instruction to all fifth-grade classrooms. Or, if it is determined that parents require more information on how to assist their students with homework, a parent group could be created to address this issue. These are examples of participation data, or enumerative data, and indicate where time is spent, with whom, and when activities occur. Your clinical log is an example of participation data.

Mindsets and Behaviors Data

The ASCA Mindsets and Behaviors for Student Success consist of 35 standards that describe the knowledge, skills, and attitudes students need in order to be proficient in academics, career- and college-readiness, and social/emotional development. The Mindset Standards consist of the psycho-social attitudes students adapt regarding their academic achievement, whereas Behavior Standards include student performance in learning strategies, self-management, and social skills. For a complete list of the Mindsets and Behaviors, see www.schoolcounselor.org/asca/media/asca/home/MindsetsBehaviors.pdf.

Conceptual Application Activity 8.3

Select a Mindset and the standard that is applicable to an identified activity you wish to explore. Next, choose a Behavior Standard to be addressed. Choose the participants who will participate in this activity and decide the method (large group, classroom, or small group) you will use to conduct this activity. Discuss this activity with your supervisor and determine how you will assess student performance. Conduct the activity, and answer the following questions:

* What went well with this activity?

  _____

* What would you do differently?

  _____

Outcome Data

Outcome data reveal the effectiveness of interventions and activities in reaching goals. Outcome results include short-term data that assess change within a few weeks or months, intermediate data measure program effectiveness for an academic year time frame, and long-term data analyze changes year after year over multiple years. Attendance reports, discipline referrals, progress reports, and unit/semester exams provide short-term data that you can use to monitor the impact of school counseling intervention programs on student behaviors, skills, and/or knowledge.

Outcome evaluations compare pre-program data with post-program data as presented in school report cards, student data management systems, and other measures of student performance. These data can be beneficial to your site supervisor in determining areas to address with the school counseling curriculum, and your efforts in collecting this information may create a legacy in the school for others to continue.

All of these primary data types are based on various means to collect information such as needs assessments, surveys, test results, and so on. Additional information regarding needs assessments can be found below.

Needs Assessments

Data from a needs assessment aids in identifying where it is essential to improve areas of student, parent, teachers, or administrator concerns. These types of assessments may be compared with other school data such as those on the school profile, and assist in determining program goals and academic, career, and social/emotional standards for student success. Figure 8.1 shows an example of the results of a needs assessment that was given to teachers by a school counseling intern. Additional examples of needs assessments that can be adapted for your particular school can be found on the ASCA website (www.school counselor.org).

In the example in Figure 8.1, elementary school teachers were asked to indicate the areas they believed were most needed by the students in their school, and the intern categorized the top needs and responses by topics which she presented on the chart. If you are unfamiliar with creating computer-generated graphs, a helpful, simplistic website that can assist you in converting data into graph form is available from the National Center for Education Statistics "Kids' Zone" at http://nces.ed.gov/nceskids/createagraph/default.aspx.

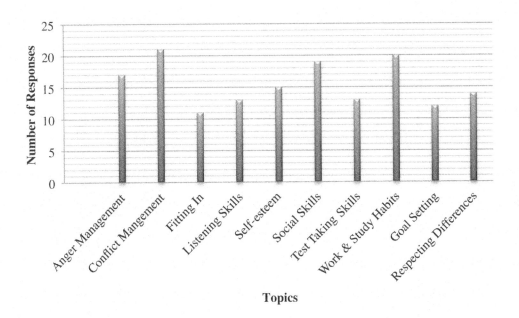

Figure 8.1 Example of a needs assessment.

Conceptual Application Activity 8.4

After analyzing the school profile and disaggregating data, look at the needs assessment examples available from the ASCA website (www.schoolcounselor.org). Design your own needs assessment to use with the stakeholders in the school in which you are interning. Show this assessment to your supervisor and administrator so that they can review it, and see if you can gain permission to distribute and analyze the results of the needs assessment. Share your results with your classmates.

Annual Data Review

Review of data based from several sources is an ongoing process in which school counselors annually identify, evaluate, and revise goals, activities, and interventions that are identified from the ASCA Mindsets and Behaviors. The SMART acronym may be used to assist in the creation of school counseling program goals based on school data which help you execute and achieve the vision and mission statement of your school counseling program. SMART goals are specific, measurable, attainable, results-oriented, and time-bound (Taylor, 2018). Several steps assist in establishing a SMART goal:

1.   Examine school, district, and state report card data to identify problem areas within the school such as academic achievement gaps between groups of students, discipline rates, attendance issues, inequitable access to resources, and so on. Other types of data include needs assessments, interviews with stakeholders, classroom observations, and pre- and post-tests. Collect data from a variety of sources to clearly identify a problem area that will be targeted using the SMART goal format.
2.   After the data have been examined and a problem is identified, the next step is to outline current interventions to target the problem, if any. In other words, what are the academic, career, and social/emotional developmental activities occurring now which correspond to this gap? Creating a comprehensive list is a concrete method for school counselors to identify what is being done, and, conversely, what is not being done to address this gap.
3.   At this stage, you will have formed a tentative and vague goal to start shaping into a refined SMART goal. However, this is an opportune time to review the school improvement plan and to discuss school goals with administrators. Aligning the goals, activities, and interventions of the school counseling program with the school's instructional accountability goals is an integral step to garner the support of stakeholders.
4.   Finally, format your SMART goals by indicating exactly how each one is:

   - *Specific*: What exact problem do you want to address and how does your goal state precisely what it will do?
   - *Measurable*: Is your goal something that can be measured or evaluated in formative or summative ways?

- **Attainable*: Is your goal realistic or possible, considering current resources and funding? What might you need to achieve your goal?
- *Results-oriented*: Does your goal promote results, based on attainability and measurability? Do you know what you want the end results of the goal to be?
- *Time-bound*: Is there a finite time period in which to achieve this goal, or will this goal permit people involved to work indefinitely? Having a finite time period increases the likelihood of successful achievement of SMART goals.

Keep in mind that SMART goals are flexible, with room for evaluation and revision after your intervention is complete. This will help to refine your goals in the future.

School Data Summary and Annual Student Outcome Goals

It may be important for you as a SCIT to peruse the school report card for the school in which you are placed. This analysis includes such information as the school's attendance, behavior, and achievement data to understand the school culture (ASCA, 2019). Investigating these data at the start of each school year serves as a basis for establishing a baseline for determining continuous program and school improvements. As a SCIT, you have an opportunity to see strengths and weaknesses in the school counseling program, and you can be instrumental in collecting and analyzing data. Learning how to make decisions based on these data will provide opportunities for you to contribute to student growth in your school setting now and will give you the skills to continue to collect this information when you transition to being a full member of the school counseling profession.

Once you have had an opportunity to analyze the school report card, determine student outcome goals that may address any school deficiencies that you notice. Compare these areas with any areas of concern you have determined through other sources of information such as the Mindsets and Behaviors. Addressing school concerns will also leave a lasting legacy at the school, and one in which your efforts will be appreciated. Look at Conceptual Application Activity 8.5 with a partner and identify an area of concern and intervention strategies for addressing this issue.

Conceptual Application Activity 8.5

High School Profile
Enrollment—1600
Grades 9–12

	2017–2018	*2018–2019*	*State Average*
Graduation rate	67%	65%	83%
College-readiness	25%	23%	53%
Race/ethnicity			
Black/African American	60%	58%	
Asian	0%	1%	
American Indian	0%	0%	
Pacific Islander	0%	0%	
White	22%	25%	

(*Continued*)

(Cont.)

	2017–2018	2018–2019	State Average
Hispanic/Latino	13%	14%	
Two or more races	4%	2%	
Students with disabilities	20%	20%	14%
Low income	3%	77%	50%
Homeless	1%	2%	2%
English learners	0%	1%	10%
Student mobility	14%	22%	13%
Chronic truancy rate	25%	17%	10%
Student attendance	87%	91%	94%

What areas of concern have you located? Brainstorm strategies for addressing this concern.

Action Plans

Action plans may be in the form of Mindsets and Behaviors and Closing-the-Gap activities. These plans are similar, in that information regarding the goals, student standards, type of activity, timeline, individuals responsible for the activities, and evaluation are developed and shared. In the contract you have developed for practicum or internship, you and your supervisors have identified various activities in which you will be involved; these tasks can be written as an action plan. As you are developing plans for your contract, or as you begin a new counseling position, you will be called upon to perform tasks that may require a lot of preparation time. It is not unusual for you to experience anxiety as you anticipate your role in implementing this task, and it is also not uncommon for you to use this as an opportunity to enhance your knowledge and skill. For instance, as stated by a former intern:

> When completing my school counseling internship, my supervisor placed me in charge of a financial aid night presentation. Fear mixed with great consternation immediately overcame me! However, this forced me to learn as much about financial aid as possible in preparation for the presentation. Not only did I learn about a subject to which I previously had little knowledge, a secondary benefit was the invaluable relationships (business and personal) that I developed with various financial aid directors at postsecondary institutions.

All individuals who are essential to the school counseling program are included in the Manage component so that all are aware of who is responsible for each activity, when and where it will occur, the evaluation means, and the supplies or equipment that are needed. As stated previously, the school counseling program does not stand alone; it is an integral component of the school mission. For example, the standards chosen from the Mindsets and Behaviors for Student Success can be addressed in a classroom in partnership with the school counselor and teacher. Or the school social worker or community human service workers may be invited into the school to discuss pertinent issues. In some cases, a written contract that identifies monetary arrangements will be needed for outside individuals who

assist with programming. Before making these types of arrangements, the building administrator, your supervisor, and/or individuals outside of the school system who are facilitating
program activities must be informed of all contractual agreements. Information regarding
materials, data, and contact personnel are in the form of a lesson plan.

Lesson Plans

A lesson plan is a written guide of how you will carry out a class lesson, and typically
includes the following:

- Mindset Standard that corresponds to student psycho-social attitudes and/or beliefs
  regarding academic work
- Behavior Standard, which includes:

  o   Learning Strategies
  o   Self-management Skills
  o   Social Skills

- instructional materials and equipment that will be used
- instructional strategies and the sequence in which they will be presented
- who will be conducting the lesson
- assessment method(s) to be used for student learning

In writing lesson plans, *goals* refer to the long-term outcome of instruction, and *objective* refers
to the specific desired outcome of a unit or lesson. One way to look at an instructional goal is to
think of it as a standard as outlined in the Mindsets and Behavior for Student Success.

Well-written lessons include four key components, sometimes referred to as the ABCDs of
learning. First is the audience (A) to whom the objective is being directed, in most cases the
students. The second is a statement of the expected behavioral (B) outcome(s) that will
result from the lesson. The third is the condition(s) (C) under which the learning will
occur. And finally, lesson objectives need to include the degree (D) of the expected performance (Erford, 2016) or the frequency with which students will demonstrate mindsets
and behaviors. An example of a lesson plan is shown in Figure 8.2.

Other examples of ASCA Mindsets and Behaviors program templates can be found at
www.schoolcounselor.org.

Mindset	Academic	Career	Social/ Emotional	Behavior Mindset	Individual conducting activity	Condition of Learning SM/LG/ Classroom	Materials	Evaluation	
M1	X	X	X	B-LS1 B-SMS1 B-SS1					
M4	X	X		B-SMS5					

Figure 8.2 Example of a lesson plan.

It is important to remember that a lesson plan is merely a guide, and not a strict "recipe" in which there has to be rigid adherence to achieve a desired outcome (Ormrod, Anderman, & Anderman, 2020). As you progress through a lesson, you may find that students are not as knowledgeable about the topic as you originally thought, or you might have to review a concept you expected students to have already mastered. You may also find that the students will show particular interest or curiosity about a particular topic that could mean spending more time than you originally intended in teaching that topic. The thing to remember in conducting a classroom lesson is to be flexible. The ultimate goal is to reach a desired outcome; how you and the students get there is a journey. You want the journey to be engaging, challenging, and rewarding for both you and the students. More information about classroom management and instruction is available in Chapter 9.

Conceptual Application Activity 8.6

Ask your site supervisor to share copies of his/her lesson plans. Note the various categories that are used to organize the information.

- Is the lesson plan written according to district policy?
- What materials are crosswalked with the Mindsets and Behaviors for Student Success?
- Are lesson plans required to be filed with the central office?

Share the information you found with your classmates, and discuss the similarities and differences.

_____

_____

August	*September*
Schedule new students	Individual student meetings with seniors
Orientation for incoming students	Order test materials
Information session for new teachers and substitutes about the school counseling program	Visit classrooms to introduce members of school counseling program
Analyze data from school report card	Design group for study skills

October	*November*
Parent conferences scheduled	Student Study Team meetings
Data collection	Parent/guardian workshop
Conduct divorce group	College night
PSAT testing	Advisory board meeting
Senior classroom programming	Analyze data

Figure 8.3 Example of events on a calendar for planning purposes, informing stakeholders of upcoming events, and documenting participation data.

Calendars

The types of calendars include the annual calendar and weekly calendar. Having a yearly calendar signifying what you will be doing throughout the academic year provides an opportunity for all interested personnel to be cognizant of when events will occur, who is involved, and responsibilities in meeting program standards. Activities are identified on a master calendar to indicate the activity, person(s) responsible, date, location, audience or recipients, and additional comments. Figure 8.3 shows an example of a calendar of events.

Keeping track of all the activities a counselor performs each day is difficult, and school counselors have learned to organize themselves according to a system that works best for them. For instance, taking time to identify dates of standardized tests such as the PSAT ahead of time and marking dates on the calendar as a reminder to order the materials prevents last-minute, stressful requisition of materials. Or, if you are planning a career day at some date in the future, indicating this event on the school district calendar in advance will also keep you organized and aware of tasks that need to be conducted prior to this date, and informs other personnel about future events.

Calendars can be in an electronic form, daily hard copy agenda, or a weekly file divided into compartments for each day of the week with the appropriate information filled in in each section. Finding available dates on calendars to schedule appointments or meetings can be problematic. However, to make scheduling easier, Doodle is a free electronic solution for scheduling events in which invited individuals are able to indicate available times and dates. It can be found at https://play.google.com/store/apps/details?id=com.doodle.android&hl=en_US

Managerial strategies that you can utilize while conducting your activities in the clinical setting include the following:

- Divide projects by those that take precedence, and categorize these tasks into priorities such as A = important and urgent, B = important but not urgent, C = urgent but not important, and D = delegate to more appropriate personnel. From the authors' experience, it seems that most counselors are good at managing A-level priorities, but are not as adept at handling B-, C-, and D-level activities.
- Other helpful time-saving organizational tools include electronic or notebook calendars, master lists, file folders, large accordion folders, and computerized systems.
- Before leaving the office at the end of the day, review all your unfinished tasks and the calendar to identify upcoming activities. Prioritize tasks that need to be addressed the next day.

Conceptual Application Activity 8.7

Ask your supervisor to show you his or her personal calendar of events. Ask how it is organized and what managerial strategies have been most helpful. For instance, some elementary counselors use a different color marker for each grade level. When that color appears on the calendar, it serves as a reminder that an activity is to occur for that particular grade. Other counselors have a different personal calendar for each grade level. In a few sentences, describe the management system used by your supervisor. Share your supervisor's technique with your peers.

_____

_____

Annual Administrative Conference

As a SCIT, you have a contract that clearly identifies the tasks in which you will be involved and evaluated. As a professional school counselor, you will hopefully have a job description or annual agreement that clarifies your duties to prevent any misunderstanding as to the expectations surrounding your role. The job description that is mutually agreed upon not only serves as a contract specifying duties, but can also be used to identify personal and professional goals that fulfill the mission and vision of the school counseling program and school community. Too often when the responsibilities of the school counselor are not clearly defined, other stakeholders will express their opinions as to what the school counselor should be doing. These impressions are often based on perceptions from interactions rather than actual knowledge of the school counselor's training.

Continually evaluating your work as a school counselor and tracking data that indicate program and professional outcomes are useful when annual professional conferences are held. In addition, concretely revealing how your time is spent and the number of students who have been impacted are useful figures to reveal how your time impacts the education of students.

Box 8.2

With the wide variety of skills school counselors implement, the use of a particular skill depends on the anticipated outcome. For instance, *informing* involves one-way communication that flows from counselor to student. *Teaching* involves two-way communication in which information is provided and students participate to apply the knowledge. *Advising* is counselor/student-centered and helps students with decision-making. *Counseling* is student-focused, and students are able to resolve personal issues with the assistance of the counselor.

Source: Gysbers & Henderson (2012).

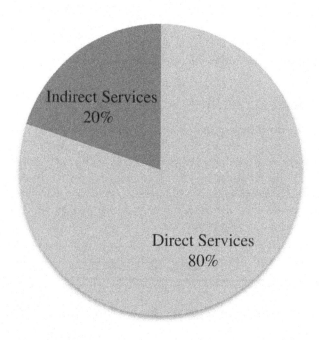

Figure 8.4 Counselors' use of time.

Use-of-Time Calculator

School counselors are required to spend 80% of their time on direct services to students that include instruction, appraisal and advisement, and counseling. These tasks are found within the Deliver component of the ASCA National Model. Indirect services are to take up 20% of the counselors' time, and include time focused on program planning and school support (ASCA, 2019).

Counselors often complain about the difficulty of tracking the myriad tasks they perform each day, and some use EZAnalyze (www.ezanalyze.com) and the Time Elapsed Analysis & Reporting System (TEARS) (www.schoolcounselor.com/tears) to calculate numbers of participants, activities, time spent in these tasks, and to offer a summary to share with stakeholders. Although these data are important, they are not enough. Mindsets and Behaviors and outcome data provide more credence to the effectiveness of the counselor's interventions.

Conceptual Application Activity 8.8

Use the technological applications mentioned above to track the time you spend each day on the various components of the ASCA National Model.

- In which areas do you spend the majority of your time?

  _____

- How does your time compare with those of your peers?

  _____

  Use the information to compare how your time is spent.

Conceptual Application Activity 8.9

Using the information in your contract, complete the following chart, or with the help of your supervisor, design one that more accurately reflects the templates adapted by the school board.

ASCA/State domain, standard	Grade level	Description of activity	Materials	Participation data	Mindsets and Behaviors data	Outcome data

Figure 8.5 Selecting a diverse advisory board helps to ensure that the needs of all students are addressed.

Source: Shutterstock.

Advisory Council

An advisory council serves as a support system for the CSC program and is composed of key stakeholder representatives. To provide credibility to these members, appointments should be supported by the administration and endorsed by the school board. It is not unusual for individual schools within the district to have an advisory council to provide feedback and concerns and to serve as liaisons to the school community. Although the school counseling advisory board serves in the same capacity, its focus is on the maintenance and evaluation of the CSC program. The advisory board is usually composed of no more than 12 individuals who characterize the diverse community and varying viewpoints. Meetings with the advisory council generally occur at the beginning of the school year, and again at the end of the school year to review, evaluate, and plan for the following year.

Conceptual Application Activity 8.10

Attend a meeting of the school counseling program advisory committee. Note the representatives who are part of this board. Discuss the advisory member composition with your peers.

- Are there similarities?
- Are there individuals who you believe should be on the board that are not represented?
- Discuss your reasons for selecting such individuals.

_____

_____

Conclusion

School counseling programs are designed to be effectively and efficiently managed, and the tools within this component provide school counselors with the ability to implement a program that assists student development in academics, careers, and social/emotional growth. The Manage component includes the program focus and program planning. Beliefs, vision, and mission statements are included in the program focus. Types of data, annual data review, school data summary, annual student outcome goals, action plans, lesson plans, calendars, annual administrative conference, use-of-time calculator, and the advisory council are elements within the Program Planning section.

Websites

- Post-it Notes with Evernote: https://help.evernote.com/hc/en-us/articles/209129077-Introduction-to-Post-it-Notes-With-Evernote

Using this auto-tag application gives users the opportunity to stamp the time, date, and person responsible for an activity. Access to your electronic calendar automatically adds the description of the activity.

- JumpStart Assessment Tools: www.jumpstart.com/parents/resources/assessment-tool

This site provides a number of resources, activities, worksheets, and assessments to use with school-aged youth in grades K–12.

- LessonPlanet: www.lessonplanet.com/search?keywords=School+Counselor&type_ids[ ]=357918&type_ids[ ]=357917&gclid=CODr2YWHpb4CFU8Q7AodbyAApA

This site provides a number of lesson plans, activities, projects, and videos for school counselors who work with students in all grades.

References

ASCA. (2019). *The ASCA National Model: A framework for school counseling programs* (4th ed.). Alexandria, VA: ASCA.

Erford, B. T. (2016). How to write learning objectives. In *Professional school counseling: A handbook of theories, programs and practices* (3rd ed.) (pp. 171–177). Austin, TX: Pro-ED.

Gysbers, N. C., & Henderson, P. (2012). *Developing & managing your school guidance & counseling program* (5th ed.). Alexandria, VA: ASCA.

Ormrod, J., Anderman, E., & Anderman, L. (2020). *Educational psychology: Developing learners* (10th ed.). Boston, MA: Allyn & Bacon.

Taylor, J. (2018). Start with a SMART goal. Retrieved from www.schoolcounselor.org/newsletters/october-2018/start-with-a-smart-goal

9 Understanding How to Deliver Your School Counseling Program Using the ASCA National Model

Jeannine R. Studer and Aaron H. Oberman

CACREP Standards

Foundations

a. models of school-based collaboration and consultation

Contextual Dimensions

b. school counselor roles in consultation with families, P-12 and postsecondary school personnel, and community agencies
k. community resources and referral sources

Practice

g. strategies to facilitate school and postsecondary transitions
m. strategies to implementing and coordinating peer intervention programs

Chapter Objectives:

- provide information on how the SCIT is able to gain experience in the Deliver component during the clinical experiences
- introduce strategies and interventions within each of the sections in the Deliver component
- identify direct and indirect student service activities

Introduction

The fourth edition of the ASCA National Model identifies the Deliver component as comprised of direct and indirect services to students, and answers the question, "What activities and strategies will be used to address student needs?"

Direct Student Services

The fourth edition of the ASCA National Model (ASCA, 2019) redefines direct student services as: (a) instruction, and (b) appraisal and advisement, and counseling.

Instruction

The school counselor provides classroom instruction by introducing activities that relate to the ASCA Mindsets and Behaviors and are integrated with the academic curriculum, which includes a lesson plan with appropriate standards and activities. All school counselors will spend time in the classroom regardless of the level in which they are assigned, with elementary and middle school counselors spending more time in the classroom than do high school counselors. Therefore, instructional awareness and familiarity with classroom management are essential parts of the job. Some state systems require aspiring school counselors to earn a teaching certificate, with some states also demanding teaching experience prior to working as school counselors. Instructional proficiency is a useful skill for conducting lessons in front of a large group, and may also assist in establishing credibility with teachers, particularly when consulting with teachers on classroom management. However, for those who do not have a teaching background, counseling skills such as reflective listening, paraphrasing, and summarizing are helpful tools. Take advantage of your role as a supervisee to learn under an experienced counselor, visit highly effective teachers in your building to gain ideas, and if possible, get experience by teaching a variety of ages in different types of settings such as in suburban, rural, and urban schools. Strategies for effective classroom management in addition to information on study skills that you can adapt to assist in classroom achievement are presented below.

Classroom Instruction and Management

Classroom management often creates difficulty for the SCIT, largely due to a lack of training and experience in leading large groups or a classroom of students. The development of inspirational, dynamic lessons can only be successful if there is effective classroom management. For novices, it is easy to lose control of a large group or classroom, and once this occurs, it is easy to become retaliatory in an attempt to regain group control, resulting in a loss of student interest and a lack of respect for you as the educator. Punitive measures typically lead to an argumentative relationship rather than the goal of creating a respectful rapport.

Knowledge and practice of effective strategies will assist you in becoming a successful large group or classroom facilitator. The following ideas and strategies are provided to help you begin to think about managing a large group or classroom:

- Give students important and active roles in the group. Meaningful roles keep students involved and engaged in learning. Students can be recorders/secretaries, summarizers, critical thinkers, timekeepers, co-facilitators, demonstrators, observers/monitors, evaluators, and so forth. Clearly explain each role and the corresponding responsibilities.
- Involve students in making rules with consequences that are predictable and consistent. Most teachers post classroom rules and involve students in making the rules; as counselors-in-training, follow their example. If you are fortunate enough to have your own designated classroom, post the rules and consequences and review them from time to time as you remind students that they were instrumentally involved in establishing the rules and consequences. Be willing to revise rules and consequences when circumstances deem it appropriate. Some school counselors find it helpful to follow the classroom rules established by the classroom teacher when visiting individual classrooms.

- When possible, arrange seating in a U-shape, circle, or other configuration so that you can see all students and students can see one another. When students sit in rows, discipline problems often occur in the back. Sitting in front helps everyone feel equally engaged and accountable.
- Use reasonable requests that are developmentally appropriate, stated positively, and specifically stated, with enough time provided for the student to perform the appropriate behavior.
- When you are teaching or facilitating, physically move around the room. If students are acting in a distracting manner, use physical closeness and approach them silently even if you are listening or talking to other students across the room.
- Develop pre-established transition rituals with time warnings that help students move from activity to activity. For example, you can clap your hands, or you can flick the lights off and on and verbally state, "We'll be shifting from large to small group activity in 5 minutes," or "Small group sharing time starts in 3 minutes, so please rearrange your chairs for small groups."
- Strategies adapted from solution-focused brief therapy accentuate what you want so that students develop a picture of acceptable behavior. Specifically identify and praise the behavior that is desired with statements such as, "Working quietly at your desk is appreciated" (Owens et al., 2017).
- Address the situation rather than the student (e.g., rather than "You were rude when I asked you to be quiet," say, "This is a time to pay attention"). Remain focused on behavior and the situation to make it less threatening, belittling, or insulting to the student.
- Point out choices and consequences. For example, say "You can either take the time to work on this assignment in class, or you will have to take it home to finish."
- Use the Premack principle, or "Grandma's rule." You have probably heard the statement, "If you eat all of your dinner, then you can have dessert." By providing an incentive as a result of performing something that may not be viewed favorably, the student is more likely to follow through on what is expected. For example, say "Choosing to work on this assignment in class will likely provide more free time when you are home."
- Find or create humor in situations, and use this humor to connect with students. By incorporating humor, the activity can be more enjoyable and motivating. Laugh with your students. Poking fun at yourself, admitting mistakes, and laughing at your errors shows students that you are human.
- Use your basic counseling skills such as attentive listening, summarizing, and open-ended questions.
- Use whole-group responses in which all students orally respond to a teacher prompt (Haydon, Marsicano, & Scott, 2013, as cited in Nagro, Fraser, & Hooks, 2019). In this situation, students hold up cards in response to a teacher-initiated prompt, or answer through the use of use of clickers (Nagro et al., 2016, as cited in Nagro et al., 2019).

Facilitating large groups is a professional activity conducted by school counselors and the SCIT in all settings. Although managing groups of students can be challenging, implementing positive and consistent group strategies can make classroom instruction fun and productive. A list of classroom management resources that you may find helpful is included at the end of this chapter.

Conceptual Application Activity 9.1

Read the following scenarios and decide on the classroom management strategy you would use in response to the situation.

You are conducting a classroom lesson on social skills in a fourth-grade classroom and you notice that Christina seems disengaged and uninterested despite the other students being actively involved in the lesson. When you quietly walk to her desk to prompt her to stay focused on the activity, she immediately starts to sob loudly and uncontrollably.

What would you do?

_____

_____

Roberto is a ninth-grader with whom you have developed rapport during the short period of time you have been interning in the high school. You are scheduled to talk about career planning in his social studies class, and as you are providing directions to the class, you notice he is talking to one of his peers. When you politely remind the class to pay attention to the instructions, Roberto yells, "This is so boring! You are wasting our time." After this outburst, the class starts snickering at his comments.

How do you handle this?

_____

_____

Learning Strategies

School counselors, like other members of the school community, have an obligation to show how their interventions support academic goals and outcomes (Zyromski, Dimmitt, Mariani, & Griffith, 2018). In fact, when we collect data and document strategies and show how our involvement assists in increasing academic performance, it is possible that unrelated tasks could be eliminated.

The ASCA Mindsets and Behaviors identify Behavior Standards that include learning strategies students utilize to assist in learning, and school counselors are able to employ a study skills curriculum that focuses on academic outcomes. Consequently, teachers may have a greater appreciation for the school counselor as student performance is improved, and an added benefit may be that teachers could be more amenable to releasing students from class. Note-taking, memory aids, and performance anxiety are discussed below for you to consider in facilitating academic achievement during your clinical experiences.

Note-Taking

The Cornell method of note-taking is often called the "T-note system" because it involves sectioning a piece of notebook paper into an upside-down T. Notes are recorded in the largest section, and next to this section is a 2½-inch cue section, with a 2-inch border at the bottom in which review notes are summarized and main points are highlighted. Templates for this system can be found at http://templatelab.com/cornell-notes/.

Memory Aids

Mnemonic devices are memory aids that assist in remembering information by helping your brain encode and recall information. Method of Loci is one method of memorizing information in which you imagine a place you are familiar with, such as your bedroom or classroom. Using the words or ideas that need to be remembered, visually imagine these concepts with objects in the room so that they are paired and associated together.

Creating an acronym is another useful memory aide. Acronyms involve looking at a list of words the student is trying to commit to memory and taking the first letter of each word to form a new word or list of letters. With the proliferation of texting and e-mailing, a common acronym is BTW, or "by the way." You can incorporate these strategies in your clinical experiences by working with individual students, through instruction in classes, or small groups. You may also want to consider developing a peer-tutoring group in which a group of students are trained to teach these strategies to their peers.

Student Activity 9.1

Are You Listening?

Some students have difficulty following directions, which leads to poorer academic growth. Teaching listening skills and how to focus on information that is provided is one strategy you can teach to students.

Materials needed: plain white paper and pencil or other writing utensil.

1. Have students find a partner. Decide who will be partner A and who will be partner B.
2. Ask students to sit back to back
3. Partner A will read the following instructions while partner B draws a picture according to the instructions. Partner B may not ask questions.

Directions to be given by Partner A:

a. Draw a small circle in the center of the paper.
b. Draw a line vertically from the inside of the circle.
c. Halfway down the line, draw a long oval shape to the left side of the line that touches the line.
d. Inside the oval, draw a square.
e. Inside the square, put a dot.

When finished, show the picture Partner B drew, and as a group discuss the following questions:

*   What was difficult about this exercise?
*   What would have made this exercise easier?
*   What does this activity teach you about listening?

Performance Anxiety

Students today have many mental health issues, with anxiety as one of the most common disorders influencing youth (Merikangas et al., 2010, as cited in Borquist-Conlon, Maynard, Brendel, & Farina, 2019). Youth as young as the age of 6 have shown debilitating and significant signs of anxiety (Niditch & Varela, 2018), and although stress is a normal part of life, debilitating stress can interfere with daily living and school performance in the form of school absences, school refusal, and lower academic achievement (Green et al., 2017). In a longitudinal study by Kraag, Van Breukelen, Kok, and Hosman (2009), 70% of high school students reported feeling anxious about schoolwork, with over 50% stating that they often or constantly worried about grades, tests, and college acceptance. In this same study, students reported that on average they spent approximately 3.07 hours on homework, with another 2 hours spent on extra-curricular activities each weekday. Stress that impacts mental and academic well-being is also reported among younger students.

A mega-analysis of school-based prevention programs designed to address mental health issues in youth have shown effective results, and as a result of participation in these groups, students revealed more positive coping, behavior, and less stress (Kraag, Zeegers, & Kok, 2006).

As a SCIT, you may consider implementing strategies that contribute to increased achievement by teaching study skills, in addition to strategies that reduce stress such as deep breathing, yoga, relaxation, and mindfulness.

Appraisal and Advisement

Individual student planning is intended to facilitate personal and/or career goal-setting through appraisal and advisement strategies. School counselors assist students in analyzing and assessing their strengths, abilities, and interests, and recommendations are made based on data such as tests and inventories. This process may take place individually, in small groups, or within a classroom setting. Although high school counselors spend more time on this area compared with middle and elementary school counselors, this activity is important for students of all ages.

Appraisal

Appraisal is an integral component of individual student planning, and generally refers to the selection of a test or assessment instrument, orientation to the instrument's purpose, administration procedures, monitoring/proctoring practices, and interpretation of the test or instrument results. School counselors are able to use the results of tests in conjunction with other sources of information (e.g. teachers, experiences, performance) to more accurately assess counselees' abilities and interests, and determine strengths and areas in which improvement is needed.

Students will be more apt to understand and take an assessment more seriously when they are told the purpose of the test in advance, as well as how the results will assist them. When students are actively involved in assessment processes, they are better able to make effective decisions specific to their needs. Furthermore, informing parents or guardians about test purposes, how results will be used, and providing an informational forum to answer questions about career and educational planning provides a partnership for educational planning. As stated by the ASCA position statement on high-stakes testing:

> The Every Student Succeeds Act (ESSA), enacted in 2015, represents a legislative move toward identifying multiple measures to assess student success. The act encourages an approach to testing that moves away from a sole focus on standardized tests to drive decisions ....

(ASCA, 2017, para. 4)

Box 9.1

Standardized testing doesn't take into account the developmental needs of children, which may result in emotional disturbances in many children. For instance, 18–20% of children may have moderate to extreme test anxiety that may manifest in forms of anger, fear, disappointment, and helplessness (Strauss, 2013).

As a SCIT, you also need to be aware of students with disabilities who struggle with traditional testing formats and may require unique testing accommodations. The Individuals with Disabilities Education Act (IDEA) and Individuals with Disabilities Education Improvement Act (IDEIA) mandate that reasonable adaptations and accommodations are available for optimal test-taking conditions. Additional information on working with students with disabilities can be found in Chapter 12.

Conceptual Application Activity 9.2

Observe your site supervisor as he or she orients students to a particular test, monitors/proctors the test, and interprets test results. What are some of the strategies that you feel are most useful in explaining test scores? Were there some areas that you think could have been explained differently?

_____

_____

Conceptual Application Activity 9.3

Take an opportunity to orient, administer, or interpret test results to one of your counselees. What were some of the particular challenges in performing this activity? Is there anything that you feel might have assisted you in this task?

_____

_____

Advisement

School counselors and school counselors-in-training often find themselves providing information to students, parents/guardians, teachers, and so forth to assist with academic, college, and career readiness, or social/emotional decision-making. Helping students and parents/guardians plan for the future while facilitating career readiness, exploring postsecondary schools well matched to the student's interests and skills, and applying to college or vocational programs are all common advising activities for school counselors, especially those at the high school level. Advisement activities can be conducted individually or in small groups, and it is wise to include school personnel and parents/guardians in the process.

In a study by Kamrath and Brooker (2018), teachers were asked to identify students to be part of a group based on high rate of absences from school, low grades, discipline problems, and the potential for academic success. The school counselor worked with these students in order to determine how well academic advisement influenced fourth- and fifth grade students in a low-performing school. The 45-minute sessions over 6 weeks included topics such as goal-setting, motivation, procrastination, managing emotions, and homework organization. The results of the study revealed the effectiveness of academic advisement intervention and the importance of parent–guardian cooperation and support (Kamrath & Brooker, 2018).

Conceptual Application Activity 9.4

Read and respond to the following scenario, and discuss your answers with your peers.

Mario is a struggling 18-year-old who has not earned the appropriate credits to be considered an eleventh-grader. He has only earned enough credits equivalent to those of a ninth-grader, and he comes to you for career information. You discuss his high school curriculum and ask him about his future career/academic goals. He indicates that he would like to attend college to become a social studies teacher, but his parents do not support this goal and are urging Mario to drop out of school to assist with the family trucking business. As Mario's father states, "After all, I don't have a high school diploma and own a successful business. You don't need a fancy college degree—you can do just fine without it."

How would you respond?

_____

_____

As students shift to higher education settings or careers, it is not unusual for school counselors to continue assisting their past graduates as they transition to other opportunities. Nor is it unusual for the school counselor to be involved with follow-up studies of graduates to gather information on how well the school counseling program assisted students in meeting their needs as they matriculated to the workforce or higher educational settings. Results of this data inform decisions about programs, offerings, activities, and needs that are not being met.

Conceptual Application Activity 9.5

Ask your supervisor to share a follow-up study that has been conducted of past graduates and his or her reactions to the study outcomes. How was the follow-up study conducted? What trends do you notice? Were there any changes that were made as a result of the results? Share and discuss what you found with your peers.

_____

_____

Counseling

Counseling is a direct student service that emphasizes individual or small-group counseling.

Box 9.2

The ASCA (2014) conducted a study to identify the concerns students struggle with the most as they enter the school. Twenty-eight percent of elementary school-aged students were most concerned about being away from parents, among middle school students, peer issues were the top concern (20%), and homework was the chief concern among high school students (20%). School counselors are instrumental in assisting students with transition concerns that could occur from grade to grade or school to school.

Small Group and Individual Counseling

According to the National Institute of Mental Health (2017), 1 in 5 children aged 13–18 have either already have been diagnosed with or will develop a mental health problem, which includes mood disorders (11%), conduct disorder (10%), or anxiety disorder (8%). In a study by Lapan, Whitcomb, and Aleman (2012, as cited in Fye, Miller, & Rainey, 2018), school counselors provided more responsive services when principals fully understood and supported the school counseling program. Participation in groups provides participants with support, coping skills, and problem-solving strategies in addition to a sense of connectiveness (Schreiber & O'Brien, 2015).

School counselors are central personnel for leading these activities, not only due to their training, but also because of their understanding of the school and culture and their fostered relationships with teachers and students. Small group counseling is a time-effective method in reaching more students experiencing similar concerns. Yet arranging for small groups and individual counseling can be problematic since some teachers are reluctant to release students from classes due to the pressure on academic achievement in subject areas. When counselors are able to demonstrate through data how these activities promote academic growth, it will more likely lead to teacher support of school counseling activities.

The school counselor provides crisis counseling to students who have directly or vicariously experienced a traumatic situation. School shootings such as that which occurred at Marjory Stoneman Douglas High School in Parkland, Florida, the death of a student or staff member, a national terrorist attack, or a natural disaster such as a flood or tornado are some of the calamities that impact our school-aged youth. The school counselor is often the only individual in the school with the training to provide counseling for traumatized students with a goal of restoring the distressed individual to an improved or at least the same level of functioning that existed before the crisis. Furthermore, the school counselor conducts classroom lessons to prepare students for critical incidents that could create long-term distress and post-traumatic stress disorder (PTSD).

Although it is nearly impossible to predict what tragedy will impact a school, prevention is key to intervening and debriefing. School counselors are able to teach preventive strategies so that students will be better prepared to cope when tragedy does strike. As you work with a student who is in crisis, ask yourself, "How do I work with this student?" and "What is my role when a crisis impacts the school?" Unfortunately, many students who display reactions to stress are inadvertently and incorrectly placed in inappropriate settings such as alternative classrooms or special education classes due to cognitive impairment that is associated with stress responses. Common stress responses are shown in Table 9.1.

Suicide

Suicide is often thought of as being on a continuum with death wishes to suicide ideation, which includes planning and/or a previous attempt; both of these are considered as basic progressive factors, with adolescents who have attempted suicide reporting more negative life events, including a greater number of interpersonal stressors such as romantic breakups.

Table 9.1 Common student responses to stress.

Physical
- agitation
- hyper-alertness
- erratic heartbeat
- difficulty breathing
- gastrointestinal distress
- sleep difficulties (excessive or inability to sleep)
- tension in the form of aches and pains

Cognitive
- negative outlook
- difficulty solving problems
- disorganization with concentration troubles
- sluggish or hyperactive thoughts
- inability to see an alternative perspective
- egocentrism

Emotional
- generalized distress
- anger or hostility
- depression
- anxiety, fear, or panic
- powerlessness
- guilt
- shame

Social/Behavioral
- substance abuse
- eating disorders
- lack of interest in activities
- inability to perform daily activities
- restricted social contacts
- questioning spiritual faith
- rigid adherence to or rejection of values

Figure 9.1 School counselor comforting a grieving student.
Source: Shutterstock.

Suicide is ranked as the second leading cause of death for individuals aged 15–24 (Save.org, 2019), with 1 in 6 adolescents reporting suicidal tendencies each year (Erbacher & Singer, 2018). A student who is contemplating suicide is one of the most difficult situations any counselor confronts, but fortunately, suicide is preventable. Talking about suicide has shown to decrease the risk; however, 80% of individuals who contemplated or completed suicide actually told someone about their intent (Shallcross, 2010). Box 9.3 explains the S-L-A-P acronym that may be used to assess present risk of suicide, and the D-I-R-T acronym (Box 9.4) is used to assess previous suicide attempts. However, remember that parents/guardians need to be contacted and this communication needs to be documented when you are working with a student who expresses suicidal ideation. In addition, be aware of the school policies regarding the protocol in reporting suicidal ideation and be sure to contact your site supervisor and program supervisor.

Box 9.3

The S-L-A-P Suicide Assessment

Specifics of the plan: Ask the student about the suicidal plan. The more specific the plan, the higher the suicide risk.

Lethality of the plan: The more lethal the suicidal plan, the higher the risk. Guns or jumping from high places are more frequently fatal methods of committing suicide.

Availability: Determine the availability of the indicated method of suicide. If guns are available in the house and the student indicates this is the means by which he/she will attempt suicide, the risk is higher .

Proximity of helping resources: Identify the significant supportive individuals in the student's life and reconnect him/her with these trusted, helpful resources.

Box 9.4

The D-I-R-T Assessment of Previous Suicide Attempt

Dangerous: Ask about previous attempts, and assess the dangerousness of these attempts.

Impression of dangerousness: Ask the student about his/her impression of the lethality of the means that was used. For instance, did the student think taking five sleeping pills would be lethal?

Rescue: In the previous attempt, did the student leave time to be discovered?

Timing: How recently did the attempt occur? The more recent the attempt, the higher the risk.

Box 9.5

National Suicide Prevention Lifeline

A 24-hour hotline is available at 1-800-273-8255, or a live chat can be accessed at www.suicidepreventionlifeline.org.

Conceptual Application Activity 9.6

Break into dyads with a member of your class. One person will take the role of a counselor, and the other will take on the role of a suicidal student or role-play the student depicted below. Role-play the following scenario using the S-L-A-P and D-I-R-T acronyms and assess for suicide using the following scenario.

Roberto is an eighth-grader who was referred to you by his health teacher. According to the teacher Roberto's grades have been dropping and he recently wrote a paper in which he discussed wanting to take his mother's blood pressure medicine to allow him to "slide into a deep sleep and never wake up." After the role-play, discuss the aspects of this role-play that were most difficult, and brainstorm solutions for these complications.

Conceptual Application Activity 9.7

Discuss with your supervisor the various types of crises that have occurred in the school and how these situations were handled. What was his or her role in these crises? Ask to see a copy of the crisis intervention plan.

_____

_____

Peer Support Programs

Peer support programs are a preventative strategy to assist students who are experiencing life problems, such as difficulty with academics, social skills, and attitudes, with most of these programs led by adults or peers who are supervised by adult leaders (Cramer, Ross, McLeod, & Jones, 2015; Goodrich, 2018). Although these programs vary among schools, the programs generally consist of peer helpers, peer mentors, peer tutors, and peer mediators.

Peer helpers commonly assist classroom teachers or school counselors with such activities as performing tasks for teachers, greeting the community at school events, serving as hosts to welcome new students into the school system, or working as office assistants. Peer mentors are able to work with their peers on social skills or assist with school transitions. Peer tutors are able to provide instruction to same-age peers who are struggling with academic issues, or assist with younger students who need additional assistance with a subject. Finally, peer mediators are trained in conflict management to resolve disputes between students, with the end goal of arriving at a resolution (Cook & Boes, 2013). Students are effective at learning and following prescribed courses of action or mediation. Typical steps for peer mediation include the following (adapted from Kittrell, Comiskey, & Carroll, 2006):

1. getting acquainted and comfortable, and establishing the rules
2. identifying the issues from all perspectives and the people directly involved
3. brainstorming all possible solution ideas without eliminating any options
4. discussing all ideas, finding commonality among ideas, and eliminating implausible or ineffective options
5. democratically choosing the best option or options
6. making an agreement or written contract among all parties to include a follow-up schedule
7. carrying out the agreement
8. following up with all involved parties and celebrating success or beginning the process again

School counselors often implement, train, monitor, and evaluate peer support programs as preventative responses to academic, career, and social/emotional issues. Peer programming takes into account the diversity and needs of the community, with attention to revising materials to reflect the needs of the peers. Appropriate peer selection, training, and supervision are necessary for the program to be successful, with attention to peers, grades, academic performance, leadership qualities, and character (Cramer et al., 2015). When students are trained to work proactively with their peers and the administration supports the program, a healthier school culture may develop.

Conceptual Application Activity 9.8

With your class members, form triads to practice mediation skills using the following scenario. Identify one person as the mediator, one person as Alysia, and one person as Marcus while practicing the steps listed earlier.

Two students, Alysia, an eighth-grade girl, and Marcus, a seventh-grade boy, are involved in a physical altercation in the middle school cafeteria during lunch period. You come into the cafeteria and observe Alysia hitting Marcus repeatedly over the head with her lunch tray. Marcus is swinging, kicking, and swearing at Alysia while she repeatedly strikes him. A group of bystanders are gathered around the pair and are chanting, "Hit him again, harder, harder!" You quickly intervene by stepping through the crowd between Alysia and Marcus. Once Alysia and Marcus see you step between them, they stop physically fighting. Marcus continues to sling verbal assaults which Alysia returns as they glare at each other. You summon a nearby female faculty member and instruct her to escort Alysia to the main office and stay with her until you arrive. You escort Marcus to your school counseling office, where you find another school counselor, inform her of the incident, and request she monitor Marcus while he sits in your office on one side of your desk to cool down. You retrieve Alysia and escort her to your office, have her sit in a chair on the opposite side of your desk from Marcus, and position yourself between the two students. You leave your door open and request that the other school counselor remain nearby in case you need her assistance.

How did the process work? Were there any instances where you were stuck? What would have helped make this process easier?

Indirect Student Services

Indirect student services refer to the work of school counselors with other stakeholders on behalf of students through such means as referrals, consultation, and collaboration. The ASCA recommends that 20% of counseling time is spent on indirect services.

Referrals

The school counselor/student ratio in most schools far exceeds the 1:250 ratio recommended by the ASCA, with a national average of one counselor for every 482 students in grades K–12 (Bray, 2017). Arizona is reported to have the highest school counselor–student ratio, with one counselor for every 924 students, and Vermont has the lowest ratio of one counselor for every 202 students. With these ratios, it is often difficult for school counselors to work effectively with students and the community, and in these situations it may be more appropriate to make a referral. When making a referral, consider the following questions:

- Do I have the competency to deal with this concern?
- Do I have enough time and energy to work with this concern?
- Is reasonable progress being made related to my counseling?

Be sure to seek advice from your supervisor as to the protocol in making referrals. For instance, in some school districts, educational personnel are not allowed to make referrals due to the concern that the school district would be responsible for covering the cost of these outside agencies. Referral sources may include community mental health agencies, employment and training centers, juvenile services, and/or social service personnel. Having a list of community resources is a helpful aid for expediting this process, and when making a referral, providing a minimum of three resources allows the parent/guardian to choose the service that will best meet the needs of the student. This process will also protect you from consequences if the referral did not work out as expected. Be sure to have a signed parental/guardian consent form to give you permission to discuss the student with outside individuals.

Consultation

School counselors consult with adults and professionals such as parents, custodial caregivers, guardians, coaches, teachers, administration, community professionals, and so forth. Today, consultation is more collaborative, where the consultant and consultee (the person with whom you are consulting) are involved in shared decision-making to determine strategies to assist in the social/emotional, academic, and career growth of school-aged youth (Cholewa, Goodman-Scott, Thomas, & Cook, 2018). Unfortunately, with the emphasis on academic growth and evidence-based strategies evident in our educational system today, consultation for social and emotional development is often overlooked (Warren & Baker, 2013). This attitude creates difficulty for school counselors who wish to emphasize the importance of social and emotional development and their impact on the whole child.

In a study by Beesley (2004, as cited in Cholewa et al., 2018), a great majority of teachers found school counselor consultation one of the school counselor's greatest strengths. In a separate study by Cholewa et al. (2018), teachers reported that when they consulted with school counselors, they valued: (a) school counselors taking the time to establish relationships with teachers and students, (b) school counselors' availability and follow-up, and (c) school counselors' knowledge and unique perspectives on issues.

As a consultant, it is sometimes difficult for teachers to understand that counselors abide by a code of ethics that includes confidentiality; be sure to communicate the importance of this ethical responsibility to all parties. Furthermore, knowing how much information to share is often tricky. One question you could ask yourself when faced with this dilemma is, "What information should be shared that will help this student at this time?"

As a consultant, be sure to strive for a relationship built on equality. You are on an equal level with the consultee, and a stronger relationship is created when you recognize individual strengths, appreciate cultural differences, and encourage new ideas for resolving an issue. When proposing an intervention that could create potential resistance, you could state something like, "You've probably already thought of this . . ." or "This might be difficult to try, but . . . ."

At times, it is difficult to be a consultant without changing into a counselor role. Keep in mind that the focus of most consultations is for the benefit of the student, not the consultee. Although counselors are trained in effective communication skills such as active listening, paraphrasing, questioning, reflecting, and summarizing which enhance an effective consultation, communication techniques that lead to individual counseling are to be avoided.

Conceptual Application Activity 9.9

Talk with your supervisor about some of the consultation concerns where he/she has served as a consultant. What were some of the most common issues that led to a need for consultation? What were some of the strategies that were most effective? Compare your responses with those of your classmates.

Collaboration

In the past, school counselors adopted an individually focused approach to assisting students and other stakeholders, yet in today's schools, a collaborative approach has been shown to be more effective due to the availability of the students' social systems and the prevalence of community resources (Gold, 2016). Quality consultation has far-reaching accountability structures when a network of individuals, services, and resources is available. According to the ASCA position statement on school–family–community partnerships (ASCA, 2016), "School counselors have an essential and unique role in promoting, facilitating and advocating for collaboration with parents/guardians and community stakeholders" (para. 1) and are essential to building, creating, and evaluating relationships that benefit students.

Conclusion

The Deliver component answers the question, "What strategies and activities will be used to address student needs?" This component consists of direct activities that are face-to-face interactions with students, and indirect activities that include interactions with others on behalf of the student. Direct activities include instruction, appraisal and advisement, and counseling. Indirect student services include referrals, consultation with other stakeholders, and collaboration.

Websites

- We Are Teachers: www.weareteachers.com/category/teaching-strategies/

This website offers strategies for classroom management and ideas for implementing classroom lessons.

- The Teacher's Guide: http://theteachersguide.com/classroommanagement.htm

This website offers organized topics that can be used in lesson planning and activities, and many are in a printable format.

References

ASCA. (2014, May/June). What do students entering your school seem to worry about or struggle with most? ASCA School Counselor, 51, 40.

ASCA. (2016). The school counselor and school-family-community partnerships. Retrieved from www.schoolcounselor.org/asca/media/asca/PositionStatements/PS_Partnerships.pdf

ASCA. (2017). The school counselor and high-stakes testing. Retrieved from www.schoolcounselor.org/asca/media/asca/PositionStatements/PS_HighStakes.pdf

ASCA. (2019). The ASCA National model: A framework for school counseling programs (4th ed.). Alexandria, VA: ASCA.

Borquist-Conlon, D. S., Maynard, B. R., Brendel, K. E., & Farina, A. S. J. (2019). Mindfulness-based interventions for youth with anxiety: A systematic review and meta-analysis. Research on Social Work Practice, 29, 195–205. doi:10.1177/1049731516684961

Bray, B. (2017, October 20). U.S. student-to-school counselor shows slight improvement. Counseling Today. Retrieved from https://ct.counseling.org/2017/10/u-s-student-school-counselor-ratio-shows-slight-improvement/

Cholewa, B., Goodman-Scot, E., Thomas, A., & Cook, J. (2018). Teachers' perceptions and experiences consulting with school counselors: A qualitative study. Professional School Counseling, 20, 77–88. doi:10.5330/1096-2409-20.1.77

Cook, J. Y., & Boes, S. R. (2013). Mediation works: An action research study evaluating the peer mediation program from the eyes of mediators and faculty. ED547782.

Cramer, E. P., Ross, A. I., McLeod, D. A., & Jones, R. (2015). The impact on peer facilitators of facilitating a school-based healthy relationship program for teens. School Social Work Journal, 40, 23–41.

Erbacher, T. A., & Singer, J. B. (2018). Suicide risk monitoring: The missing piece in suicide risk assessment. Contemporary School Psychology, 22, 186–194.

Fye, H. J., Miller, L. G., & Rainey, J. S. (2018). Predicting school counselors' supports and challenges when implementing the ASCA national model. Professional School Counseling, 21, 1–11. doi:10.1177/2156759X18777671

Gold, J. (2016). Humanistic intentionality in clinical collaboration. International Journal of Advanced Counseling, 38, 115–122. doi:10.1007/s10447-016-9260-0

Goodrich, A. (2018). Peer mentoring and peer tutoring among K–12 students: A literature review. National Association for Music Education, 36, 13–21. doi:10.1177/8755123317708765

Green, J. G., Comer, J. S., Donaldson, A. R., Elkins, R. M., Nadeau, M. S., Reid, G., & Pincus, D. B. (2017). School-based accommodations by treatment-seeking anxious children. Journal of Emotional and Behavioral Disorders, 25, 220–232. doi:10.1177/1063426616664328

Kamrath, B., & Brooker, T. (2018). Improved attitude and achievement: A case study of an elementary school academic advisement intervention. Professional School Counselor, 21, 60–69. doi:10.5330/1096-2409-21.1.60

Kittrell, J., Comiskey, J., & Carroll, L. (2006, February). Establishing peer mediation in middle and high schools. Presentation at the University of Tennessee, Knoxville, TN.

Kraag, G., Van Breukelen, G. J. P., Kok, G., & Hosman, C. (2009). "Learn young, learn fair", a stress management program for fifth and sixth graders: Longitudinal results from an experimental study. Journal of Child Psychology and Psychiatry, 50, 1185–1195. doi:10.111/j.1469-7610.2009.02088.x

Kraag, G., Zeegers, M. P., & Kok, G. (2006). School programs targeting stress management in children and adolescents: A meta-analysis. Journal of School Psychology, 44, 449–472. doi:10.1016/j.jsp.2006.07.001

Nagro, S. A., Fraser, D. W., & Hooks, S. D. (2019). Lesson planning with engagement in mind: Proactive classroom management strategies for curriculum instruction. Intervention in School and Clinic, 54, 131–140. doi:10.1177/105345121876790

National Institute of Mental Health. (2017, November). Transforming the understanding and treatment of mental illnesses. Retrieved from www.nimh.nih.gov/health/statistics/mental-illness.shtml

Niditch, L. A., & Varela, R. E. (2018). A longitudinal study of inhibited temperament, effortful control, gender, and anxiety in early childhood. Child Youth Care Forum, 47, 463–479. doi:10.1007/s10566-018-9447-0

Owens, J. S., Holdaway, A. S., Smith, J., Evans, S. W., Himawan, L. K., Coles, E. K., … Dawson, A. E. (2017). Rates of common classroom behavior management strategies and their associations with challenging student behavior in elementary school. Journal of Emotional and Behavioral Disorders, 26(3), 156–169. doi:10.1177/1063426617712501

Save.org. (2019). Suicide facts. Retrieved from https://save.org/about-suicide/suicide-facts/

Schreiber, J. K., & O'Brien, K. H. (2015). Training and supervision of counselors at a residential grief camp. Social Work with Groups, 38, 56–67. doi:10.1080/01609513.2014.931664

Shallcross, L. (2010, July 25). Confronting the threat of suicide. Counseling Today. Retrieved from https://ct.counseling.org/2010/07/confronting-the-threat-of-suicide/

Strauss, V. (2013, February 13). Test anxiety: Why is it increasing and 3 ways to curb it. The Washington Post. Retrieved from www.washingtonpost.com/news/answer-sheet/wp/2013/02/10/test-anxiety-why-it-is-increasing-and-3-ways-to-curb-it/

Warren, J. M., & Baker, S. B. (2013). School counselor consultation: Enhancing teacher performance through rational emotive-social behavioral consultation. VISTAS online. Retrieved from www.counsel ing.org/docs/default-source/vistas/school-counselor-consultation-enhancing-teacher-performance.pdf

Zyromski, B., Dimmitt, C., Mariani, M., & Griffith, C. (2018). Evidence-based school counseling: Models for integrated practice and school counselor education. Professional School Counseling, 2, 1–12.

10 Understanding How to Assess Your School Counseling Program Using the ASCA National Model

Aaron H. Oberman and Jeannine R. Studer

CACREP Standards

Foundations

e.   assessments specific to P-12 education

Practice

i.   approaches to increase promotion and graduation rates
n.   use of accountability data to inform decision-making
o.   use of data to advocate for programs and students

Chapter Objectives:

*   introduce the importance of program and school counselor assessment and appraisal
*   present various strategies for collecting program effectiveness data
*   describe data analysis techniques

Introduction

In this age of educational reform, all members of the school community have a responsibility to show how their efforts have made a difference in the lives of school-aged youth. School counselors are no exception. Assessment practices are especially critical at a time when a struggling economy and resulting budget cuts may cause programs to be negatively impacted. Programs that lack proof of progress or effectiveness are more likely to be seen as lacking value, and therefore more vulnerable to public scrutiny and possible elimination. School counseling programs continue to be considered as one of the areas targeted for reduction, resource reallocation, or elimination in the continuing trend of smaller education finances and budgets. Despite these potential threats to school counseling programs, some school counselors still resist the need to be accountable to those they serve (Stone & Dahir, 2011). Further evidence of this lack of commitment to the Assess component was found in a study that investigated where school counselors-in-training spend their time during the internship experience. School counselors-in-training at all levels concentrated their time on components of the ASCA National Model, with little time spent on the Assess component (Oberman & Studer, 2016).

Your reasons for entering the school counseling profession probably did not include a vision of operationally defining goals and objectives, tracking progress, and "crunching the numbers," or analyzing data as part of your job description. Did any of your reasons for entering the school counseling profession include any aspect of school counselor assessment? If so, assessment may be an easier task for you. If not, assessment may be more challenging for you as a SCIT, and later as a professional school counselor. Regardless of your level of affinity toward assessment and regardless of your educational experience, you are still professionally responsible for revealing how you make a difference in the growth of students. Two of the sections that follow, "Program Assessment" and "School Counselor Assessment and Appraisal," emphasize the Assess component.

Program Assessment

Assessment encompasses analyzing data that are created based on classroom and group Mindsets and Behaviors, as well as closing-the-gap measures to address the changes that occur as a result of your efforts within the school counseling program. The professional school counselor and the school community benefit when your assessment documentation reveals how you achieved the goals as part of a comprehensive program. Graduation from your school counseling training program does not make you an expert school counselor, but instead demonstrates that you have met the minimum standards to begin your career as a professional school counselor. Being able to provide outcome evidence to your stakeholders that you are positively impacting the student body displays your value to the educational community.

There are various methods by which you are able to record your activities and the impact of these activities on student achievement. These data can be in the form of qualitative or quantitative results.

Quantitative data are expressed using numbers. Examples include rank ordering 10 items from least desired (ranked 10) to most desired (ranked 1), choosing a point on a Likert scale from 1 to 6, or assigning a categorized number (e.g., 1–3, weak; 4–6, moderate; 7–10, strong). Relatively simple quantitative analyses such as means, medians, and modes are popular ways to summarize data so that they are easily understood by the school's stakeholders.

Qualitative data are expressed through words. An open-ended written summary of a student expressing how individual counseling helped him/her improve his/her schoolwork, a third-party observer's feedback critiquing your classroom lesson, the results of a focus group, or a parent's handwritten note thanking you for your input in developing her son's Individualized Education Plan (IEP) are a few examples of qualitative data.

Describing numbers of participants in interventions, reporting Mindsets and Behaviors data, reporting yearly results on achievement, attendance, and discipline, and collecting data over a specified period of time are types of documents for examining how students have grown as a result of program and classroom counseling instruction interventions.

Experimental Action Research

An experimental action research approach can be used to measure the effectiveness of an intervention on similar groups of students. As an example, one group would be considered as a treatment/experimental group, and the other as a control group. The treatment/experimental group would receive the treatment or intervention, while the control group would not receive the treatment/intervention (or would be delayed in receiving the treatment/intervention). For this approach to be most effective, students should be randomly assigned to each group (each student should have an equal chance of being selected into either group).

For instance, suppose you want to determine whether the study skills lesson you are teaching students is improving their test-taking abilities. Using an experimental approach, you could collect data from teachers of two fifth-grade classes. (These would be convenience groupings, but not randomly assigned groups.) Ideally, you would collect pre-intervention data on both groups to establish a baseline average test score for each group. Following the pre-test, one class would receive a series of classroom lessons on study skills, while the other class would receive no lessons during this time. The group receiving the study skills lesson is considered the treatment/experimental group, while the class not receiving instruction is the control group. After the sessions are completed, you would assess the post-treatment/intervention test scores of both groups and compare these scores to their pre-test scores to see whether there was any improvement or difference between the two groups' test scores. If the change between pre-test and post-test scores for the treatment/intervention group improved significantly more than did those for the control group, you have an indicator that your study skills lessons may have had a positive impact on test score improvement (note that you would need to conduct a statistical analysis such as a t-test to determine whether or not the change between the two groups is considered to be significant). When evidence suggests that a strategy was effective, you have an ethical responsibility to provide this treatment to all students. In this case, the fifth-graders who did not receive the study skills intervention would now have the opportunity to receive the same lessons on study skills.

At times, school counselors are hesitant to engage in research due to: (1) the results not turning out as expected, (2) lack of confidence in research or statistical abilities, and (3) fear that positive outcomes will generate additional responsibilities. However, even if the results did not turn out as anticipated, it may simply mean that the activities, goals, or procedures need to be altered. Furthermore, counselor educators are often looking for practitioners with whom they can partner to conduct research. Connect with a professor at a nearby college or university to assist you in research methodologies.

Conceptual Application Activity 10.1

Ask your supervisor to assist you in developing an experimental action-based assessment in which you can collect data to compare groups. Discuss your assessment and intervention with your peers, and debate the pros and cons of developing this type of intervention and assessment.

Now that you are apprised as to how data can indicate program and curricular areas of strength and areas that need attention using an experimental design, you may also consider using action research to address these areas. The MEASURE program is a systematic approach for identifying and addressing a problematic area.

MEASURE

Stone and Dahir (2011) developed the MEASURE action research protocol. The MEASURE acronym stands for Mission, Elements, Analyze, Stakeholders–Unite, Reanalyze, and Educate.

Table 10.1 Overview of the MEASURE assessment tool.

Mission—The school counseling program is connected to the school mission.	The school counseling mission statement addresses the three Ps (purpose, practice, and principles). What are the student needs? How do school counselors address these needs? What beliefs guide this work?
Elements—Identify elements that impede student growth	Critical analysis of information attained through data assists in identifying an issue to address.
Analysis—What are the data that indicate an issue to address?	Disaggregating data may provide a more comprehensive picture of factors that are impeding student growth.
Stakeholders–Unite	Identification of individuals who are able to address the issue. This could mean community members, teachers, school board members, etc.
Reanalyze, Reflect, and Revise	Data are addressed while an intervention occurs to make necessary changes (formative assessment), and again at the end of the intervention to determine how well the strategy met the identified goal (summative).
Educate	Documenting and sharing results of the intervention educates stakeholders as to how the school counselor is essential to the school environment.

Stone and Dahir (2011) maintain that school counselors should first align their role in the school with the school's mission. Second, school counselors need to determine what elements they are trying to impact or change. Next, school counselors are to examine and analyze the data to establish goals for the counseling program. After analyzing the data, counselors collaborate with the school's stakeholders and unite them to create an action plan that will address the needs of the school. Fifth, counselors reanalyze the data to see whether any changes have taken place and make modifications as needed. Finally, school counselors use a report card to reveal program effectiveness and areas that need attention. This report educates stakeholders as to how the school counselor promotes students, is integral to the academic mission, and provides direction for future goals.

Conceptual Application Activity 10.2

Use the MEASURE assessment system to target an identified area for improvement in the school where you are an intern. With the assistance of your supervisor, determine strategies for improving this target area. Compare your system with those of your peers.

At times, an assessment instrument is necessary to show evidence of program or intervention effectiveness. Since there are very few ready-made instruments that will meet all of your programmatic needs, it is likely that you will need to design an instrument. Similar to the awareness of the demand to be accountable to your stakeholders, creating an assessment instrument can seem like a daunting task for school counselors, yet the following section may address some of your concerns.

Assessment Instruments to Measure Effectiveness

As a SCIT, you do not receive extensive training in data collection and analysis; therefore you may feel like you do not have the training required to conduct sophisticated assessments or research (Gladding, 2013). To develop an effective assessment instrument, you first need to determine what is being assessed and how the results will be used. It is also important to consider where and when the assessment will happen. Certain times during the academic year may be better than others to conduct various lessons and to collect evaluative information pertinent to your counseling program. Moreover, it is important to constantly revise the instrument to make sure the data being collected are in line with your school counseling program's established goals. A pilot group of individuals who are similar to the target population you will be assessing can take the instrument you have designed and provide feedback on it. Revisions can then be made based on their feedback.

Some of the questions to consider when designing your instrument include the type of data to collect, how to collect the data, the types of questions or items that will yield accurate and meaningful results, analysis methods, and the manner in which to share the information with stakeholders. Observational forms, pre- and post-test instruments, surveys, and retrospective assessments are examples of assessment tools. Refer to Figure 10.1 for a sample assessment instrument checklist.

Observations

Observations are used when you want to document behavioral patterns without interfering with the behavior you wish to observe. This assessment includes selecting the behavior to be observed, developing a system for documentation, and then deciding whether an intervention is needed. For instance, suppose a teacher is concerned about anger outbursts from a fifth-grade student. You would observe in the classroom or other designated place to determine baseline data on the number of times this identified behavior occurs in a determined time frame. Based on this observation, an intervention can be created, and a follow-up observation of the behavior in the same environment will be tallied to assess how well the intervention worked. See Figure 10.2 for an example of an observation form.

---

1. Why is the assessment being done?

2. Who is being surveyed?

3. What is the best method for data collection?

4. What is the best time to conduct this assessment?

5. Where will the assessment take place?

6. How will you share the information in an easy-to-understand format?

Figure 10.1 Sample checklist to create an assessment tool.

Location_____   Name_____   Date_____

Definition of Behavior to be Observed _____

_____

_____

Time   Tally   Description of Behaviors

_____   _____   _____

_____   _____   _____

_____   _____   _____

Summary _____

Signature of Observer _____

Figure 10.2 Observation form.

Figure 10.3 School counselor observing student behavior during a classroom activity.
Source: Shutterstock.

Conceptual Application Activity 10.3

Ask a teacher whether you can sit in the classroom to observe student behavior. Select a student you would like to observe, and make note of the behaviors this individual exhibits in a certain amount of time. Choose one of the behaviors, and use the observation form in Figure 10.2 to note numbers of times this behavior occurs.

Pre- and Post-Test

One method for collecting information about a strategy is to conduct a pre-test assessment prior to completing an activity, and a similar post-test assessment after a task or intervention has been completed. The information gathered from this type of assessment would be compared to determine whether the activity was successful. For example, suppose you wanted to conduct a six-session counseling group focused on helping middle school students build social skills and friendships. To gather data, you could give a pre-test to the group participants at the beginning of the first session to determine knowledge, skills, or attitudes toward social skills and friendship. After conducting the six sessions, you could give the same assessment as a post-test during the last group session. Pre- and post-test data would be compared to determine whether the information and activities resulted in an increase in the students' knowledge, skills, or attitudes related to social skills and building friendships with peers at school. See Figure 10.4 for an example of a pre-test/post-test.

Conceptual Application Activity 10.4

Talk with your site supervisor about implementing an upcoming school counseling activity that is based on an identified school counseling program standard. Design a pre- and post-test that allows you to assess changes in student knowledge, attitudes, or behavior. Compare your activity and assessment with those developed by your peers. Discuss the successes and challenges in performing this activity assessment.

_____

_____

Surveys

Another method of gathering data is through the use of surveys that could be given to students, teachers, parents, and/or administrators. These instruments can be oral or written, and may be distributed by surface mail, email, online, or in person. As an example, suppose that you wanted to learn what your stakeholders believe are the most critical concerns impacting students. Survey items could include open- and closed-ended questions, multiple-choice, rank order, and short-answer items. Open-ended items allow for more comments from your stakeholders, while closed-ended or multiple-choice questions could be used to target feedback on a specific issue. See Figure 10.5 for examples of each type of question.

Scale: 1 = never, 2 = rarely, 3 = sometimes, 4 = most of the time, 5 = always

1.   I know how to be a friend.
    1 2 3 4 5

2.   I know what qualities to look for in a friend.
    1 2 3 4 5

3.   I only talk to classmates I know.
    1 2 3 4 5

4.   I feel comfortable introducing myself to new people.
    1 2 3 4 5

5.   I know how to react if someone doesn't want to be my friend.
    1 2 3 4 5

6.   I would like to make friends with people who are different than me.
    1 2 3 4 5

7.   I know what is appropriate to share with others about my friendships.
    1 2 3 4 5

8.   I must have a best friend.
    1 2 3 4 5

9.   I can tell my family about my friendships.
    1 2 3 4 5

Figure 10.4 Friendship group.

Conceptual Application Activity 10.5

Ask your site supervisor about surveys he or she has designed, adapted, borrowed, or purchased. Bring one of these surveys to class to compare it with those of your peers, and talk about the advantages and disadvantages of each of the formats.

The information described above will assist in creating annual results in the form of revealing classroom and group Mindsets and Behavior analyses and reporting outcome data and behaviors over several years. Remember to use graphs to concretely indicate how your program contributes to student success.

Open Questions

1. This year I would like to learn more about ...
2. The school counselor should focus his/her time on ...

Closed Questions

1. Do students need more help with study skills? Yes or No
2. Does the school counselor meet your needs? Yes or No

Multiple-Choice Items

1. Which of the following groups would you be most likely to participate in?
    a. Anger management
    b. Friendship
    c. Bullying
    d. Divorce
    e. Study skills
2. Which of the following topics are most needed in your class?
    a. Time management
    b. Stress
    c. Career development
    d. Anger management
    e. Other _____

Figure 10.5 Sample survey questions.

School Counselor Assessment and Appraisal

The ASCA School Counselor Professional Standards and Competencies Assessment is a self-evaluation to identify the mindsets and behaviors that are needed to lead a successful school counseling program. The evaluative criteria that will be used to assess your skills as a supervisee are outlined prior to beginning your clinical experiences, and are a topic of conversation between you and your supervisors so that everyone is aware of the criteria that will be used for this evaluation. Receiving and applying feedback is crucial to your training, as the supervisors have your best interests in mind and want you to succeed as a school counselor. Rather than being upset if the feedback you receive is not as favorable as you would like it to be, instead recognize that utilizing this advice will facilitate your transition into the profession. Therefore, embrace this experience and use this feedback as an opportunity for growth.

Box 10.1

Marilee was an intelligent, motivated SCIT. However, she had no real work experience as she spent her summers in academic camps throughout her high school years and took summer classes while she was in her bachelor's program at a major university. Furthermore, her parents, although well-meaning, bought her a condominium and car and gave her an allowance to cover all her living expenses so that she would have more time to study. The result was a student who had difficulty relating to her classmates and had problems understanding different lifestyles and issues related to diversity.

Marilee's challenging dispositions were apparent during her clinical experiences, when she would observe her supervisor conduct classroom lessons and automatically wrote down what the supervisor said and did, word for word. The result was Marilee mimicking her supervisor with little effort to create her own lessons, and with a reluctance to engage in group and individual counseling for fear that she wasn't "doing it right." During the middle of the semester, the supervisor decided that Marilee just wasn't reaching the appropriate developmental markers previous supervisees had attained at this point in their internships. Although the supervisor had discussed her concerns with Marilee throughout the weeks, little improvement had been noted, and a meeting involving the faculty supervisor, Marilee, and the site supervisor was scheduled.

When Marilee listened to the concerns her supervisors presented, she immediately became defensive, cried uncontrollably, and raced out of the room, saying, "None of these statements are true—I have done everything everyone has asked." The next day, she contacted an attorney who threatened legal action if the supervisors continued to be uncooperative. Unfortunately, the end result of this situation was a poorly trained supervisee and supervisors who refused to provide a recommendation for her.

In the example above, the SCIT was unable to listen graciously to feedback and make appropriate changes to address the concerns that were presented. Instead, she chose to blame the school, supervisors, and program rather than reflectively looking inward. Take advantage of the assessments your supervisors provide. They are in a position to guide you to facilitate your transition into being an effective school counselor. As you gain more experience, hopefully you will continue to reflect on your values, motives, and knowledge so that you can learn from your mistakes and successes and enhance the lives of the students with whom you interact.

School Counselor Professional Standards and Competencies Assessment

Use the School Counselor Professional Standards and Competencies Assessment to self-evaluate your knowledge, abilities, skills, and attitudes at this stage of your career. If you use this assessment on a regular basis, you will be able to monitor your professional growth and annually evaluate your abilities, as well as use it as a basis for personal goal-setting.

Conceptual Application Activity 10.6

Talk with your supervisor about the evaluation instrument that is used to evaluate his/her performance and whether or not this assessment is a favorable indication of the work your supervisor performs. What suggestions does your supervisor have for improvement?

_____

_____

The school counselor performance appraisal template is based on the ASCA National Model, and includes such areas as the school counselor's ability to manage, define, deliver, and assess a comprehensive school counseling program. Although this instrument is a useful tool that is compatible with the role and function of a 21st-century counselor, there are other evaluative forms that may be used as a SCIT or as a professional school counselor. The following section describes peer, student, self, and portfolio assessment strategies.

Peer Assessment

Peer assessment is one strategy for determining your performance as a supervisee, and could be a valuable evaluative method for you when you become a professional school counselor. As a SCIT, your site and faculty supervisors will evaluate you, and in some instances your school counseling peers may also provide you with personal feedback. More likely than not, while you are a student training for the counseling profession, this will be the last time you will be provided feedback on your clinical skills. As a professional school counselor, it is most likely that a school administrator will evaluate you, and in many cases this individual will not have a background in counseling. Yet group and individual counseling are significant parts of your job, and receiving feedback on your counseling skills facilitates your development. Seeking someone who is considered an expert to observe and evaluate your clinical skills, such as the district school counselor director, school counselors within the district, or local counselor educators, is a step toward enhancing these skills. Having an open dialogue with your evaluator as to your training and education and how your counseling skills and data collection competence can be utilized to improve student growth is an advocacy skill that promotes professional understanding.

Student Assessment

A student assessment is another useful form of evaluation. Not only are you able to receive qualitative feedback regarding your counseling interventions, you can also receive quantitative data from the students to determine changes in their knowledge, skills, or attitudes due to their participation in school counseling interventions. These results can be documented in the Classroom and Group Mindsets and Behaviors Results Report Analysis and/or Closing the Gap Results Report for program assessment and improvement information (ASCA, 2019).

A more straightforward method for requesting student feedback is through a rating scale. Incorporating a basic rating scale from 1 (poor) to 5 (excellent) is a simple technique for tracking how the students experienced the counseling or group school counseling session. Although this method can give you a basic understanding of how students felt about the sessions, other methods could be implemented to determine the extent to which thoughts, feelings, or behaviors changed. For instance, subjective case notes provide a means for school counselors and SCIT to refresh their memory on what occurred in counseling so that future counseling sessions may continue seamlessly. You may want to familiarize yourself with the SOAP (Subjective, Objective, Analysis, Plan) method of writing case notes to assist in remembering the specific concerns each counselee brings to counseling (Cameron & Turtle-Song, 2002). Figure 10.6 provides an outline of the SOAP acronym that can be adapted for your personal case note needs.

Although confidentiality is a cornerstone of the profession, confidentiality in counseling sessions for a supervisee cannot be guaranteed, because it is generally a program requirement to audio- or video-record sessions and to keep case notes on counselees for supervision purposes. However, once a person has become a professional school counselor, there is debate as to the wisdom of keeping case notes. Two cautionary suggestions in keeping these records

---

Confidential

Student Counselor-in-Training _____

Student Counselee (first name or initials) _____

Date of Session _____

Session # _____ Type of Session _____

Start Time _____ End Time _____

Subjective Impressions

How did the counselee present self (e.g., affect, behavior, nervousness)

What were your subjective reactions to the counselee?

Objective Impressions

What are the facts that were discussed during counseling?

What did you say?

What did the counselee say?

What was the presenting issue?

Analysis

How did the session address the goals of counseling?

Plan

What are your goals for the next scssion?

What do you need to prepare to address these goals?

What aspect of the problem needs continued focus?

Figure 10.6 The SOAP method of writing case notes.

Note: S = subjective impressions; O = objective impressions; A = analysis; P = plan.

Counselor-in-Training _____

Date _____

Counselee Initials and Grade Level: _____

Counselee's Presenting Problem:

Session Goals:

What were your feelings regarding the counselee?

What detracted from working most effectively with the student?

What was your theoretical model in working with this student?

What techniques did you implement in the session? Why?

What strategies did you use to evaluate the session?

What were your strengths in the session?

What areas would you like to improve?

Plans for next session:

Rate yourself on the session from 1 (needs improvement) to 5 (excellent). Explain your rating.

Figure 10.7 Counselor-in-training tape review form.

are: (a) any information that is shared is no longer private and becomes part of the student records, and (b) the school counselor's personal notes (and yours, as a supervisee) can be subpoenaed. Although your school counseling training program has probably provided you with forms to use in conjunction with this requirement, a sample form is provided in Figure 10.7. EZAnalyze is an Excel-based tool with which you can track your activities, create graphs, and analyze your data. You can download this tool for free at www.ezanalyze.com/.

Box 10.2

I use Google.docs to create templates for spreadsheets and graphs. Although making templates takes a little practice, after you get the hang of it, it is easy to use. When I first started as a school counselor, I felt so lonely trying to collect data by myself, but eventually I learned to collaborate with faculty, parents, and even my students. I learned to start small, and it was fun seeing the results that were generated with the help of others.

Source: Elementary school counselor

Self-assessment

Identifying and setting professional and personal goals at the beginning of the school year and self-evaluating at the end of the year is another method of determining your effectiveness in the educational system. As mentioned earlier, one helpful self-evaluation strategy is

Name _____   Date _____

Total number of hours for week _____   Direct _____   Indirect_____

Summarize the activities in which you were involved this week:

On a scale of 1 to 10, with 1 indicating a stressful, anxiety-filled week and 10 indicating a productive, successful week, what number best indicates your weekly experience? _____ Explain.

What were some of the most difficult challenges you faced this week, and discuss what made these events difficult.

What were some of your accomplishments and successes? Explain.

What do you need from supervision this week?

What are your professional goals for next week?

What are your personal goals for next week?

Any questions or concerns?

Student's Signature: _____

Figure 10.8 Practicum and internship weekly journal reflections.

to utilize the School Counselor Performance Appraisal Template as a checklist (ASCA, 2019). Although personal goals are helpful for improving your role and function within the school, they are often not objective, and therefore do not have the same evaluative weight as assessments conducted by a third-party stakeholder.

In addition, your clinical training program may require you to journal your weekly thoughts, feelings, and behaviors to track and assess your progress from the beginning of the clinical experience until you have completed the program requirements. Self-reflection of your work with students as well as the overall program is helpful for both school counselors and as a SCIT in order to process the identified goals and objectives set for the program. Figure 10.8 provides an example of prompts that may assist you with this process.

Portfolio

As a SCIT, you may be required to submit a portfolio that will be reviewed by your faculty members before graduation. A portfolio is a working document that typically includes an accumulation of documents or artifacts that demonstrate your acquired competencies during your graduate school counselor training. A portfolio is considered a capstone assignment, and could be in the form of a large binder filled with information or in an electronic format that summarizes your training experience. Artifacts you might include in your portfolio include your philosophy of school counseling, current résumé, samples of lessons or group plans, an outline of a CSC program you developed as a class assignment, media displaying your skills, and other types of data that document your progress as a SCIT. If you are interviewing for a position, you can bring this document to the interviewer's office or provide the interviewer a link in advance to access your electronic portfolio before the interview.

Program Goal Analysis

The professional school counselor thoughtfully analyzes the data that have been collected throughout the school year, carefully scrutinizes the results of the interventions, and intentionally facilitates goal development for the following school year. As discussed in Chapter 8, the ASCA uses the SMART acronym as a tool for goal-setting (S = specific; M = measurable; A = attainable; R = realistic; T = time-bound). In other words, the goal needs to be specific and worded in such a way that it is easy to evaluate. An attainable, realistic goal is one that can be reached by the students for whom the goal is established, and a description of the time frame sets a specific time for when the intervention or program is to occur.

Conclusion

As a professional school counselor in the 21st century, it is imperative to demonstrate how your program impacts the student body and other stakeholders. Analyzing the school report card is one method by which school counselors are able to determine areas that need to be improved, data collection reveals the number of participants that were involved in an intervention, and what these individuals know, believe, or can perform describes participation and behaviors and mindsets data. In addition, outcome data show the success of the intervention. Action research through the use of the MEASURE acronym describes a method in which you are able to systematically engage in assessment procedures. Observational forms, pre- and post-test instruments, surveys, and retrospective assessments are examples of assessment tools. It is possible that you may need to design your own assessment instruments if a standardized instrument is not available.

School counselor assessment can occur through a standardized form that is adapted by the school district, or through the ASCA School Counselor Competencies Assessment and Performance Appraisal. Peer, student, self, and portfolio assessment strategies are additional evaluative tools to measure school counselor performance.

Website

- *Accountability Through Documentation: What Are Best Practices for School Counselors?*: https://files.eric.ed.gov/fulltext/EJ914267.pdf

This article describes best practices in school counselor assessment.

References

ASCA. (2019). *The ASCA National Model: A framework for school counseling programs* (4th ed.). Alexandria, VA: ASCA.

Cameron, S., & Turtle-Song, I. (2002). Learning to write case notes using the SOAP format. *Journal of Counseling and Development, 80,* 286–292.

Gladding, S. T. (2013). *Counseling: A comprehensive profession* (8th ed.). Upper Saddle River, NJ: Merrill Prentice Hall.

Oberman, A., & Studer, J. (2016). An exploratory study of the tasks performed by school counselor trainees in internship. *Georgia School Counseling Association Journal, 23,* 6–15.

Stone, C. B., & Dahir, C. A. (2011). *School counselor accountability: A MEASURE of student success* (3rd ed.). Upper Saddle River, NJ: Merrill Prentice Hall.

11 Applying the ASCA Ethical and Legal Standards in Your Clinical Experiences

Carolyn Stone

CACREP Standards

Contextual Dimensions

2b. school counselor roles in consultation with families, P-12 and postsecondary school personnel, and community agencies
5e. school counselor roles and responsibilities in relation to the school emergency management plans, and crises, disasters, and trauma
11k. community resources and referral sources

Practice

11k. strategies to promote equity in student achievement and college access

Chapter Objectives:

* explore in detail the various implications of confidentiality in education settings
* understand the principles of legal behavior for school counselors through the application of federal statutes and court cases
* examine the values/philosophies in ethical decision-making
* explain the contextual nature of school counseling and the need for professionals to be tolerant of ambiguity
* learn how to avoid negligence lawsuits, administrative hearings, and criminal proceedings
* review the 2016 ASCA Code of Ethics and Standards of Practice

School Counselors and the Legal and Ethical Complications

School counselors' work is more complicated legally and ethically than counselors in agency or private practice because their clients are minors in an academic setting, and not one specifically intended for counseling (ASCA, 2017). To further complicate the legal and ethical imperative, school counselors owe parents an obligation even though their primary client is a student. Unless parents choose to home school or participate in private schooling for their child, the 50 states demand that parents relinquish physical control of their child to educators (Alexander & Alexander, 2019; Iyer & Baxter-MacGregor, 2010). The *in loco parentis* position mandated by the states requires that educators are careful not to impede parents' rights and demands considerable finesse on the school counselor's part when parents want information on their child, carefully balancing parental rights with the trusting relationship students deserve and the profession holds in high regard (Iyer & Baxter-MacGregor, 2010; Stone, 2017).

The unique nature of counseling in schools is complicated by critical factors that can be summarized by the acronym COMPLICATIONS (Stone, 2017). The acronym stands for:

Counselor's values
Obligations beyond the student
Minors' developmental and chronological levels
Privacy rights of minors
Legal status of minors
In loco parentis
Community and institutional standards
Academic instruction
Trusting relationship
Informed consent
Opacity of laws and ethical codes
Number of student clients
Standard of care

Counselor's Values

School counselors are unable to separate themselves from their values (Stone, 2017). It is impossible to shed one's values at the schoolhouse door, but checking to make certain you do not impose your values on someone else's child is part of the ethical behavior expected of school counselors. Since it is impossible to do value-free counseling, school counselors must know those parts of themselves that have the potential to interfere with parents' and students' rights. Prejudices such as racism, sexism, and homophobism are sometimes grouped together and referred to as "isms" (ASCA, 2016b; Lee & Park, 2013). More than anyone else under the schoolhouse roof, school counselors must examine and eradicate, or at a minimum soften, their "isms" (ASCA, 2016b; Lee & Park, 2013). This intentionality is necessary to practice with confidence that you are not consciously or unconsciously oppressing students. School counselors have the greatest potential for harm given the nature of their work. Counseling is intimate in nature, as the professional sits knees to knees, eyeball to eyeball, often behind closed doors, hearing the personal stories and needs of students. The very nature and function of the profession can wield great sway. A counselor's values are far more at play than if teaching algebra or English.

The courts have recently addressed three cases involving counselors and their values which found their way into their work. *Cash v. Missouri State University* (Roberts, 2016) is the most recent of the cases, preceded by *Ward v. Wilbanks* (Case No. 09-CV-11237 (E.D. Mich. Dec. 13, 2010)) and *Keeton v. Anderson-Wiley* (United States Court of Appeals for the Eleventh Circuit 664 F.3d 865 (2011)).

Andrew Cash's federal lawsuit against Missouri State University involved 51 internship hours he accrued at the Christian counseling center he directed. The center refused to counsel gay couples, and Cash concurred, citing his religious beliefs. He was required to change sites and denied the 51 hours accrued. Cash was eventually dismissed from the preparation program, and the university eventually settled out of court for $25,000 in 2017.

In *Ward v. Wilbanks,* Julea Ward, a school counseling candidate, was dismissed from Eastern Michigan University after she refused to counsel an EMU student whose presenting problem was his same-sex relationship. Ward, citing her religious beliefs, said she needed to refer this student as she would work with gay students on a number of subjects, but not to affirm their same-sex relationships. The university, citing failure to adhere to the profession's code of ethics, dismissed her, and she sued with the help of the Alliance Defense Fund, whose clients believe they had been wronged by institutions or individuals stepping on family values. EMU settled with Ms. Ward for $75,000 (Lambda Legal, 2012).

The marked difference between the *Cash* case and the *Ward* case is that Cash was preparing for the mental health field, in which it is easier to determine a fit between counselor and client. Ward, on the other hand, was going to be a school counselor, and they do not get to choose their student clients. Students are assigned to counselors by grade level or alphabet. The potential to do great harm is present in both the mental health and school counseling arenas, but considerably heightened when a vulnerable student seeks the only help that might be available to him/her and is rebuffed, however skillfully, because of who he/she is as a person (Stone, 2017). The onus is on the school counselor to work to eradicate or soften biases so that students are not systematically referred to other counselors. Ward had a list of topics she was unwilling to help students negotiate (Lambda Legal, 2012). Ethical school counselors engage in pointed opportunities for exposure to other opinions and viewpoints in order to be able to affirm all students in their charge.

The third case out of Georgia involved Jennifer Keeton, whose case against Augusta State University was dismissed. She was required to complete a remediation plan, which included attending diversity workshops and reading articles about counseling LGBTQ students, or leave the program. Keeton had made remarks about using reparative therapy, which is considered unethical and archaic in the counseling world (American Counseling Association, 2013). She refused to comply with the attendance requirements at events she considered were promoting immoral behavior, citing her religious views. The profession requires school counselors to seek supervision, participate in continuing education, and practice deliberate self-examination given the nature and function of the counseling relationship.

School counselors refrain from referring students based solely on school counselors' personal beliefs or values rooted in their religion, culture, ethnicity, or personal worldview. School counselors maintain the highest respect for student diversity. School counselors should pursue additional training and supervision in areas where they are at risk of imposing their values on students, especially when the school counselor's values are discriminatory in nature. School counselors do not impose their values on students and/or families when making referrals to outside resources for student and/or family support (ASCA, 2016a, A.6.e.).

School counselors hold personal values rooted in their religion, but they must ensure they do not expose their values verbally or nonverbally, in word or deed, if they risk putting up barriers to students' ability to explore their own beliefs (ASCA, 2016b, 2016c, 2016d; Lee & Park, 2013).

Obligations beyond the Student

The multiplicity of obligations school counselors have extends to parents, but also to other educators who are able to support students if apprised of critical, timely information that the educators might need to attend to the personal, social, emotional needs of the student (Stone, 2017; Stone & Dahir, 2016). School counselors' loyalty is first and foremost to the student, but standing behind that student are other educators and parents to whom we owe allegiance given the nature and function of schools.

The Supreme Court of the United States continually vests in parents the right to be the guiding voice in their children's lives, especially in value-laden issues. In *Bellotti v. Baird* (443 US 622 (1979)), the court upheld states' rights to require parental involvement in minors' abortion decisions.

The ASCA Ethical Standards includes an entire section on respecting the rights of parents/guardians:

B.1. Responsibilities to Parents/Guardians

School counselors:

a. Recognize that providing services to minors in a school setting requires school counselors to collaborate with students' parents/guardians as appropriate.

b. Respect the rights and responsibilities of custodial and noncustodial parents/guardians and, as appropriate, establish a collaborative relationship with parents/guardians to facilitate students' maximum development.

c. Adhere to laws, local guidelines and ethical practice when assisting parents/guardians experiencing family difficulties interfering with the student's welfare.

d. Are culturally competent and sensitive to diversity among families. Recognize that all parents/guardians, custodial and noncustodial, are vested with certain rights and responsibilities for their children's welfare by their role and according to law.

e. Inform parents of the mission of the school counseling program and program standards in academic, career and social/emotional domains that promote and enhance the learning process for all students.

f. Inform parents/guardians of the confidential nature of the school counseling relationship between the school counselor and student.

g. Respect the confidentiality of parents/guardians as appropriate and in accordance with the student's best interests.

h. Provide parents/guardians with accurate, comprehensive and relevant information in an objective and caring manner, as is appropriate and consistent with ethical and legal responsibilities to the student and parent.

i. In cases of divorce or separation, follow the directions and stipulations of the legal documentation, maintaining focus on the student. School counselors avoid supporting one parent over another.

(ASCA, 2016a)

Sometimes a student's values or needs do not coincide with their parents' values. For example, if a student is in a state that requires parental permission for their minor child's abortion and the student is afraid to tell her parents about her pregnancy for fear they will not approve her need for an abortion, can the school counselor share with the student her right to go before a judge for a judicial bypass? A judicial bypass is a process in which minors can get state approval to have an abortion without parental involvement (*Bellotti v. Baird*, 1979). In this case, a judge made an exception called judicial bypass that can occur once the minor demonstrates the maturity to make the decision to abort and can articulate an understanding of the health risks and possible emotional consequences.

The New Hampshire Supreme Court in Appeal of Farmington School District (No. 2015-0032 (N.H. 2016)) reinstated a school counselor whose contract was not renewed after she became entangled with a student's need to require a judicial bypass and the principal's determination that her parents should be notified of her pregnancy. The counselor, who obtained a restraining order, muted the principal from telling the girl's mother about her pregnancy (Walsh, 2016). The court agreed that there was adverse action against the school counselor, who was acting within her professional capacity. However, this case could easily have gone the other way. Pregnancy and abortion as an option might well be the most value-laden topic a school counselor is called on by a student to help them navigate. School counselors try to remain neutral in value-laden issues, and stand ready to defend themselves by maintaining that they did not push one way or another. The courts continually vest parents/guardians with legal rights to be the guiding voice in their children's lives, especially in value-laden issues.

The trusting relationship school counselors owe to students must be balanced against the United States Supreme Court-endowed rights given to parents to have the authority to raise their children and to be the pre-eminent voice in their children's lives in value-laden issues (Alexander & Alexander, 2019). Counselors owe parents/guardians an ethical obligation as well as a legal one to create collaborative relationships with parents/guardians and to increase their sense of trust in the counselor.

Minors' Developmental and Chronological Levels

School counselors most often must use the developmental levels of their students as their guide rather than being able to rely on the students chronological age. Research indicates that counselors implicitly endorse such a developmentally based approach when faced with the dilemma of whether to breach confidentiality (Stone & Isaacs, 2002a, 2002b). Consider that statutory and case law make distinctions in crime and penalties based on developmental levels, not just chronological levels.

The courts are regarding the developmental levels as critical in cases involving children. Defendant children under the age of 18 are generally considered for juvenile court, although some states put the age at 16 or 17 years. Depending on the crime, the child might be tried as an adult. Just one case in point was Joshua Phillips, who at 14 was accused of killing his 8-year-old neighbor and hiding her under his bed. In 2012, the Supreme Court declared mandatory life sentences without parole for juveniles unconstitutional (*Miller v. Alabama*, Case No. 10-9646, 567 US 460 (2012)). In 2016, the Supreme Court ruled that the court's decision must be applied retroactively to what juvenile advocates estimate are 1,200–1,500 cases primarily in Pennsylvania, Louisiana, and Michigan where the 2012 ruling has not been retroactive.

Privacy Rights of Minors

The Family Educational Rights and Privacy Act (FERPA) (20 USC §1232g (1974)) and Protection of Pupil Rights Amendment (PPRA) are two primary federal laws that govern privacy for students from the United States Department of Education (USDOE): Any information a district maintains on a student is protected by FERPA, and any information the district might want to obtain from a student that should be considered private is protected by the PPRA (USDOE, 2002).

The Family Educational Rights and Privacy Act gives parents privacy rights over their child's educational records. Students have an ethical right to privacy and confidentiality in the counseling relationship, and the legal right for privacy belongs to their parents or guardians (USDOE, Family Policy Compliance Office, 2008). A few states afford students privacy in counseling in statute, but FERPA supersedes if case notes and educational records are at odds. Confidentiality and privacy for students is a complicated ethical imperative to negotiate given the competing interest with parental rights (ASCA, 2014).

The PPRA protects eight areas for students. Students should not be made to reveal their political affiliations, beliefs, or mental or psychological problems, or the student's family, their religion, income, sexual behavior. The PPRA means parents have "certain rights regarding the conduct of surveys, collection and use of information for marketing purposes, and certain physical exams." Schools cannot reveal:

1. political affiliations or beliefs of the student or student's parent
2. mental or psychological problems of the student or student's family
3. sexual behavior or attitudes
4. illegal, anti-social, self-incriminating, or demeaning behavior
5. critical appraisals of others with whom respondents have close family relationships
6. legally recognized privileged relationships, such as with lawyers, doctors, or ministers
7. religious practices, affiliations, or beliefs of the student or student's parent
8. income, other than as required by law to determine program eligibility (US Department of Education, 2002)

Students do not leave their constitutionally protected privacy right at the school house door. They have a privacy right, freedom of expression, and freedom to assemble and to be protected from illegal searches and seizures (Alexander & Alexander, 2019). However, minors' legal status differs significantly from that of adults if the educators need to supersede the students legal right to improve the students' educational opportunities. Even 18-year-olds do not have the same legal rights as adults if they are still in a secondary setting. For example, FERPA allows educators to contact parents of 18-year-olds for health and safety reasons (US Department of Education, 2007).

Most jobs for youth require the federal minimum wage of $7.25 per hour, depending on what and where the job is; states can also provide greater protection, but they cannot abridge federal laws. State-by-state laws for minors for everything from age of consent to emancipation can be found at https://statelaws.findlaw.com/family-laws/legal-ages.html.

Privacy rights can be a very difficult to navigate. A school counselor was rightly upset when the administration wanted to put a camera in her office along with dozens of others installed around the school. Legally, this is allowed without encroaching on the student's privacy rights (Alexander & Alexander, 2019). Locker rooms are different because of the expectation of privacy when changing one's clothing. Ethically, the counselor can argue that students who come to see a school counselor should be afforded the expectation of privacy and that this expectation is reasonable. The school can show a nexus or link between student safety and the installation of a camera in the school counselor's office. The cameras are everywhere for school safety. The counselor must argue that the right to privacy in counseling supersedes safety concerns—a hard argument to win. The better argument might be to work towards an agreement that the tapes will only be used in the event there is a safety concern (USDOE, Family Policy Compliance Office, 2007).

Rust observed:

> FERPA represents the floor, not the ceiling of privacy laws impacting academic advising. FERPA generally imposes less onerous requirements regarding maintenance and disclosure of education records than what state privacy laws and institutional policies require.

Additionally, the penalties for non-compliance with FERPA are generally not as intimidating as those associated with state privacy laws.

(Rust, 2014)

This means that states can create laws much more stringent than FERPA, but they cannot soften FERPA.

In Loco Parentis

The government's interest in having an educated populace supersedes the custodial authority of parents (Alexander & Alexander, 2019). Parents are forced (unless they choose an alternative approach such as home schooling) to relinquish physical control of their children because the states say they must be educated (Alexander & Alexander, 2019). This has tremendous implications for confidentiality in the world of school counseling.

Mandated state control with parents having a very limited voice brings with it tremendous *in loco parentis* legal responsibilities for educators toward students. *In loco parentis* means "in place of the parent." The courts never intended that school authorities, teachers, or school counselors would fully stand in place of parents in relationship to their children (Alexander & Alexander, 2019), but they must do so for safety needs. The courts are generally reluctant to interfere with the *in loco parentis* authority of educators. Educators who are acting within a state's statutes are supported by the courts because of the responsibilities involved in the difficult job of school administration (Alexander & Alexander, 2019). In *Nguon v. Wolf*, a principal outed a student as gay to her mother after she was caught kissing her girlfriend on several occasions in the hallways. Principal Wolf, the district and the other individual defendants claimed they were entitled to immunity based on the fact the suit against them involved their capacities and their actions were not ministerial (meaning they must happen in a certain way), but discretionary, and the principal and district won their case. Governmental immunity (from sovereign immunity, meaning you cannot sue the king) exists for educators for liability for discretionary acts performed in the exercise of their discretion as long as the state allows for governmental immunity (Alexander & Alexander, 2019).

Community and Institutional Standards

School counselors apply ethical standards in context of the larger community and the individual school (ASCA, 2016a). Ethics are not a one size fits all, but ethics depend on the situation and context. This does not mean we accept without challenge when the prevailing community standards stratify our student's opportunities, it means we work politically astutely to make change when needed. As Elie Wiesel said: "There may be times when we are powerless to prevent injustice, but there must never be a time when we fail to protest."

This context-driven ethics means school counselors are attuned to the prevailing community standards. For example, New York differs considerably from Utah in its approach to minors' confidentiality rights. A child in California can have an abortion in absence of parental involvement, but cannot in 44 other states.

Community standards have been cited in court judgments involving school counselors, as was the case when a school counselor said she was fired because of her religion, not because she discarded the district's sex education curriculum in the garbage. The deciding judge in

Grossman v. South Shore Public School District (507 F.3d 1097 (7th Cir. 2007)), Judge Posner, said: "With 838 churches (116 of them Lutheran—the plaintiff's denomination, though there are different sects within Lutheranism) within about 40 miles of tiny Port Wing, it can hardly be a region hostile to Christianity."

Academic Instruction

Schools are not mental health sites, and this dramatically defines the difference between confidentiality in school counseling and confidentiality in mental health sites (ASCA, 2014, 2017). Parents bring children to mental health agencies where they sign intake forms and have confidentiality and the intent of counseling explained to them. The intent for schools is dramatically different, and the way school counselors receive their clients/students ranges from a teacher sending a student for counseling to student self-referral. Even when parents call and ask that their child receive counseling, it is different as the counseling takes place in a setting designed for reading, writing, and arithmetic. The imperative to keep a student's trust and guard his/her confidentiality is just as strong in school, but the setting limits the legal muscle to do so (ASCA, 2014).

Trusting Relationship

The counselor–student relationship is built on trust. A student might come under the guise of discussing a banal topic, when in reality he or she is sizing up the school counselor to determine whether it is safe to talk about the real presenting issue which is a highly sensitive topic. A student must develop confidence in the trusting relationship to broach highly sensitive information about his/her family's domestic violence, the bullying he/she is enduring, his/her brother's recent suicide, his/her sister's rape, and on the list goes. It is very difficult for some students to open up and discuss personal issues, but trusting and connecting with the school counselor, believing he/she cares and will listen and not judge, builds what is referred to as the therapeutic alliance (Rogers, 1957). Unconditional positive regard, affirming the students when we cannot affirm their behavior, builds trust. When school counselors breach confidentiality, they do it in the least intrusive way appropriate to the situation in order to promote a trusting relationship.

Informed Consent

Informed consent means the counselor explains the limits of confidentiality, the intent of the counseling, and the student's rights (ASCA, 2016a; Stone, 2017). Informed consent requires that students are knowledgeable about informed consent, are voluntarily in counseling, and are competent to understand the implications of entering counseling. School counselors strive to obtain informed consent, but recognize it is not possible with students at some developmental levels. Even when a student signs up to be in a group, counselors work diligently to respect the student's confidences except when there is serious and foreseeable harm for the student or others (ASCA, 2016a). One way to effectively approach the ethics of informed consent is to view it as an on-going process rather than trying to cover every possible consideration in the first meeting. In addition, tailoring informed consent practices to a student's developmental level is critical. It is good practice to discuss examples of where the counselor may need to disclose confidential information to the student's parents/guardians or to school personnel. Best practice is to notify parents if ongoing counseling will occur (ASCA, 2016a). Notification does not imply written parental permission, but school districts require this. Students have a right to say "no" to counseling, and school counselors generally respect parents' rights to refuse counseling for their child. When students sign up to be in a counseling group and reveal personal information that makes its way into the hallways and social media, therefore, we say informed consent is not something we can rely upon.

Opacity of Laws and Ethical Codes

The courts and legislators define ministerial duty, and often agree that school counselors can exercise discretion in reporting to parents their child's suicidal ideation. However, let's remind ourselves that the law is the floor, or the minimum, and the courts and statutes might not hold the school counselor to a ministerial duty to report to parents suicidal ideation, but ethically, the profession believes it is a ministerial duty. As a profession, regardless of whether we have a clear state statute to guide our behavior, we must make certain that everyone in our profession understands that calling parents whenever we are placed on notice that suicide is even a remote possibility is not an option or judgment call, but an absolute duty. If you are a counselor educator, a school counseling department head, the lone counselor in your school, or one colleague among many, advocate to all to avoid the fatal mistake of not informing parents about their child's reported or rumored suicidal ideation.

School counselor state associations can advocate for appropriate state statutes that support counselors' role as reporters of suicide. The Virginia Code 22.1–272.1 A states:

> Any person licensed as administrative or instructional personnel by the Board of Education and employed by a local school board who, in the scope of his employment, has reason to believe, as a result of direct communication from a student, that such student is at imminent risk of suicide, shall, as soon as practicable, contact at least one of such student's parents to ask whether such parent is aware of the student's mental state and whether the parent wishes to obtain or has already obtained counseling for such student.

While on the surface the law reads soundly, it is out of date. The law does not require reporting unless the student self-reports he/she is suicidal. The research is clear that peer reports hold more truth than students' self-reports (Suicide Prevention Resource Center, 2020), therefore the profession pays close attention to peers and to its ministerial duty to call parents.

Number of Student Clients

The sheer number of students whom the professional is assigned to affects the counselor's legal and ethical obligations. The demands placed on school counselors, including career and academic advising, paperwork, and individual counseling, increase the importance of school counselor assignment to deliver services via the most effective, efficient, and equitable means possible (Akos, Schuldt, & Walendin, 2009; ASCA, 2017). In May 2019, the ASCA reported the current student-to-counselor ratio was 455:1 for the 2016–2017 school year (ASCA, 2019). Key findings include Alabama as the most improved state, gaining 269 new school counselors. Idaho, California, New York, Indiana, and Virginia also had notable improvements. Although the national average has decreased, it is still nearly twice the ASCA's recommended ratio of 250 students per school counselor (ASCA, 2019, p. 1). Caseloads do not spell the difference between a counselor who behaves professionally, ethically and legally and one who does not; however, caseloads influence the thoroughness school counselors can devote to each case (Akos et al., 2009).

Standard of Care

If all the school counselors in America were faced with a similar issue, how would the overwhelming majority of them respond? This is standard of care. Standard of care is what the reasonable competent school counselor would do. It is what the courts try to determine when finding for negligence. The question is, "Did the counselor adhere to the standard for the profession, or did the counselor step away from the standard?" In a recent presentation given by the author, a court case involving illegal search and seizure by a counselor who requested that students take a pregnancy test and provided them with one, a counselor commented that he does this all the time and sees no harm. He went on to explain this was the culture and climate of the school, and there was a long history of doing this. Although the courts will always look at the context and culture of a school and school district, the fact remains this counselor and his colleagues are extraordinarily far outside the standard of care for the profession. Just as the standard of care is greater for a teacher in a chemistry lab with dangerous chemicals, the standard of care for school counselors is greater because of the personal, social, and emotional overlay of their work.

Standard of care also applies to the developmental level of our students. You might not react if you saw one of your 17-year-old students smoking off school grounds, but most assuredly you would react if you passed one of your 7-year-old students smoking.

The legal duty of standard of care also applies to the foreseeability of danger. A peer reporting that his/her social media friend he/she has never met except online has been talking about suicide but the friend's comments last night were most concerning means that any reasonable, prudent counselor knows to contact the parents and the student even if the peer who reports is not even one of his/her students or in his/her school. The standard of care for the profession is that counselors always err on the side of caution with regard to suicide.

Ethical Codes

Our ethical codes matter. In every court case involving a school counselor as defendant since 1984, the ethical standards are considered if the court is trying to determine the standard of care for the profession. Ethics help guide us, but rarely hold the answers. Ethical codes are not concrete answers, but are used in consultation in the decision-making process. Our work is context-driven, and there is no single right answer. Ethical standards are aspirational. Unlike the law, which is the minimum standard society or the floor, the codes are the ceiling. *Ethics is knowing the difference between what you have a right to do and what is right to do.* As Potter Stewart, Associate Justice of the United States Supreme Court, said: "Ethics is knowing the difference between what you have a right to do and what is right to do."

The 2016 revision of the ASCA Ethical Standards for School Counselors was the fifth revision since their adoption in 1984, and has been on a six-year revision cycle since 1998. The 2016 codes represent a significant departure from the historical approach of using a small committee to do all the revisions. The 2016 codes represent a year-long process involving all 50 state school counseling associations. State leaders from 37 states sent in feedback. The approach to securing input from as many people as possible was important because the standards guide our work and protect the integrity of the profession. The standards are the values, norms, and customs that undergird our ethical practice.

The major changes in the 2016 ethical standards were efforts to strengthen the urgency and demand for advocacy and equity. Strong equity has been part of every revision since 2004, and in this version of the standards cultural competence became a focus:

> Advocate for equitable school and school counseling programs policies and practices for every student and all stakeholders including use of translators and bilingual/multilingual school counseling program materials that represent all languages used by families in the school community, and advocate for appropriate accommodations and accessibility for students with disabilities.
>
> (ASCA, 2016a, E.2.d.)

Counselors apply Kitchener's (1984) moral principles of beneficence, non-maleficence, loyalty, justice, and the promotion of student's autonomy to the ethical work they do. The 2016 codes have cultural competence front and center and infused throughout as we increase our understanding of our imperative to examine how systemic and individual issues can limit students' opportunities:

> Monitor and expand personal multicultural and social-justice advocacy awareness, knowledge and skills to be an effective culturally competent school counselor. Understand how prejudice, privilege and various forms of oppression based on ethnicity, racial identity, age, economic status, abilities/disabilities, language, immigration status, sexual orientation, gender, gender identity expression, family type, religious/spiritual identity, appearance and living situations (e.g., foster care, homelessness, incarceration) affect students and stakeholders.
>
> (ASCA, 2016a, B.3.i.)

The standards work to support transgender and gender-nonconforming students:

> Students are to: Be respected, be treated with dignity and have access to a comprehensive school counseling program that advocates for and affirms all students from diverse populations including but not limited to: ethnic/racial identity, nationality, age, social class, economic status, abilities/disabilities, language, immigration status, sexual orientation, gender, gender identity/expression, family type, religious/spiritual identity, emancipated minors, wards of the state, homeless youth and incarcerated youth. School counselors as social-justice advocates support students from all backgrounds and circumstances and consult when their competence level requires additional support . . .. Privacy that should be honored to the greatest extent possible, while balancing other competing interests (e.g., best interests of students, safety of others, parental rights) and adhering to laws, policies and ethical standards pertaining to confidentiality and disclosure in the school setting.
>
> (ASCA, 2016a, Preamble)

Data-informed programs became an emphasis, and the codes read in part:

a. Collaborate with administration, teachers, staff and decision makers around school-improvement goals.
b. Provide students with a comprehensive school counseling program that ensures equitable academic, career and social/emotional development opportunities for all students.
c. Review school and student data to assess needs including, but not limited to, data on disparities that may exist related to gender, race, ethnicity, socio-economic status and/or other relevant classifications.
d. Use data to determine needed interventions, which are then delivered to help close the information, attainment, achievement and opportunity gaps.
e. Collect process, perception and outcome data and analyze the data to determine the progress and effectiveness of the school counseling program. School counselors ensure the school counseling program's goals and action plans are aligned with district's school improvement goals.

(ASCA, 2016a, A.3)

Court cases informed the profession of needed changes in the ethical standards. In addition to the previously noted addition of standard A.6.e., the *Ward v. Wilbanks* court case was responsible for underscoring the need to better define ethical practice around marginalized youth:

Refrain from refusing services to students based solely on the school counselor's personally held beliefs or values rooted in one's religion, culture or ethnicity. School counselors respect the diversity of students and seek training and supervision when prejudice or biases interfere with providing comprehensive services to all students.

(ASCA, 2016a, B.3.j.)

Legislative changes impacted revisions. Title IX, governed by the USDOE Office of Civil Rights, requires equal access to education. The 2016 standards added:

Report to the administration all incidents of bullying, dating violence and sexual harassment as most fall under Title IX of the Education Amendments of 1972 or other federal and state laws as being illegal and require administrator interventions. School counselors provide services to victims and perpetrator as appropriate, which may include a safety plan and reasonable accommodations such as schedule change, but school counselors defer to administration for all discipline issues for this or any other federal, state or school board violation.

(ASCA, 2016a, A.11.a.)

Many other areas, such as confidentiality, were enlarged upon, and managing boundaries was strengthened (ASCA, 2016a, A.5). Site supervisors and their critical roles in preparing candidates were heightened (ASCA, 2016a, D), and the ASCA's appropriate duties were given ethical weight (ASCA, 2016a, B.2).

The standards are applied in context with careful consultation with other professionals; it is then that the professional can determine how to apply the codes. The definition of a professional includes the fact that he/she has ethical standards, a professional organization, and that he/she abides by the standards and is a member of his/her professional organization. In the case of school counselors, this adherence is to the American School Counselor Association Ethical Standards (ASCA, 2016a). The codes are aspirational, whereas the law, procedures, and legislation represent the floor, or the minimum standard society will tolerate. Anyone can be legal, but in our highly charged, high-stakes profession, it is not enough for us to be legal, we must also aspire to a high ethical standard. Ethics are aspirational. As Supreme Court Justice Potter Stewart said: "Ethics is knowing the difference between what you have a right to do and what is right to do."

Conclusion

School counselors have numerous responsibilities in which they have obligations to legal and ethical codes. The acronym COMPLICATIONS assists school counselors in making decisions that are in the best interests of their students and numerous stakeholders. The ASCA Ethical Codes were revised in 2016 and were written with the feedback of practitioners throughout the nation with attention to values, norms, and customs, and emphasized advocacy and equity while enlarging and strengthening the definition of confidentiality.

References

Akos, P., Schuldt, H., & Walendin, M. (2009). School counselor assignment in secondary schools. *Professional School Counseling, 13*(1), 23–29.

Alexander, K., & Alexander, M. D. (2019). *American public school law* (9th ed.). Belmont, CA: Thomson West.

American Counseling Association. (2013). Ethical issues related to conversion or reparative therapy. Retrieved from www.counseling.org/news/updates/2013/01/16/ethical-issues-related-to-conversion-or-reparative-therapy

ASCA. (2017). *ASCA position statement: The school counselor and individual student planning for postsecondary preparation*. Retrieved from www.schoolcounselor.org/asca/media/asca/PositionStatements/PS_IndStudentPlanning.pdf

ASCA. (2014). *ASCA position statement: The school counselor and confidentiality*. Retrieved from www.schoolcounselor.org/asca/media/asca/PositionStatements/PS_Confidentiality.pdf

ASCA. (2016a). *ASCA ethical standards for school counselors*. Retrieved from www.schoolcounselor.org/asca/media/asca/Ethics/EthicalStandards2016.pdf

ASCA. (2016b). *ASCA position statement: The school counselor and LGBTQ youth*. Retrieved from www.schoolcounselor.org/asca/media/asca/PositionStatements/PS_LGBTQ.pdf

ASCA. (2016c). *ASCA position statement: The promotion of safe schools through conflict resolution and bullying/harassment prevention*. Retrieved from www.schoolcounselor.org/asca/media/asca/PositionStatements/PS_Bullying.pdf

ASCA. (2016d). *ASCA position statement: The school counselor and transgender/gender nonconforming youth*. Retrieved from www.schoolcounselor.org/asca/media/asca/PositionStatements/PS_Transgender.pdf

ASCA. (2019). ASCA releases updated student-to-school-counselor ratio data. Retrieved from www.schoolcounselor.org/asca/media/asca/Press%20releases/ASCA-Student-to-SC-Ratios-Press-Release-5_2019.pdf

Iyer, N. N., & Baxter-MacGregor, J. (2010). Ethical dilemmas for the school counselor: Balancing student confidentiality and parents' right to know. *NERA Conference Proceedings 2010*. Paper 15. Retrieved from http://digitalcommons.uconn.edu/cgi/viewcontent.cgi?article=1017&context=nera_2010

Kitchener, K. S. (1984). Intuition, critical evaluation and ethical principles: The foundation for ethical decisions in counseling psychology. *Counseling Psychologist, 12*(3), 43–55.

Lambda Legal. (2012). Amicus brief of Parents, Families and Friends of Lesbians and Gays ("PFLAG"), Gay, Lesbian and Straight Education Network ("GLSEN"), Affirmations, and Ruth Ellis Center in Support of Defendant-Appellee for Affirmance, Ward v. Wilbanks, 667 F.3d 727 (2012). Retrieved from www.lambdalegal.org/in-court/legal-docs/ward_mi_20110211_amicus-pflag-et-al

Lee, C. C., & Park, D. (2013). A conceptual framework for counseling across cultures. In C. C. Lee (Ed.), *Multicultural issues in counseling: New approaches to diversity* (4th ed.). Alexandria, VA: American Counseling Association.

Ramer, H. (2016). Court: Advisor who helped girl get abortion should keep job. Associated Press. Retrieved from www.concordmonitor.com/News/State/Court-Adviser-who-helped-girl-get-abortion-should-keep-job-1403877

Roberts, N. (2016). Former student sues MSU for wrongful dismissal from counseling master's program. Retrieved from www.the-standard.org/news/former-student-sues-msu-for-wrongful-dismissal-from-counseling-master/article_942ed568-0963-11e6-9a89-afcb0727d981.html

Rogers, C. R. (1957). The necessary and sufficient conditions of therapeutic personality change. *Journal of Consulting Psychology, 21*, 95–103.

Rust, M. M. (2014). FERPA and its implications for academic advising practice. Retrieved from www.nacada.ksu.edu/Resources/Clearinghouse/View-Articles/FERPA-overview.aspx

Stone, C. (2017). *School counseling principles: Ethics and law* (4th ed.). Alexandria, VA: ASCA.

Stone, C., & Dahir, C. (2016). *The transformed school counselor* (3rd ed.). Belmont, CA: Brooks/Cole, Cengage Learning.

Stone, C., & Isaacs, M. (2002a). Confidentiality with minors: The effects of Columbine on counselor attitudes regarding breaching confidentiality. *Journal of Educational Research, 96*(2), 140–150.

Stone, C., & Isaacs, M. (2002b). Involving students in violence prevention: Anonymous reporting and the need to promote and protect confidences. *National Association of Secondary School Principals Bulletin, 86*(633), 54–65. doi:10.1177/019263650208663305

Suicide Prevention Resource Center (2020). Evidence based prevention. Retrieved from: www.nimh.nih.gov/health/topics/suicide-prevention/index.shtml

USDOE. (2002) *Recent changes affecting Protection of Pupil Rights Amendment (PPRA)*. Retrieved from www.fldoe.org/safeschools/pdf/ppra_recent_changes.pdf

USDOE, Family Policy Compliance Office. (2007). *Balancing student privacy and school safety: A guide to the Family Educational Rights and Privacy Act for elementary and secondary schools*. Retrieved from www2.ed.gov/policy/gen/guid/fpco/brochures/elsec.html

USDOE, Family Policy Compliance Office. (2008). *Family Educational Rights and Privacy Act (FERPA) final rule 34 CFR part 99: Section-by-section analysis*. Retrieved from https://www2.ed.gov/policy/gen/guid/fpco/pdf/ht12-17-08-att.pdf

Walsh, M. (2016, April 8). N.H. Supreme Court backs school counselor on abortion advice [Blog post]. Retrieved from http://blogs.edweek.org/edweek/school_law/2016/04/nh_supreme_court_backs_school_.html

Part III

Diversity and Developmental Issues among School-Aged Youth

Guidelines for School Counselors-in-Training

12 Cross-Cultural Competence in the Schools

Jolie Ziomek-Daigle

CACREP Standards

Contextual Dimensions

a. School counselors as leaders, advocates, and systems change agents in P-12 settings
d. School counselor roles in school leadership and multidisciplinary teams
k. Community resources and referral sources

Practice

h. Skills to critically examine the connections between social, familial, emotional, and behavior problems and academic achievement
k. Strategies to promote equity in student achievement and college access
o. Use of data to advocate for programs and students

Chapter Objectives:

*   assess SCIT awareness, knowledge, and skills in regard to counseling diverse student populations
*   gain experience with creating a school profile to help identify the needs of the school, students, and gaps related to achievement, attainment, and opportunities
*   expand competence around student cultural and ethnic diversity issues, increase knowledge and skills related to gender differences between students, and develop sensitivity to the needs of students of various levels of socioeconomic status
*   increase competence of trainees to counsel students with disabilities
*   add competence to counsel gifted students and understand the interactions among various aspects of identity for students who have multiple exceptionalities
*   gain competence to counsel and advocate for students in regard to sexual orientation and gender expression
*   develop competence related to students who are English language learners
*   increase skills for working with youth who have socioeconomic differences

Introduction

In this chapter, you will assess your cross-cultural competency (i.e., awareness, knowledge, and skills), learn how to develop and assess a school profile to better understand your school's students, recognize multiple identities among people in your school (e.g., multicultural, students with disabilities, students with giftedness, students with various sexual orientations), appreciate leadership opportunities to advocate for and on behalf of your students, and apply various scenarios and activities to practice developing your counseling competence and advocacy skills.

Becoming an advocate for students and being a culturally competent counselor in the schools begin with understanding ourselves in relation to others and our student populations. The population of the United States can be described as multiethnic, multicultural, and multilingual (Holcomb-McCoy & Chen-Hayes, 2019). The diversity that is represented in the United States and most likely represented in the schools can be broadly defined to include (a) race/ethnicity, (b) gender, (c) physical or mental ability, (d) sexual orientation/gender expression, (e) socioeconomic status, and (f) other characteristics of background or group membership (Lee & Hipolito-Delgado, 2007). Moreover, it is estimated that while the non-Hispanic white population in the United States is still the largest major racial and ethnic group, the growth of this group is slowing, while the Latino, Asian American, and African American populations are growing rapidly (Lee, 2014). With the knowledge that student populations will be as diverse as ever, school counselors-in-training can begin with an assessment of their own awareness, knowledge, and skills in relation to working with diverse populations.

Assessment of SCIT Awareness, Knowledge, and Skills

In terms of assessing multicultural competence, faculty members and your supervisors will determine whether you have gained competence (i.e., awareness, knowledge, and skills) to work with diverse student populations in the school setting. At this juncture in your graduate training, you most likely have gained multicultural awareness and knowledge through foundational courses such as cross-cultural counseling and other courses where multiculturalism and advocacy are infused. These skills will be further assessed during clinical placements like practicum and internship. Therefore, you should graduate with a sufficient competency related to issues of diversity as well as advanced skills such as advocacy that are consistently in a state of refinement.

Holcomb-McCoy and Chen-Hayes (2019) suggest ways you can increase your multicultural competence, including: (a) investigate your own cultural or ethnic heritage; (b) attend workshops and events on multicultural and diversity issues; (c) join counseling organizations focused on cultural and diversity issues, such as Counselors for Social Justice (CSJ), the Association for Multicultural Counseling and Development (AMCD), and the Association for Lesbian, Gay, Bisexual, Transgender Issues in Counseling (ALGBTIC); (d) read literature by culturally diverse authors; and (e) become immersed in multicultural and diversity-focused literature such as journals from the aforementioned associations. It is important for you to realize that professional development extends throughout the career of a school counselor, and does not stop at graduation. By utilizing the ways mentioned earlier, you can further develop your diversity awareness and multicultural competence to remain lifelong, reflective practitioners.

This section is intended to advance your competence as you embark on practicum and internship experiences. Holcomb-McCoy (2004) created a multicultural checklist containing nine sections (multicultural counseling, multicultural consultation, understanding racism and student resistance, understanding racial and/or ethnic identity development, multicultural assessment, multicultural family counseling, social advocacy, developing school–family–community partnerships, and understanding cross-cultural interpersonal interactions) with 51 items in total. To provide you with a better understanding of your multicultural competence and areas you need to address, complete the School Counselor Multicultural Competence Checklist in Table 12.1.

Table 12.1 School counselor multicultural competence checklist.

Competence

I. Counselor Awareness of Own Cultural Values and Biases

A. *Attitudes and Beliefs*   Met   Unmet

1. I am aware and sensitive to my own cultural heritage and to valuing and respecting differences.
2. I am aware of my own cultural backgrounds and experiences and attitudes, values, and biases that influence psychological processes.
3. I am able to recognize the limits of my own competencies and expertise.
4. I am comfortable with differences that exist between myself and my students in terms of race, ethnicity, culture, and beliefs.

B. *Knowledge*   Met   Unmet

1. I have specific knowledge about my own racial and cultural heritage and how it personally and professionally affects my definitions of normality-abnormality and the process of counseling.
2. I have knowledge and understanding about how oppression, racism, discrimination, and stereotyping affect me personally and in my work.
3. I possess knowledge about my social impact on others, including communication style differences and how this style may clash or foster the counseling process.

C. *Skills*   Met   Unmet

1. I seek out educational, consultative, and training experience to improve my understanding and effectiveness in working with culturally different populations. I am able to recognize the limits of my competencies and (a) seek consultation, (b) seek further training or education, (c) make referrals to more qualified individuals or resources, or (d) engage in a combination of these.
2. I seek to understand myself as a racial and cultural being and am actively seeking a nonracist identity.

II. Counselor Awareness of Student's Worldview

A. *Attitudes and Beliefs*   Met   Unmet

1. I am aware of my negative emotional reactions toward other racial and ethnic groups that may prove detrimental to my students in counseling. I am willing to contrast my own beliefs and attitudes with those of my culturally different students in a nonjudgmental fashion.
2. I am aware of stereotypes and preconceived notions that I may hold toward other racial and ethnic minority groups.

B. *Knowledge*   Met   Unmet

1. I possess specific knowledge and information about the particular group I am working with. I am aware of the life experiences, cultural heritage, and historical background of culturally different students.
2. I understand how race, culture, ethnicity, and so forth may affect personality formation, vocational choices, manifestation of psychological disorders, help-seeking behavior, and the appropriateness or inappropriateness of counseling approaches.
3. I understand and have knowledge about sociopolitical influences that impinge upon the life of racial and ethnic minorities.

C. *Skills*   Met   Unmet

1. I familiarize myself with relevant research and the latest findings regarding mental health and mental disorders of various ethnic and racial groups. I actively seek out educational experiences that foster their knowledge, understanding, and cross-cultural skills.

(*Continued*)

Table 12.1 (Cont.)

Competence		

2. I am actively involved with minority individuals outside of the counseling setting (community events, social and political functions, etc.) so that my perspective of minorities is more than an academic or helping exercise.

III. Culturally Appropriate Intervention Strategies

A. Attitudes and Beliefs   Met Unmet

1. I respect students' religious and/or spiritual beliefs and values, including attributions and taboos, because they affect worldview, psychosocial functioning, and expressions of distress.
2. I respect indigenous helping practices and respect minority community intrinsic help-giving networks.
3. I value bilingualism and do not view another language as an impediment to counseling.

B. Knowledge   Met Unmet

1. I have a clear and explicit knowledge and understanding of the generic characteristics of counseling and therapy and how they may clash with the cultural values of minority groups.
2. I am aware of institutional barriers that present minorities from using mental health services.
3. I have knowledge of the potential bias in assessment instruments and use procedures and interpret findings keeping in mind the cultural and linguistic characteristics of the students.
4. I have knowledge of minority family structures, hierarchies, values, and beliefs. I am knowledgeable about the community characteristics and the resources in the community as well as the family.
5. I am aware of relevant discriminatory practices at the social and community level that may be affecting the psychological welfare of the population being served.

C. Skills   Met Unmet

1. I am able to engage in a variety of *verbal* and *nonverbal* helping responses. I am able to send and receive both verbal and nonverbal messages *accurately* and *appropriately*. I am not tied to only one method or approach to helping but recognize that helping styles and approaches may be culture bound.
2. I am able to exercise institutional intervention skills on behalf of my students. I can help students determine whether a "problem" stems from racism or bias in others so that students do not inappropriately personalize problems.
3. I am not averse to seeking consultation with traditional healers and religious and spiritual leaders and practitioners in the treatment of culturally different students when appropriate.
4. I take responsibility for interacting in the language requested by the student and, if not feasible, make appropriate referral. If appropriate I will (a) seek a translator with cultural knowledge and appropriate professional background and (b) refer to a knowledgeable and competent bilingual counselor.
5. I have the training and expertise in the use of traditional assessment and testing instruments. I not only understand the technical aspects of the instruments but I am also aware of the cultural limitations.
6. I attend to as well as work to eliminate biases, prejudices, and discriminatory practices. I am cognizant of sociopolitical contexts in conducting evaluation and providing interventions and develop sensitivity.
7. I take responsibility in educating my students to the processes of psychological intervention, such as goals, expectations, legal rights, and the counselor's orientation.

Source: Gysbers and Henderson (2014), printed with permission.

Conceptual Application Activity 12.1

Using the Multicultural Checklist (Table 12.1), respond to the following questions and process your answers in small groups with your peers.

1. What are my strengths and stated competencies?
    _____
    _____

2. In what areas do I need to gain competence?
    _____
    _____

3. In using my strengths and competencies, how can I guide other professionals in gaining competence?
    _____
    _____

4. In reviewing the areas in which I need to gain competence, how can I work with other professionals to get there?
    _____
    _____

Assessment of School Site and Developing a School Profile

You can assess a school site to better understand not only the needs of individual students, but those of the student body as well. School profiles provide a backdrop of the school based on accessible, existing data. The material in Chapter 8 on managing your school counseling program provides a background of school data summarization, yet these data present rich potential for disaggregating data to identify students who may be overlooked. Information that is revealed from a school profile may include gaps in achievement, attainment, funding and opportunities, and certain student groups that may be isolated and not receiving the full range of services from the school. School profiles provide the data for school counselors-in-training and school counselors to take action in terms of better defining their comprehensive school counseling program and the direct and indirect services that are offered. Baseline data are to be collected on an ongoing basis to monitor the progress of student groups and emerging needs (ASCA, 2019). Some baseline data needed to determine potential areas of discrimination could include:

*   percentage of students enrolled in the free or reduced lunch program
*   percentage of students who have passed or failed state standardized tests
*   percentage of students who scored at or above the national averages on the ACT and SAT
*   percentage of students who are homeless
*   percentage of students enrolled in the special education program

- percentage of students enrolled in the gifted education program
- percentage of students who are bilingual and enrolled in the English for Speakers of Other Languages (ESOL) program
- school's daily and weekly attendance/tardiness rate
- school's daily and weekly suspension rate
- school's daily and weekly behavior referrals rate
- school's dropout rate or school completion rate

Conceptual Application Activity 12.2

Look at the demographic profile of the school in which you are completing your practicum or internship experience and determine the numbers of students who fit into the baseline data categories. These data can be obtained by looking at school district or state websites. Compare your list with those of your peers.

_____

_____

Culturally and Ethnically Diverse Students

We are different, but also share similarities. In an attempt to categorize these differences and similarities, key aspects of who we are have been identified and used to help people understand one another culturally. Race, ethnicity, age, gender, sexual orientation, gender expression, disability, socioeconomic status, and disability are some aspects of culture. Culture, however, incorporates much more than these variables. Cultural considerations also include, but are not limited to, views and practices related to individualism versus collectivism, masculinity and feminism, communication practices, physical proximity and closeness, religion/spirituality, language(s) spoken, structure and predictability, work ethic, political views, holidays recognized and celebrated, geographic region in which one is reared or lives, food and music preferences, value placed on education, family status, and so on. Our focus in this section will remain on increasing your awareness of cultural and diverse student populations. As discussed earlier, the development or review of an existing school profile will help you understand the backdrop and unique needs of the school and certain student groups. Understandably, a school profile may also reveal equity gaps that a multiculturally competent school counselor will need to work toward reconciling. These gaps are usually most noticeable in achievement, attainment, funding, and other opportunities (Holcomb-McCoy & Chen-Hayes, 2019).

Conceptual Application Activity 12.3

Read the following scenarios, answer the questions that appear at the end of each scenario, and then discuss your answers in small groups with your peers.

Sara is a first-year school counselor in an inner-city setting. The student population consists of the following: 82% African American, 12% Latino/a, and 6% biracial. Ninety-five percent of the students are enrolled in the free or reduced lunch program. Sara is white and from a middle- to upper-class background. Her dad worked while her mom stayed at home. She does not speak a second language because her parents did not "like the idea" of her taking a world language while she was in school and it was not required. Her school did not have a free or reduced lunch program that she knew of, and generally she socialized with people who looked and acted similarly to the way she did. While in graduate school, Sara took one course on cross-cultural counseling and completed her practicum and internship at a rural, white, working-class high school.

In regard to Sara's new position, how can she assess her multicultural competence?

_____

_____

Where and how can she begin this work?

_____

_____

What could be her goals in this area as a school counselor?

_____

_____

What could be her specific outreach strategies to students, parents, administrators, teachers, and community members?

_____

_____

Veronica is a first-year school counseling student. She is African American, grew up in a rural area in a Southern state, and was raised by her aunt. Because of her aunt's influence, Veronica was committed to her schoolwork and rose to the top of her class in high school. She was enrolled in the gifted education program, and knew the program would help her to reach her educational goals, but she did not like being the only student of color with others who grew up in very different circumstances. Veronica is now deciding on practicum and internship placements, and has this awareness in mind. She is considering interning at a middle-upper-class high school because she wants to work on her biases against upper-class families and her thinking that "those families" have problems. Veronica knows that all families do have problems and that all students struggle at some point, so she wants to push herself to experience something different than what she already knows.

How should Veronica proceed in identifying her clinical placements?

_____

_____

With whom should she consult on a consistent basis?

_____

_____

How can she become familiar with the school culture and the lives of her students and families?

_____

_____

Although universities are doing a better job in the recruitment and retention of diverse students, many school counseling graduates continue to be white, female, and middle-class. Given that people of European descent have been the dominant group throughout the years of formalized education in the United States, it would benefit you to gain an understanding of oppression and privilege. An extension of Conceptual Application Activity 12.2 can be devoted to further understanding the influences of power and prejudice as they relate to oppression. In addition, you can begin by interviewing your own family members to better understand their histories. Holcomb-McCoy and Chen-Hayes (2019) suggest that school counselors-in-training read Howard Zinn's *A People's History of the United States* or excerpts from the book so that they can analyze the information and messages they received in school or within the family while growing up.

Box 12.1

Under-age migrants from South and Central America are entering the United States in record numbers. Many leave of their own volition for more opportunities. Undocumented children and adolescents account for approximately 15% of the immigrants living in our country, and are often referred to as the "1.5 generation" due to their fit somewhere between the first and second generation. Although these children were not born in this country, many have received much of their education here, but without a method for legalizing their status. This undocumented status makes it difficult for these youth to obtain higher education or enter the workforce.

Students with Disabilities

Until the 1960s and 1970s, students with disabilities such as mental illness or mental disability were commonly institutionalized and held separate from the rest of society (Hallahan & Kauffman, 2006). It was not until the last decade that these students were integrated into mainstream classrooms and schools. Additionally, there have been several legislative movements such as Section 504 of the Rehabilitation Act of 1973, the Education for All Handicapped Children Act (PL 94-142) in 1975, the Individuals with Disabilities Education Act (IDEA) in 1990, the Americans with Disabilities Act (ADA) in 1990, and the reauthorized and renamed Individuals with Disabilities Education Improvement Act (IDEIA) in 2004. These directives have greatly shaped the role and function of school personnel (including school counselors and school counselors-in-training) in working with students with disabilities. Though these legislative acts have been helpful in providing accommodations to students, school counselors must also recognize where legislation for disabilities may or may not overlap. For example, a student with attention-deficit hyperactivity disorder (ADHD) may qualify for accommodations either under IDEA, under Section 504, or under neither Act depending upon the nature of the student's disability and other health conditions (Lockhart, 2003).

Disabilities that are often present in school settings are listed in Table 12.2. These terms can be used as a reference as you work with various school-aged children, as it is important for you to realize that the terminology used for certain disabilities or disorders in schools may be different from the terminology used by non-school mental health professionals; for example, depression is commonly classified in schools as an emotional or behavioral disorder

Table 12.2 Common disabilities present in school settings.

Common disabilities	Standard accommodations and interventions
Traumatic brain injury	Recording lessons
Hard of hearing/deaf	Allow extra time for testing/amplifications devices/sign interpretation
Visual impairment	Seating near teacher and away from sources that create distractions/auditory description of content/color contrast such as overlays
Communication disorders	Tutoring
Students with ADD or ADHD	Masking templates to block off content not of immediate concern to the student/visual cues for time on task/self-monitoring systems/permit overactivity
Orthopedic impairments	Large pencils or utensils for gripping/minimize or eliminate board copying
Intellectual disabilities	Tutoring/have students repeat directions
Emotional or behavioral disorders	Tutoring/communication in a supportive manner/establish clear expectations
Autism spectrum disorders	Repetition of instruction/positive reinforcement/picture schedules
Learning disabilities	Teach adaptive skills

(EBD; Hallahan & Kauffman, 2006). Furthermore, some states use different terminology to describe the same classification.

Although much research to date in working with students with disabilities has focused on a deficit- or pathology-based model, other researchers have suggested that a strengths-based approach may be beneficial. Dykens (2006) cites research findings that families with children who have intellectual disabilities may have stressors related to raising such a child, but may also find the experience of having a child with disabilities in the family leads to a more fulfilling life. For example, the family of a child with a disability may find that they are better able to accept differences in other people, are more socially and politically active and aware, and are connected emotionally (Hallahan & Kauffman, 2006).

The American School Counselor Association (ASCA, 2016a) has provided a position statement on working with students with disabilities. In addition to providing direct counseling services to these students, the ASCA calls school counselors to collaborate with the school professionals in the delivery of services. The work of these teams typically results in written Individualized Education Programs (IEPs), 504 plans, transition planning, and other documentation. The statement also urges school counselors to be aware of community support resources for referrals, both while the student is in school as well as for postsecondary employment and education options. The ASCA's statement also advises school counselors to not serve in certain supervisory or administrative roles in the planning for students with disabilities that would better be served by school administrators or special education coordinators. Such inappropriate roles include the school counselor making the sole determination as to a student's placement or retention, coordinating a 504 team, and supervising the actual implementation of the student's plan.

The incorporation of Response to Intervention (RtI) in schools is now a legal mandate. Although RtI is viewed as a general education initiative, IDEA was the original impetus behind this mandate (Shepard, Shahidullah, & Carlson, 2013). RtI is a process in which students who may be identified as having learning-related problems or other special needs or concerns like behavior are given instructional and behavioral interventions and monitored for how they respond to such interventions. RtI requires that the interventions utilized with students be evidence-based and measurable with respect to their outcomes. In addition to being utilized with students who may be identified to have disabilities, the RtI process involves universal to targeted approaches to determine which students may be in need of more intensive services such as IEPs, 504 plans, wrap around, etc. (Klotz & Canter, 2006). RtI is commonly referred to as a multi-tiered approach (usually depicted as a pyramid). Tier 1 (the base of the pyramid) consists of more universal, classroom-based instruction, screening, and large-group interventions such as consistent reinforcement, preferential seating, guided choices, and untimed tests. Tier 2 includes more specialized interventions for students who are identified as needing more targeted strategies such as smaller-group or more intensive instruction in reading or math, as in an extended learning time block. Tier 3 (the highest level of the multi-tiered pyramid) consists of the most intensive set of interventions for students who do not respond to interventions provided at Tier 1 or 2. In Tier 3, students may be considered for and formally identified as needing special education services and/or provided additional assessments (National Center for Learning Disabilities, 2013).

More importantly, RtI in conjunction with IDEA provides increased flexibility in terms of serving students who may not necessarily be identified as having a severe discrepancy between intellectual ability and achievement (as has traditionally been used to identify students with learning disorders), but may also be used with students who may not meet such criteria but nevertheless have a need for specialized services. As such, it eliminates the need for a "wait to fail" approach to identifying and serving students who may have special needs (Klotz & Canter, 2006).

In serving students with special needs, school counselors should be aware of the differences among these various forms of serving students, including RtI, IEPs, Section 504 plans, and transition plans. RtI is more of a general framework or process that involves universal screenings and interventions at the lowest (Tier 1) level up to more specialized services (including formal identification for special education services) at the highest level (Tier 3). An IEP may be considered as part of the RtI process and is typically only implemented at higher levels of intervention in the RtI process, or may only be mandated for students who are formally identified as qualifying for IDEA services (Tilly, 2013).

Section 504 plans are similar to IEPs in that both were developed under civil rights statutes in order to help serve students with special needs; specifically, IEPs were developed under the IDEIA of 2004, and 504 plans were developed under Section 504 of the Rehabilitation Act of 1973. Zirkel (2009b, p. 68) refers to IDEA and Section 504 as "sister civil rights statutes." However, Zirkel points out that there are differences between IEPs and Section 504 plans, particularly with the implementation of the more recent Americans with Disabilities Act Amendment (ADAA) in 2009. In particular, Zirkel discusses that 504 plans generally cover a wider range of both mental and physical health issues, such as ADHD, dyslexia, food allergies, and diabetes, than would typically fall under the purview of an IEP. The passage of the ADAA provided for a broader set of criteria that would allow students to qualify for a 504 plan if their impairment affects a "major life activity to a substantial extent" (Zirkel, 2009b, p. 68). For example, not only would students qualify for a 504 plan for mental or cognitive impairments such as difficulty with concentrating, but they may also qualify for more physical health-related problems that impact learning, such as irritable bowel syndrome and Crohn's disease. As Zirkel (2009b) states regarding the revised standards, "the overall effect is obviously to expand the number and range of students eligible under Section 504" (p. 69). School counselors should be aware, then, that in the past they may have been encouraged to use a Section 504 plan as a "consolation prize" (p. 69) for students who would not qualify for an IEP under IDEA, and that in the past "Section 504 has taken a backseat to the IDEA in public schools" (Zirkel, 2009a, p. 211). However, at present, the expanded qualifying criteria for Section 504 plans make them equally valid and robust options in terms of serving students who may have disabilities.

In addition to the overall process of RtI and specific documentation such as IEPs and 504 plans, an important aspect of awareness for school counselors in working with students with disabilities is how to best support them in transitioning from the K–12 environment to postsecondary educational options such as college. The transition for students from high school to college is known to be particularly difficult for all students who make this transition, but in particular for students with disabilities (Lapan, Tucker, Se-Kang Kim, & Kosciulek, 2003). From a legal standpoint, the Americans with Disabilities Act (ADA) and Section 504 both provide provisions not only for K–12 education, but also for students in postsecondary settings (US Department of Education, 2011b). As such, school counselors should be aware from both a legal and a professional standpoint of the need to support students with disabilities through the postsecondary transition process. IEPs often include a section related to planning for postsecondary transitions and may document current levels of functioning, but school counselors should be aware that an IEP or 504 plan by itself may not serve as sufficient documentation for a student to receive necessary disability accommodations in a college setting (although it may be helpful in partially substantiating such needs) (US Department of Education, 2011b). Students transitioning to college may require more formal documentation of a disability through means such as formal psychological testing. Additionally, school counselors may be able to help students with disabilities be more successful with their postsecondary transitions by paying particular attention to conducting career development activities with high school students (Lapan et al., 2003).

Conceptual Application Activity 12.4

Read and respond to the following questions, then process the questions with your peers in small groups.

1. From your clinical placement experiences, how closely do school counselors work with the special education coordinator or teachers? How involved are the school counselors in working with the special education population in general? What are the specific practices that you have observed?

   _____

   _____

2. What unique issues would students face with comorbid disabilities or disabilities that also overlap with other identities discussed in this chapter (e.g., a student with both a learning disability [LD] and ADHD, a student with intellectual disabilities who is Hispanic, a student with a reading disorder who identifies as transgender)?

   _____

   _____

3. What considerations should you, as a school counselor-in-training, think about in terms of a student with disabilities' transition to college, the workforce, or adulthood?

   _____

   _____

4. Do you think that all students with disabilities or other special needs require accommodations? Why, or why not?

_____

_____

5. Many students with disabilities have a significant physical health component of their condition. As a school counselor-in-training, how could you make yourself more aware of the physical and medical needs of these students?

_____

_____

Students Who Are Gifted

Oftentimes, school counselors will not be required to identify gifted students, but may need to help facilitate the process for parents and teachers. Consultation with the gifted education teacher or the district office in terms of how you can partner in servicing this student group would be helpful to you as a SCIT. School counselors often work with these students through such means as connecting parents to the gifted education teacher or school district office for possible testing, counseling students individually or in small groups, conducting a classroom unit for the gifted, facilitating curriculum changes, and discussing postsecondary options based on student academic strengths.

According to the National Association for Gifted Children (2008), gifted children may have characteristics that include general intellectual ability, specific academic aptitude, creative thinking and production, leadership, psychomotor ability, and talent in visual and performing arts. Conversely, according to Delisle and Galbraith (2002), some misconceptions of gifted students may include that all are white and from middle- to upper-class families, are loved by teachers, excel in all subjects, enjoy school and learning, and will succeed no matter the circumstances. Further, Wood (2008) suggests that asynchronous development, affective regulation, and being from a marginalized population (e.g., a student of color, LGBTQ, lower socioeconomic status) can present additional unique challenges for the gifted student population.

Conceptual Application Activity 12.5

Read and respond to the question at the end of the following scenario, and in small groups process your answer with your peers.

Mr. Stevens is a social studies teacher at Anytown High School. He is also the father of Greg, a 15-year-old freshman who just started at Anytown this school year. Mr. Stevens has been good friends with one of the school counselors, Mr. Sheetz, for several years since the two started working together at the high school. Mr. Stevens and Mr. Sheetz work out at the local gym together and share their love of adventure sports through their frequent rock climbing and whitewater kayaking trips. As luck would have it, Greg happens to be one of the students whom Mr. Sheetz is assigned to counsel. Mr. Sheetz was concerned about this at first, but since he feels he already knew Greg and Mr. Stevens fairly well, he did not anticipate Greg to be a frequent visitor to his office. He knew Greg to have had a few disciplinary problems in middle school and that Greg was a somewhat sensitive and emotional teenager in general, but Mr. Stevens had always said that Greg had persevered and done well in school. One afternoon while Mr. Sheetz and Mr. Stevens are on bus duty together, Mr. Stevens has a concerned look on his face. "You know I keep putting pressure on Greg's teachers to have him evaluated for gifted classes," Mr. Stevens tells Mr. Sheetz. "I am aware that Greg is in regular classes but I think the gifted and advanced coursework would challenge him more." Mr. Sheetz knows Greg's test scores and grades and does not see how he can support or endorse a gifted evaluation for Gregg.

How should Mr. Sheetz proceed?

What data should Mr. Sheetz have available if a meeting was scheduled?

How do professionals have boundaries about their roles, responsibilities, and relationships in the school setting?

School counselors have a responsibility to monitor the total development of gifted students in the social/emotional domain, not just in academics. An example would be the development of characteristics related to the happiness, well-being, life satisfaction, self-regulation (Peterson, 2006), and peer relations of gifted students. Additionally, school counselors need to be aware of and actively engage in updated identification and retention practices so that all students from diverse gender, racial, ethnic, socioeconomic, and disability backgrounds benefit from the services a gifted education program can offer should they qualify. Gifted programs may look different from state to state, district to district, and possibly school to school. Most likely, a school counselor will be asked to serve on the gifted placement committee to review student referrals for evaluation and reevaluation. Certain instruments are used that provide data to help committee members make a recommendation through the use of certain criteria and multiple assessments. For example, in the Clarke County (Georgia) School District (Clarke County, 2019), students are evaluated in the areas of mental ability, achievement, creativity, and motivation. Students must receive a score or a certain percentile in three of the four categories to be placed in a gifted program.

Conceptual Application Activity 12.6

Read and respond to the question at the end of each of the following scenarios and discuss your answers in small groups with your peers.

Karl is a tenth-grader and enrolled in the gifted education program. He is African American and from a middle-class family. Karl did not want to enroll in the gifted program and have to make new friends in the classes, but his parents insisted, stating, "If you got it, use it." Karl is one of two students of color and has to sit by himself during lunch because all of his old friends eat lunch at a different time. He is having trouble with the accelerated pace in his new classes and does not finish all of his nightly homework. Karl's grades have slipped slightly, and he is not used to receiving B's. He volunteers after school and helps the technology teacher update the school computers and has aspirations to become a computer technician. You are providing career counseling to him during your internship, and Karl's parents called and want you to get him more motivated to succeed.

How would you proceed?

_____

_____

Delia is in ninth grade and is classified as twice exceptional. She has cerebral palsy and uses an electric wheelchair at school. Delia is also enrolled in the gifted education program, and her talents are in math and science. It has been a hard semester for her, and she has not liked the transition to high school. Delia has to leave the ninth-grade hall twice a day to rush across campus to the gifted classes. She runs into other students and has to use ramps that take time to maneuver around. She is late to all of her classes almost every day. Delia also gets self-conscious when she interrupts the class by being late. She loves being in the gifted classes because she is learning new things, making friends, feels inspired, and knows she wants to be a civil engineer. As a SCIT, you are also learning about the school culture and want to help Delia.

How can you assist her?

_____

_____

The following strategies illustrate ways of working with students who are gifted within the academic, career, and social/emotional domains (Wood, 2008).

Academic Counseling Domain

- Facilitate gifted identification and placement, and allow for flexible plans.
- Assess for decision-making, organization, and time-management skills.
- Provide inventories that help students understand learning styles, learning preferences personality characteristics, and personal/social (renamed social/emotional) domains.

Career Counseling Domain

- Explore possible careers as an extension of talents through inventories and the Internet.
- Help connect students to job shadowing, apprenticeships, and internships.
- Explore leisure and free-time activities.
- Encourage contribution to society via service-learning or volunteering.

Social/Emotional Counseling Domain

- Normalize student feelings, experiences, and the unique characteristics of giftedness.
- Validate feelings of loneliness, uniqueness, being different than others.

- Work on regulation of emotions and negative thinking.
- Consider stress-reducing activities, relaxation techniques, and mindfulness.
- Include expressive arts such as play, music, bibliotherapy, journaling, and drama.

Gender Differences among Students

School counselors should be aware of both the similarities and differences between the male and female students they serve. Some available data indicate that males and females were enrolled in school in similar numbers in pre-K and kindergarten programs nationally as of 2001 (NCES, 2012). However, the same source also exposed other data suggesting educational inequities between males and females. For example, the report by the National Center for Education Statistics (NCES) describes that females repeat grades and drop out of school at lower rates than males. Males are also believed to have more behavioral problems at school. In terms of specific subjects taught at school, the report also states that females have historically outperformed their male student counterparts in reading and writing, while in other areas such as math and science male students outperformed females (although this gap appears to be narrowing). As a result, school counselors should be aware of the differences in perception and expectations their male and female students may experience and that these differences may play themselves out in the counseling context, particularly with respect to potential career aspirations for these students.

Legislative mandates also require school counselors and school counseling trainees to be sensitive to gender differences and to inequities in opportunities presented to their students. Title IX of the Education Amendments of 1972 prohibits discrimination on the basis of sex in programs that receive federal funding (including public schools). Some data that have been tracked in recent years in relation to Title IX compliance have shown that gaps in educational opportunities have been closing between males and females, such as the increased number of female students who successfully obtain postsecondary degrees and the increased number of female athletes in postsecondary settings (NCES, 2013a). However, while this gap is narrowing, there still exist differences in opportunities available to male and female students, and we have an obligation to support all students of all genders.

Further differences exist between males and females in terms of their social behaviors, some of which are particularly relevant to the context of counseling. Crick, Casas, and Nelson (2002) denote the differences between different forms of aggression that youth and their peers may exhibit toward one another. While some forms of aggression are more physical in nature, more recently Crick et al. (2002) studied relational forms of aggression, such as excluding a victim from a peer social group, withdrawing a friendship, or other forms of affection based upon a perceived slight. With regard to gender differences and how these manifest themselves in aggressive acts, the authors cite that while males tend to be more frequently the victims of physical aggression, females tend to be more frequently the victims of relational aggression. Just as physical forms of aggression are harmful to students, social and relational forms of aggression also deprive the affected victims of peer relationships, feelings of acceptance, and other factors associated with positive well-being for youth. School counselors should be aware of gender differences with respect to different forms of aggression and bullying, as negative consequences may be experienced. School counselors can help both the victims as well as the perpetrators of these offenses to be more understanding toward one another and create an overall more positive school climate for students of all genders.

Children and adolescents may also experience other forms of discrimination related to their gender, particularly for those who do not conform to societal expectations of their expected and perceived gender identity and expression. Wyss (2004) qualitatively explored the experiences of gender queer, transgender, and other gender non-conforming high school youth. Through this research, Wyss elicited common themes of experiences of homophobia and transphobia. For example, Wyss provides examples of the discrimination experienced by biologically female teens who do not comply with societal expectations related to dating males, who present with more of a "tomboyish" image, and wear clothes inconsistent with dominant culture views of beauty. Similarly, for biological male teens, those who may display more feminine forms of self-expression (such as clothing) may experience discrimination as well. Be aware of the pressures faced by gender non-conforming youth and help advocate for their well-being and acceptance by others.

Students Who are Lesbian, Gay, Bisexual, Transgender, and Queer (LGBTQ)

In January 2005, White County High School junior Kerry Pacer made national headlines from the small town of Cleveland, Georgia. She asked the administration of her high school if she could form a Gay-Straight Alliance (GSA) club. The organization, named Peers Rising in Diverse Education (PRIDE), was initially allowed to meet, but quickly drew controversy and protests (Yoo, 2005). Soon afterward, the county school board passed a ruling that all non-academically related clubs, including Pacer's, would not be allowed to meet, although other non-academic clubs such as a dance club and a shooting club were still permitted to meet at the school. The American Civil Liberties Union (ACLU) represented Pacer and other students in a lawsuit against the school board that stated that the students' rights had been violated and that the club should be allowed to meet (Ghezzi, 2006). In July 2006, a federal district judge ruled in the ACLU and Pacer's favor, allowing the organization to meet (Scott, 2006).

The preceding example from recent news headlines illustrates that LGBTQ students may experience institutionalized discrimination in the schools. The Gay, Lesbian and Straight Education Network (GLSEN, 2019) noted that 73.6% of LGBTQ students often or frequently heard homophobic remarks at school. The majority of the students expressed being verbally harassed due to their sexual orientation (86.2%) or gender expression (66.5%). Unfortunately, the report also stated that 22.1% of the students reported being physically assaulted due to sexual orientation, and 14.2% due to gender expression. Even more disturbing is that the report found that even after such students reported incidents of harassment or assault to school staff, almost one third said that the staff did nothing to respond to their complaint. The report also found higher levels of school absenteeism and lowered pursuit of postsecondary education among LGBTQ students compared with a national sample of students.

School counselors may be reluctant to work with this population of students (Pollock, 2006), and training in counseling programs is sparse (Pearson, 2003). LGBTQ students have a higher rate of victimization, mental health disorders, suicide, and dropping out (Callahan, 2001; Varjas et al., 2007), and school counselors are in a unique position to provide services to LGBTQ students, but often recoil from the opportunities (Callahan, 2001). Some explanations may include: (a) incongruence with personal, religious, and political beliefs, (b) concerns with legal age, parental notification, and consent, and (c) lack of professional development (ADD). However, the ethics, professionalism, and efficacy of school counselors might be called into question if they are not advocating for and providing services for all youth, including those identified as LGBTQ.

You should be aware of the discrimination and difficulties that face LGBTQ youth in schools, and discuss this issue with your site supervisor. Such issues may present themselves in terms of difficulty with "coming out," increased class absences, negative self-esteem, increased bullying, and issues related to school disengagement and dropping out. The ASCA's position statement on working with LGBT youth (ASCA, 2016b) calls for professional school counselors to support and affirm students of all sexual orientations and gender identities, as well as to recognize how their own views of these subjects may affect their work with students. In addition to working with individual students, the position statement describes the role of professional school counselors as advocates against discriminatory policies (such as those presented in the introduction to this section) as well as educators for faculty and staff in schools about the importance of diversity in schools, including that of LGBTQ students.

Legal Implications of Working (or Not Working) with LGBTQ Students (Adapted from McFarland & Dupuis, 2003)

As noted in the introduction to this section, several instances of legal action have taken place against administrators and schools that have failed to protect the rights of LGBTQ students. Legal precedent has shown that school administrators must provide equal access and protection to students regardless of gender or sexual orientation. For example, in the 1996 case of *Nabozny v. Podlesny*, a student named Jamie Nabozny was subjected to verbal and severe physical abuse by other students and sued the principals and school district. In his suit, Nabozny stated that the school had treated him differently from other students who had been sexually harassed by failing to take action against the perpetrators of the abuse. The principals settled the suit, costing them nearly $1 million. In 1997, the Office of Civil Rights of the Department of Education specified under its Title IX guidelines that gay and lesbian students should be protected from sexual harassment. The guidelines were used in the 1998 court case of *Wagner v. Fayetteville Public Schools*, in which the school district was mandated by the Department of Education to integrate policies around sexual harassment related to sexual orientation. The Lambda Legal Defense and Education Fund (a link to its website is provided at the end of this chapter) is an organization dedicated to legal issues for LGBTQ persons, and monitors these and many other cases. School counselors, then, must be aware of the legal implications for unfair treatment of and failure to protect LGBTQ students, particularly with regard to sexual harassment in schools.

Conceptual Application Activity 12.7

Answer the following questions, and discuss your responses with your peers in small groups.

1. In light of the introductory story of a high school student trying to start a Gay-Straight Alliance at her school, what would be your reaction if one of your students approached you about starting such an organization at your school and wanted you to serve as a sponsor?

   _____

   _____

2. What unique concerns do you think LGBTQ students of color face in terms of their multiple identities (e.g., a black woman who identifies as lesbian, or a person with a disability who identifies as transgender)?

---

3. How do you think the coming out experience of a transgender student would differ from the coming out experience of a gay student? Discuss the complexity.

---

4. How appropriate do you think it is for a school counselor to self-disclose his or her own sexual orientation or gender expression to an LGBTQ student he or she is counseling?

Language and terms are important, as they help people communicate complex ideas in mutually understood words and phrases. Within the LGBTQ community there are a number of terms and acronyms used to communicate aspects unique to that subculture. As a school counselor-in-training, it would be beneficial to familiarize yourself with some of these terms. Table 12.3 provides an alphabetical list of terms and definitions that may help you get started.

Conceptual Application Activity 12.8

Read and respond to the following scenario, and discuss your answers with your peers in small groups.

Ms. Johnson is a second-semester school counseling intern at Anytown Middle School. She has recently attended a diversity training seminar at her university that focused on LGBTQ issues among university students. The seminar is part of the university's Safe Space program, in which participants identify themselves as LGBTQ allies by placing a rainbow-colored sticker in their rooms or offices. Ms. Johnson is very excited about the program and decides to put one of the stickers in the window to her office at Anytown Middle. Her supervisor, Mr. Hood, says that he is supportive of this decision. Ms. Johnson is pleased that several of her students who come in for individual counseling appointments notice the new sticker and ask her what it means. One day, Ms. Johnson arrives at school and finds a note on her door from the principal, Dr. Smith. In the note, Dr. Smith requests that Ms. Johnson remove the sticker from her window, stating that the parents of some students had called the office saying that "the school is no such place for controversial displays." As she finishes reading the note, Dr. Smith enters the counseling suite. What should Ms. Johnson do?

Table 12.3 Commonly used terms in the LGBTQ community.

Term	Definition
Ally	A person who advocates for or supports LGBTQ people; many allies often identify themselves as straight/heterosexual
Biological sex	Sex as determined by chromosomes, hormones, internal/external genitalia
Bisexual	A person who is attracted to both men and women
Coming out	A lifelong process of declaring one's identity to another individual, to a group of people, or in a public setting
Gay	A person who is attracted only to people of the same sex; this term can be used for both men and women, although the term *lesbian* is typically used for gay women, and the term *gay* by itself typically refers to gay men
Gender identity	How we perceive or call ourselves as "male" or "female"; gender identity may or may not correspond with a person's biological sex
Gender queer	A person who identifies his/her gender to be either between or outside of the male/female dichotomy
Intersexual	A person born with biological aspects of both male and female; about 1.7% of the population can be defined as intersexual
Lesbian	A woman who is only attracted to other women
LGBTQ	An acronym for lesbian, gay, bisexual, transgender, and queer
LGBTQQI	An acronym for lesbian, gay, bisexual, transgender, queer, questioning, and intersexual
Queer	Although this term was historically considered negative when used against LGBTQ people, it has been reclaimed as an umbrella term to refer to people who do not conform to traditional gender or sexual identities or roles; this term frequently appears in a political context
Questioning	Refers to people who are questioning or unsure of their sexual orientation or gender identity
Sexual identity	What we call ourselves or how we perceive ourselves to be; this may include gay, lesbian, bisexual, bi, queer, etc.
Sexual	A person's orientation as related to his/her sexual and emotional attraction; this may include homosexual, bisexual, heterosexual
Transgender	A person who expresses his/her gender differently from the way that society would traditionally identify that person; "transgender" is an umbrella term for several other terms, which may include transsexuals, drag kings, drag queens, cross-dressers, etc.
Transsexual	A person who surgically/hormonally changes sex to match gender identity

Source: Adapted from *The 2015 National School Climate Survey: Executive Summary* (GLSEN, 2015) and *Safe Space Kit: A Guide to Supporting Lesbian, Gay, Bisexual, Transgender, and Queer Students in Your School* (GLSEN, 2019)

Students Who Are English Language Learners

The National Center for Education Statistics of the US Department of Education estimates that during the 2010–2011 academic year, approximately 10% (approximately 4.7 million) of US public school students were English language learner (ELL) students (NCES, 2013b). This represents an increase from an estimated 4.1 million (9%) ELL students in 2002–2003. Geographic and other considerations are also correlated with the relative percentages of ELL students that are served in various regions of the US. For example, the NCES (2013b) provides data that western states (such as Oregon, Hawaii, Alaska, Colorado, Texas, New Mexico, Nevada, and California) have higher percentages of ELL students relative to other regions of the country. ELL students may also be clustered within other areas of the US based upon where their families have settled. For example, in Barrow County, Georgia (a rural area east of Atlanta), Hmong students represent the second largest ELL student population in the district after Hispanic students, and it is believed that this may be due to refugee resettlement efforts that sponsored Hmong families to move to this part of the Southeastern US (Hatcher, 2003; Poole, 2004). As such, school counselors-in-training should be aware that potentially a significant number of their students may be ELL students, and that depending upon the geographic location of their field placement, they may be working with a particularly concentrated number of ELL students.

Several factors are important for school counselors and school counseling trainees to take into account when engaging in counseling work with both ELL students and their families. For example, family context may be of particular importance to working with these students. Thompson and Henderson (2010) discuss that counselors should familiarize themselves with the "customs, styles, symbols, and standards of behavior of these diverse group" (p. 378). Therefore, those working with ELL students and their families should take into account the roles the students and their family members may play within their own families and within the larger community, and understand the stressors these students may face in light of balancing maintenance of their native culture with acculturating to the dominant culture. Or, as Thompson and Henderson write on the example of working with immigrant parents, "the key is to reframe the situation with respect to the clients' roots and solve the problem without molding the couple to behave like the dominant culture" (p. 379).

In addition to the roles that may be played by students' parents and other members of their families, be aware that oftentimes students who are English language learners may find themselves placed in leadership roles within their families, particularly with respect to interfacing with and translating information between the students' families and the English-speaking communities they live in based upon their own relative proficiency in English compared with their families'. Be sensitive to these roles, and recognize that ELL students placed in the role of translators for counseling purposes may create issues related to role confusion, power differentials, and potential ethical concerns with respect to confidentiality (Council of National Psychological Associations for the Advancement of Ethnic Minority Interests, 2003). Furthermore, even when school counselors and their trainees have access to professional translators or outsourced language translation resources such as telephone language line services, it is important that such translators be fluent in counseling-related topics, as otherwise the "nuances and intensity of psychological symptoms and concerns" may be lost (p. 20). Also, keep in mind that ELL students may express their verbalizations of emotions differently in English than in their native language. For example, Santiago-Rivera and Altarriba (2002) write that individuals in counseling may feel less anxiety in expressing potentially embarrassing or taboo subjects in their non-dominant or second language than in their native language because this gives these clients a means of distancing themselves from topics that they may otherwise choose to avoid or feel uncomfortable expressing in their native language. The authors also cite the viewpoint that bilingualism should be considered "a client strength rather than a deficit" (p. 30). As such, school counseling trainees may benefit from honoring the experience of ELL students to utilize both English and their native language in counseling work, knowing that in some situations the student may find it more comfortable to use English, and in other situations the student may prefer to express him/herself in the native language.

Other considerations to take into account when working with ELL students include adjustment issues these students may face with respect to living in a new geographic environment, particularly if they and their families have recently immigrated to the country. School counselors may also wish to explore with these students their expectations for themselves in terms of academic achievement, maintaining contact with their relatives in their native country, how they typically ask for help with social or emotional concerns, and what resources they perceive are available to them in their schools and communities.

Socioeconomic Differences

Forms of diversity arise not only from racial, ethnic, and other forms of identity, but also from economic and financial differences among students. Legislation and federal forms of assistance such as Title I, Part A (Title I) of the Elementary and Secondary Education Act (US Department of Education, 2011a) provide funding for schools which have a significant number of their students coming from low-income families. Despite such forms of assistance, school counselors and school counselors-in-training should recognize that students from low-income families may have special challenges and opportunities. For example, data demonstrate that certain ethnic groups have higher levels of poverty than the national average. For example, US Census data from 2018 described an overall poverty rate (i.e., an annual household income below the poverty threshold at the time for a family of four of $24, 465) of 11.8% for the entire US population, but that several racial/ethnic groups, such as blacks and Hispanics, had significantly higher rates of poverty. Furthermore, data suggest that youth with low socioeconomic status tend to be associated with higher levels of mental illness, stress, unemployment, and less education compared with peers who do not grow up in impoverished homes (Koball & Jiang, 2018). This may be due to lack of access to health care from living in a rural community and/or financial strain. In the case of students in the school setting, this may mean not only that the students from low-income families may experience higher rates of mental illness, but that they are also more likely to have family members or an extended family history of mental illness. Awareness of the socioeconomic context of students and how this may affect the way other students perceive them, the effects of poverty on the student, and the student's family is a critical consideration.

Box 12.2

School counselors have a responsibility to work with all students and to recognize students who are not accessing services. Unfortunately, although there have been many initiatives to provide equitable services to students, inequities still exist. Classes in STEM (science, technology, engineering, and mathematics) are considered critical for today's global economy. Yet there is a significant lack of access for students of color in these core classes. Furthermore, students of color are more likely to attend schools with teachers with less experience than are their more privileged peers.

Source: Hefling (2014).

Students with Multiple Exceptionalities

Finally, with student populations becoming increasingly diverse, school counselors and their trainees are more likely to encounter students who have not only one form of exceptionality or minority identity, but multiple forms of exceptionality with respect to their identities. For example, school counselors may work with a student who identifies as both Latinx and transgender. A trainee may work with a student with a learning disorder who is from a family of low socioeconomic status. Or a school counselor may encounter a student with a physical disability such as cerebral palsy who identifies as gender queer and is also gifted.

Constantine (2002) discusses the limitations for counselors who view various forms of identity such as race, ethnicity, gender, and social class individually and in isolation rather than developing an integrated sense of the counseling client. She proposes that these various aspects of identity are to be perceived in a dynamic, interactive context rather than in isolation. As Constantine (2002) states, "Current models of mental health care often do not allow for the processes by which individuals with multiple oppressed identities arrive at a positive overall sense of cultural identity" (p. 211). This is also referred to as intersectionality.

Models of incorporating multiple aspects of a person's identity are available which may help one better understand how to integrate the various forms of identity claimed by a student. For example, Ridley (2005) provides a model of integrated identity that resembles

Figure 12.1 A flower with aspects of identity displayed on petals is one model for recognizing an integrated identity.

Source: Shutterstock.

a flower, of which each petal represents an aspect of identity (e.g., race, ethnicity, socioeconomic status, gender, sexual preference), with the individual at the center.

Such models also suggest that at various times in students' educational careers, certain aspects of their identity may be more salient than others. For example, a student who identifies as both gay and black may find himself being more discriminated against by others for his gay identity in certain settings, and in other settings may be more discriminated against for his more physically visible black identity. Therefore, take into account the complete picture of your students' identities and understand where the intersectionality of these various aspects of identity may create challenges for students, but may also be understood to create unique forms of strength and personal identity for these same students.

Conclusion

This chapter explored student differences. Although the focus of this chapter was specifically students, it is important to remember that many of these differences also apply to administrators, staff, faculty, parents, and other stakeholders in the school. You were given an opportunity to assess your diversity competency, looked at components of a school profile to better understand your school's students, reviewed differences among students in your school, and used various scenarios and activities to practice developing your counseling competence. Cross-cultural competence begins with understanding that there is always more to learn, understand, and respect when considering all of your counselees—those who share similarities, and those who are different from you.

Acknowledgment

Special thanks to Michael Jay Manalo for contributing to the first two editions of this chapter.

Websites

Multicultural Differences

- "When educators understand race and racism": www.tolerance.org/magazine/when-educators-understand-race-and-racism

This article was written by Melinda Anderson to expand educators' cultural competence.

Students with Disabilities

- "Teaching Special Kids: Online Resources for Teachers": www.educationworld.com/a_curr/curr139.shtml

This link will take you to online information about resources that can help you better understand students with disabilities.

- "Adaptations and Modifications for Students with Special Needs": www.teachervision.com/special-education/resource/5347.html

This link provides easy modifications to incorporate into the curriculum for students with disabilities.

- RtI Action Network: www.rtinetwork.org/

This link provides information, resources, and example forms that may be used for understanding and implementing Response to Intervention.

- "National Center for Learning Disabilities": www.ncld.org/

This link provides information for parents and educators regarding learning disabilities, IEPs, and Section 504 plans.

Students Who Are Gifted

- "Working with Gifted & Talented Students": www.teachersfirst.com/gifted.cfm

This web page provides a list of traits that are frequent indicators of students who are gifted, strategies and ideas that can be utilized to ensure that students who are gifted use their abilities to the greatest potential, and a list of resources.

- "Gifted Children": www.educationworld.com/parents/special/gifted.shtml

This webpage provides links to articles and resources for working with students who are gifted.

Gender Differences among Students

- "Why Gender Matters in the Classroom: The Differences between Boys and Girls": www.teachhub.com/why-gender-matters-classroom

Students Who Are Lesbian, Gay, Bisexual, Transgender, and Queer

- The Gay, Lesbian and Straight Education Network (GLSEN) provides research and statistics on LGBTQ students: www.glsen.org
- PFLAG (Parents, Families, and Friends of Lesbians and Gays): www.pflag.org
- ASCA Position Statement on Gay, Lesbian, Bisexual, Transgender, and Questioning Youth:

  www.schoolcounselor.org/asca/media/asca/PositionStatements/PS_LGBTQ.pdf

- The Human Rights Campaign is an organization dedicated to political advocacy for LGBTQ people: www.hrc.org/
- Lambda Legal is an organization dedicated to LGBTQ legal issues: www.lambdalegal.org/

Students Who Are English Language Learners

- Helping English language learners in the classroom: www.glencoe.com/sec/literature/ellevate/section1.html

This web page provides information, strategies, and considerations in working with ELL students.

Students of Various Socioeconomic Statuses

- American Psychological Association factsheet on "Education and Socioeconomic Status": www.apa.org/pi/ses/resources/publications/factsheet-education.aspx

This factsheet includes statistics for consideration regarding the effects of socioeconomic status on education.

Students of Multiple Exceptionalities

- "Teaching Students with Multiple Disabilities or Handicaps": http://specialed.about.com/od/multipledisabilities/a/multiple.htm

This article explores strategies for working with students who may have more than one disability.

References

ASCA. (2016a). *The professional school counselor and students with disabilities*. Retrieved from https://schoolcounselor.org/asca/media/asca/PositionStatements/PS_Disabilities.pdf

ASCA. (2016b). *The professional school counselor at LGBTQ youth*. Retrieved from www.schoolcounselor.org/asca/media/asca/PositionStatements/PS_LGBTQ.pdf

ASCA. (2019). *The ASCA National Model: A framework for school counseling programs* (4th ed.). Alexandria, VA: Author.

Callahan, C. (2001). Protecting and counseling gay and lesbian students. *Journal of Humanistic Counseling, 40*(1), 5–10.

Chen-Hays, S., & Getch, Y. (2015). Leadership and advocacy for every student's achievement and opportunity. In B. Erford (Ed.), *Transforming the school counseling profession* (pp. 194–218). London, UK: Pearson.

Clarke County School District. (2019). *Georgia's gifted eligibility rule*. Retrieved from www.clarke.k12.ga.us/Page/943

Constantine, M. G. (2002). The intersection of race, ethnicity, gender, and social class in counseling: Examining selves in cultural contexts. *Journal of Multicultural Counseling and Development, 30*(4), 210–215. doi:10.1002/j.2161-1912.2002.tb00520.x

Council of National Psychological Associations for the Advancement of Ethnic Minority Interests. (2003). *Psychological treatment of ethnic minority populations*. Washington, DC: Association of Black Psychologists.

Crick, N. R., Casas, J. F., & Nelson, D. A. (2002). Toward a more comprehensive understanding of peer maltreatment: Studies of relational victimization. *Current Directions in Psychological Science, 11*(3), 98–101. doi:10.1111/1467-8721.00177

Delisle, J., & Galbraith, J. (2002). *When gifted kids don't have all the answers: How to meet their social and emotional needs*. Minneapolis, MN: Free Spirit Publishing.

Dykens, E. M. (2006). Toward a positive psychology of mental retardation. *American Journal of Orthopsychiatry, 76*(2), 185–193.

Ghezzi, P. (2006, February 28). ACLU files suit vs. district over school clubs rule; gay support group seeks right to meet. *Atlanta Journal-Constitution*, 3B.

GLSEN. (2015). *The 2015 national school climate survey: Executive summary*. New York, NY: Gay, Lesbian and Straight Education Network. Retrieved from www.glsen.org/article/2015-national-school-climate-survey

GLSEN. (2019). *Safe space kit: A guide to supporting lesbian, gay, bisexual, transgender, and queer students in your school*. Retrieved from www.glsen.org/sites/default/files/2019-11/GLSEN English Safe Space Book Text Updated 2019.pdf

Gysbers, N., & Henderson, P. (2014). *Developing & managing your school guidance program* (5th ed.). Alexandria, VA: American Counseling Association.

Hallahan, D. P., & Kauffman, J. M. (2006). *Exceptional learners: Introduction to special education* (10th ed.). Boston, MA: Pearson/Allyn & Bacon.

Hatcher, B. (2003, November 10). Diversity abounds in Barrow County. *Athens* [Georgia] *Banner-Herald*.

Hefling, K. (2014, March 23). New data show gaps in education for minorities. *Knoxville Sentinel*, 19A.

Holcomb-McCoy, C. (2004). Assessing the multicultural competence of school counselors: A checklist. *Professional School Counseling, 7*, 178–186.

Holcomb-McCoy, C., & Chen-Hayes, S. F. (2019). Multiculturally competent school counselors: Affirming diversity through challenging oppression. In B. T. Erford (Ed.), *Transforming the school counseling profession* (5th ed.) (pp. 173–193). Upper Saddle River, NJ: Pearson Merrill/Prentice Hall.

Klotz, M. B., & Canter, A. (2006). *Response to Intervention (RTI): A primer for parents*. Bethesda, MD: National Association of School Psychologists. Retrieved from www.ldonline.org/article/15857/

Koball, H., & Jiang, Y. (2018). *Basic facts about low-income children: Children under 18 Years, 2016*. New York, NY: National Center for Children in Poverty, Columbia University Mailman School of Public Health.

Lapan, R. T., Tucker, B., Kim, S.-K., & Kosciulek, J. F. (2003). Preparing rural adolescents for post-high school transitions. *Journal of Counseling & Development, 81*(3), 329.

Lee, C. C. (2014). *Multicultural issues in counseling: New approaches to diversity* (4th ed.). Alexandria, VA: American Counseling Association.

Lee, C. C., & Hipolito-Delgado, C. (2007). Counselors as agents of social justice. In C. C. Lee (Ed.), *Counseling for social justice* (pp. 302–340). Alexandria, VA: American Counseling Association.

Lockhart, E. J. (2003). Students with disabilities. In B. T. Erford (Ed.), *Transforming the school counseling profession* (pp. 357–409). Upper Saddle River, NJ: Merrill Education/Prentice Hall.

McFarland, W. P., & Dupuis, M. (2003). The legal duty to protect gay and lesbian students from violence in school. In T. P. Remley, M. A. Hermann, & W. C. Huey (Eds.), *Ethical & legal issues in school counseling* (2nd ed.) (pp. 341–357). Alexandria, VA: American School Counselor Association.

National Association for Gifted Children. (2008). *Characteristics checklists for gifted children*. Retrieved from web.archive.org/web/20120202210846/www.austega.com/gifted/9-gifted/22-characteristics.html

National Center for Learning Disabilities. (2013). *What is RTI?* Retrieved from www.rtinetwork.org/learn/what/whatisrti

NCES. (2013a). *Fast facts: Title IX*. Retrieved from http://nces.ed.gov/fastfacts/display.asp?id=93

NCES. (2013b). *English language learners*. Retrieved from http://nces.ed.gov/programs/coe/indicator_cgf.asp

NCES. (2012). *Percentage of 3-, 4-, and 5-year-old children enrolled in preprimary programs, by attendance status, level of program, and selected child and family characteristics*. Washington, DC: National Center for Education Statistics.

Pearson, Q. M. (2003). Breaking the silence in the counselor education classroom: A training seminar on counseling sexual minority clients. *Journal of Counseling and Development, 81*, 292–300.

Peterson, C. (2006). *A primer in positive psychology*. New York, NY: Oxford University Press.

Pollock, S. L. (2006). Counselor roles in dealing with bullies and their LGBT victims. *Middle School Journal, 38*(2), 94–102.

Poole, S. M. (2004, August 4). Hmong refugees to settle in area; an old war debt is being repaid to the Laotian ethnic group, which has been exiled in Thailand for decades. *Atlanta Journal-Constitution*, 1F.

Ridley, C. R. (2005). *Overcoming unintentional racism in counseling and therapy: A practitioner's guide to intentional intervention* (2nd ed.). Thousand Oaks, CA: SAGE Publications.

Santiago-Rivera, A., & Altarriba, J. (2002). The role of language in therapy with the Spanish-English bilingual client. *Professional Psychology: Research and Practice, 33*(1), 30–38. doi:10.1037/0735-7028.33.1.30

Scott, J. (2006, July 15). Judge rules gay group can use school. *Atlanta Journal-Constitution*, 3E.

Shepard, J. M., Shahidullah, J. D., & Carlson, J. S. (2013). *Counseling students in levels 2 and 3: A PBIS/RTI guide.* Thousand Oaks, CA: Corwin.

Thompson, C. L., & Henderson, D. A. (2010). *Counseling children* (8th ed.). Belmont, CA: Thomson/Brooks/Cole.

Tilly, W. D. (2013). *What are the differences between an IEP and RTI?* Retrieved from www.rtinetwork. org/index2.php?option=com_content&task=emailform&id=366&itemid=202

US Department of Education. (2011a). *Improving basic programs operated by local educational agencies (Title I, Part A).* Retrieved from www2.ed.gov/programs/titleiparta/index.html

US Department of Education. (2011b). *Transition of students with disabilities to postsecondary education: A guide for high school educators.* Retrieved from www2.ed.gov/about/offices/list/ocr/transition guide.html

Varjas, K., Graybill, E., Mahan, W., Meyers, J., Dew, B., Marshall, M., . . . Birckbichler, L. (2007). Urban service providers' perspectives on school responses to gay, lesbian, and questioning students: An exploratory study. *Professional School Counseling, 11*(2), 113–119.

Wood, S. (2008, March). *Counseling gifted students.* Paper presented at the meeting of the American Counseling Association, Honolulu, Hawaii.

Wyss, S. E. (2004). "This was my hell": The violence experienced by gender non-conforming youth in US high schools. *International Journal of Qualitative Studies in Education, 17*(5), 709–730.

Yoo, C. (2005, May 8). Gay teens seek support and safety; White county has become center of emotional clash over equal rights. *Atlanta Journal-Constitution,* 1C.

Zirkel, P. A. (2009a). Section 504: Student eligibility update. *Clearing House, 82*(5), 209–211.

Zirkel, P. A. (2009b). What does the law say? New Section 504 student eligibility standards. *Teaching Exceptional Children, 41*(4), 68–71.

13 Developmental Issues of Students

Brittany L. Pollard, Sibyl Cato West, and Kaitlyn M. Figurelli

CACREP Standards

Contextual Dimensions

g. characteristics, risk factors, and warning signs of students at risk for mental health and behavioral disorders
i. signs and symptoms of substance abuse in children and adolescents as well as the signs and symptoms of living in a home where substance use occurs

Chapter Objectives:

*   review human development as it relates to school counseling
*   introduce developmental themes and concepts
*   discuss major developmental theories
*   consider the impact of basic forces in human development
*   provide scenarios to help the reader consider strategies for working with students in academic settings

Introduction

School counselor training programs are required to teach concepts surrounding human growth and development. Although you have probably taken a course that highlights developmental issues across the lifespan, this chapter is intended not only to serve as a review of conceptual considerations, but also to present ideas to consider while assisting school-aged youth with issues they bring to your counseling setting.

Developmental Themes and Concepts

Because human development addresses every aspect of the lifespan, the concepts and themes discussed in existing literature play a particularly important role in understanding those students with whom school counselors work. The themes of nature versus nurture, continuity versus discontinuity, universal versus context-specific, and normative influences are a few developmental concepts for you to review as you apply these concepts during your practicum and internship experiences.

Nature versus Nurture

Nature versus nurture involves the degree to which genetic or hereditary influences (nature) and/or environmental influences (nurture) determine personal attributes and characteristics. For years, a multitude of research has been conducted to determine which of these influences most directly impacts individual development. It has been consistently found that development is not due exclusively to either; rather, it is shaped by both, therefore both are considered interactive influences. For example, a student may be predisposed to heart disease based on heredity and genetics (nature), but with healthy lifestyle choices, proper diet, and exercise, heart disease may be prevented (nurture).

Continuity versus Discontinuity

Continuity is a concept indicating that development is a smooth progression throughout the lifespan. Continuity indicates that if a person develops certain characteristics early in life (e.g., a student who is shy or timid), these characteristics will continue throughout life (e.g., the student becomes a shy and timid adult). Discontinuity indicates that development has a series of abrupt shifts which influence changes that may occur. For example, a shy, timid child is taught social skills by his/her parents, and is provided with opportunities to utilize these skills. As a result, changes can occur in the child's personality, and he/she may become more social and outgoing over time.

Universal versus Context-Specific

Human growth and development experts consider the path of development as either universal (one similar path for all people) or context-specific (different paths related to environmental factors). Many developmental tasks occur similarly and within the same time frame (e.g., language development across different cultures); however, context or environment (e.g., the fact that the child learns the language[s] to which he/she is exposed) can also impact the developmental process.

Normative Influences

Many developmental tasks are normative, based on characteristics generally considered to be "typical" or "average." However, developmental tasks can also be affected by age, history, and atypical occurrences. When considering age-graded normative influences, developmental tasks are affected by events that are related to particular age groups, generations, or cohorts (i.e., birth group). Living generations and cohorts include GIs, Baby Boomers, Generation Xers, Millennials, Generation Zers, and those children currently belonging to Generation Alpha. Normative history-graded influences describe the impact historical events can have on development. For example, the tragic events of September 11, 2001 have had a major impact on several of the aforementioned generations, and may indirectly affect the development of generations yet to be born.

Keep these developmental themes and concepts in mind when you work with students. They provide constructs from which to view and understand student temperament, behavior, and characteristics. They can also be used as reframing tools when counseling students who may use these developmental ideas to reflect on and better understand their own journeys and the journeys of their peers.

Theories of Development

Psychodynamic Theory

From a human growth and development perspective, a theory is defined as "an inter-related, coherent set of ideas that help to explain phenomena and make predictions" (Santrock, 2012). Theories of development can be divided according to perspectives. Some of the broader perspectives that are more pertinent to school settings include psy-chodynamic, learning, cognitive, and systems theories. Although there are numerous add-itional developmental theories, each of the aforementioned perspectives is reviewed briefly here.

According to Seligman and Reichenberg (2014), the roots of present problems are a result of past incidents, and exploration and interpretation of these incidents are essential for understanding identified problems. Psychodynamic theories are typically stage-based, in that one's personal development is based on sequences of stages. Erikson (1950, 1968) developed a theory that explained human development in terms of the impact of social demands on the individual. Erikson's psychosocial theory is composed of eight stages, with each stage typically emerging at a particular age. Within these stages, the person is met with a developmental task or interpersonal challenge, with the outcome dependent on whether the person meets the challenge successfully. If the person is successful at each stage, there is a positive outcome; if he/she is not successful, then there is a negative out-come (see Tables 13.1 and 13.2). Remember that each person accomplishes the task some-where along this continuum.

Table 13.1 Erikson's eight stages of psychosocial development.

Developmental task/ interpersonal challenge	Age	Positive outcome	Negative outcome
Trust vs. mistrust	Birth to 1 year	Hope	Fear and mistrust of others
Autonomy vs. shame and doubt	1–3 years	Self-sufficiency if exploration encouraged	Doubts about self, lack of independence
Initiative vs. guilt	3–6 years	Discovery of ways to initiate actions	Guilt from actions and thoughts
Industry vs. inferiority	6 years to adolescence	Development of sense of competence	Feelings of inferiority, no sense of mastery
Identity vs. role confusion	Adolescence	Awareness of uniqueness of self, knowledge of role to be followed	Inability to identify appropriate roles in life
Intimacy vs. isolation	Early adulthood	Development of loving, sexual rela-tionships and close friendships	Fear of relationships with others
Generativity vs. stagnation	Middle adulthood	Sense of contribution to continuity of life	Trivialization of one's activities
Ego integrity vs. despair	Late adulthood	Sense of unity in life's accomplishments	Regret over lost oppor-tunities of life

Conceptual Application Activity 13.1

Think back to some of the students you have counseled in your practicum or internship experiences. Identify which of Erikson's stages best fits the students you have selected. Keeping confidentiality in mind, describe the students you chose and the stages you identified, and discuss your reasoning with your peers.

- How might you use stage-based information to help you in counseling students?
- How might you use the stage models described here to consult with other school community stakeholders and facilitate positive therapeutic outcomes?

_____

_____

Learning Theory

Whereas psychodynamic theories focus on the influence of motives and drives, learning theories focus on the ways in which learning influences a person's development. According to social learning theory, this learning emphasis includes the importance of modeling, or the person's ability to learn from others. Albert Bandura's (1977, 1986) social cognitive theory integrates both cognitive and social influences. Bandura believed that people attempt to understand the world around them, as well as their place in the world (cognitive). In addition, Bandura considered the influence of others an important force of development (social). For instance, to better understand the students with whom you are working, consider the influences of their parents/guardians on social process.

Conceptual Application Activity 13.2

Read and respond to the following scenarios, and discuss your answers with your peers.

Angelina is a second-grader at a local elementary school. Over the years, she has shown tremendous anxiety whenever a thunderstorm occurs, often crying uncontrollably and demanding that her mother be called to pick her up. Her teachers and the school counselor are very puzzled by her behavior, and Angelina does not seem to understand why she reacts to storms this way. During a brief meeting with the school counselor, Angelina's mother reports that her own childhood home was destroyed by a tornado, and that whenever there is a report of inclement weather, she insists they all get in the closet to protect themselves.

- How may Angelina's mother's childhood experience have affected Angelina's present-day thinking (cognitive) about and reactions (behavior) to thunderstorms?
- With this new information, how might you work with Angelina to calm her fears?
- Which of the American School Counselor Association (ASCA, 2014) Mindsets and Behaviors apply to Angelina's situation?

_____

_____

Janicia is a sixth-grader at a local middle school who has made an appointment to see the school counselor. During the visit, Janicia reveals she has recently been diagnosed with diabetes and is having to take daily shots for her condition. With Janicia's permission, the school counselor schedules a consultation with the school nurse to learn what she can do to help Janicia. The school nurse reports that Janicia has *not* been diagnosed with the condition. After meeting with Janicia again, the school counselor learns that Janicia's mothers were recently divorced. Janicia attended a school assembly where an eighth-grader recently diagnosed with diabetes was joined by her parents on stage to help the school understand how to deal with diabetes. Janicia believes that if she develops a similar illness, her mothers will reconcile.

- How did her experience at the assembly influence Janicia's beliefs about her parents' divorce?
- How can you assist Janicia from a developmental perspective?
- How might the ASCA Category 2 Behavior Standards B-SS 5 and B-SS 9 apply here?

Parents/Guardians and Other Social Influences

Parents or primary caregivers are the most influential social models for children. Working alongside and supporting parents or primary caregivers is one way that you, as a school counselor, can greatly impact a student. Parenting style has a deep impact on the social and emotional well-being of children. Positive parenting styles have been linked to high self-esteem, emotional self-regulation, academic achievement, prosocial skills, and friendship development, as well as low levels of aggressive behavior and negative social skills (Santrock, 2012). Negative parenting styles have been linked to low self-esteem, aggressive behavior, anxiety, anger, poor social skills, and possibly more susceptibility to bullying.

Baumrind (1971) identified four parenting styles based on the quality of parenting: (a) authoritative, (b) authoritarian, (c) permissive, and (d) rejecting–neglecting. The authoritative style is considered the most positive form of parenting, in that it provides both nurturing and discipline, in addition to giving children freedom while they adhere to consistent rules and limits. Authoritarian parents are inflexible, rigid, and often cold, establishing rules which require unquestionable obedience. Children of authoritarian parents may have difficulty expressing emotions due to the fact that a negative emotional environment is the norm in their lives. Permissive parents are the exact opposite of authoritarian parents, and are typically very loving, but provide few rules. Discipline is not a priority with these parents. Children of permissive parents may have high self-esteem, but may be less self-reliant than other children, and may exhibit impulsive and aggressive behavior. Rejecting–neglecting parents are the most flawed parental type, providing little nurturing and discipline. These parents spend little time with their children, and tend to be less affectionate. Children of rejecting–neglecting parents are neglected and ignored, often leading to significant depression and aggressive tendencies.

Conceptual Application Activity 13.3

Two scenarios are offered in this exercise. Read each scenario and respond to the questions. Compare your answers with those of your peers.

Tyler is 14 years old, and has recently been getting in trouble with other classmates. He is easily frustrated, and takes out his frustration on his peers. When talking to you, the SCIT, he reveals that his father beats him almost every day and never lets him make decisions for himself. He also says that he is criticized for everything he does and that his father often threatens to send him away if he does not do what his father says.

- What steps would you first take to secure Tyler's safety?
- With whom would you need to consult?
- What kind of parenting style is Tyler's father using?
- How would you intervene in this situation?
- Which of the ASCA (2014) Mindsets and Behaviors would apply in your work with Tyler?

Carolina's parents recently divorced after her mother caught her father cheating. Carolina and her two younger brothers are currently in her mother's custody, but Mom seems disengaged and unmotivated to care for the children. She often sits in her room, depressed because she feels alone and overwhelmed. When Carolina and her brothers try to spend time with Mom, she tells them to go away.

- What might Carolina be experiencing, and what kind of parenting style is Carolina's mom currently using?
- How is this likely impacting Carolina and her two brothers?
- How might you work with Carolina and her family?
- Which of the ASCA Category 2 Behavior Standards Self-Management Skills might you work on with Carolina?

Although awareness of parenting styles can help school counselors understand the dynamics between students and their parents, we must acknowledge that other factors may also affect children's development, including genetics, gender, differing beliefs of the parents, culture, and personal temperament. It is expected that school counselors will encounter each of these parenting styles in their careers. Engaging in parent education may be an appropriate activity for you to consider during your clinical experiences while learning about the school counselor's role in working with parents/guardians.

Table 13.2 Piaget's four stages of cognitive development.

Stage	Age	Description
Sensorimotor	Birth to 2 years	Infants know the world through their senses and through their actions. For example, they learn what dogs look like and what petting them feels like.
Preoperational	2–7 years	Toddlers and young children acquire the ability to internally represent the world through language and mental imagery. They also begin to be able to see the world from other people's perspectives, not just from their own.
Concrete operational	7–12 years	Children become able to think logically, not just intuitively. They now can classify objects into coherent categories and understand that events are often influenced by multiple factors, not just one.
Formal operational	12 years and older	Adolescents can think systematically and reason about what might be as well as what is. This allows them to understand politics, ethics, and science fiction, as well as to engage in scientific reasoning.

Source: Lefrancois (1996)

Cognitive Theories

Cognitive theories focus on the influence of thought processes on one's development, particularly in terms of how people think and how their thinking changes over time. Piaget (1926, 1929, 1972; Piaget & Inhelder, 1969) developed one of the most influential cognitive theories, known as cognitive development theory. Piaget's theory focused on cognitive development in childhood and adolescence, emphasizing primarily the construction of knowledge and thought pattern changes that occur over time. Piaget believed that it is the natural inclination of children to try to understand their world, and that significant cognitive changes occur three times in a person's life: at 2 years old, at 7 years old, and right before adolescence. Each change is based on a child's ability to understand and organize his/her environment as cognition becomes increasingly more sophisticated. Piaget's theory is based on four stages: sensorimotor, preoperational thought, concrete operational thought, and formal operational thought (see Table 13.2).

Conceptual Application Activity 13.4

Read and respond to the following situation. Compare your answers with those of your peers.

Dante, a middle-schooler, is told a short story by his teacher and then asked to respond to a few related questions at the end. The teacher says that a mailwoman was bitten by a dog at one of her routine neighborhood stops. She gives no other details, and asks Dante to tell her why the postal worker might have been bitten. Dante replies with several ideas about why this may have occurred—maybe the dog was scared, maybe the mailwoman was mean, and maybe the dog was just trying to get her attention are just a few of his answers.

- What stage of Piaget's cognitive development is Dante likely in?

- How do you know?

  _____

  _____

- Identify three specific strategies that school counselors may be able to use to engage students who are in this stage of development.
- Which of the ASCA (2014) Mindsets and Behaviors apply to this application activity?

  _____

  _____

Box 13.1

Neurologists have discovered that the brain is continually adapting to new input. Meditating daily improves the area in the brain that is essential for focus, memory, and compassion. School counselors can teach students meditation and mindfulness strategies to alter the physical structure of the brain (Weaver, 2014).

Sociocultural Perspective

Russian psychologist and theorist Lev Vygotsky (1986) developed the theory of human cultural and biosocial development, in which several important concepts, such as scaffolding, help school counselors to understand how children learn. Scaffolding is the process by which a more accomplished learner (parent, teacher, or peer) provides direct instruction using prompts and cues to assist learning, slowly providing less instruction as the child's knowledge increases. Scaffolding requires the advanced learner to enter the child's *zone of proximal development*, defined as the difference between the child's ability to solve problems and his/her ability to be taught by another person. These two concepts can be particularly significant for you to remember as a SCIT, as you will be involved in the direct instruction of social/emotional knowledge and problem-solving skills related to personal situations. Additionally, you may assist teachers in the instruction of study skills within the academic domain. You can enter the child's zone of proximal development and use scaffolding to help the child learn how to deal with peers, adjust his/her emotional reactions, and navigate the challenges associated with such diagnoses as attention-deficit hyperactivity disorder (ADHD). As a supervisee, you may also consider applying this concept by creating a mentorship program in which older students who understand and can model concepts are paired with younger students to help enhance their academic and social skills.

Conceptual Application Activity 13.5

As a SCIT, what are two specific scenarios in which you could apply the concept of scaffolding in your current school setting? For each of these scenarios, select a Mindset Standard from Category 1 of the ASCA (2014) Mindsets and Behaviors that could be applied.

_____

_____

Systems Theories

Systems theories are often referred to as ecological theories due to their environmental focus on development. Bronfenbrenner's (1979) ecological systems theory is based on the idea that development stems from the interaction of various systems in the person's life. According to Bronfenbrenner's theory, the environment is divided into four systems: the microsystem, meso-system, exosystem, and macrosystem. The microsystem is defined as including the person's immediate environment (e.g., parents, children, daycare, schools, church), which has a significant influence on his/her development. The mesosystem refers to the interaction between the person's microsystems and any modification that can occur based on this inter-action. The exosystem is defined as the social settings that influence the person, either directly or indirectly (e.g., extended family, media, job/work environment, neighbors), through

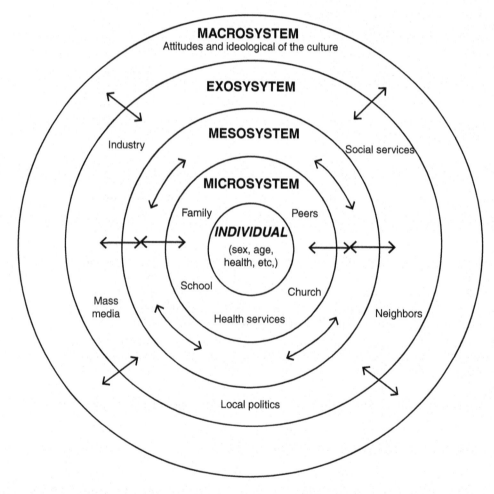

Figure 13.1 Four systemic levels, according to Bronfenbrenner's theory.

Source: Illustration by Hchokr, 2012: https://commons.wikimedia.org/wiki/File:Bronfenbrenner%27s_Eco
logical_Theory_of_Development_(English).jpg. Licensed under the Creative Commons Attribution-Share
Alike 3.0 Unported license: https://creativecommons.org/licenses/by-sa/3.0/deed.en.

a trickle-down effect. The macrosystem is considered to be the broadest of the four systems and involves cultural influences on a person's development (see Figure 13.1).

Conceptual Application Activity 13.6

Lydia is an 8-year old girl who lives with her mother and grandmother. She and her mother moved in with her grandmother after Lydia's father died. Lydia's father was a soldier who was killed during combat in Afghanistan. There are two cousins who live with Lydia's grandmother, as well as her uncle. Since the death of her father, Lydia's family has been attending church regularly to deal with their grief. Her mother also takes Lydia to a local support group for children who have lost a parent. The family recently attended a memorial service held by the community to honor local soldiers who had died while serving in the military. Lydia is very proud of her father, and believes that serving in the military is very noble. She is considering joining the military when she is older.

- Which system(s) can you, as a supervisee, access to assist in Lydia's development?
- How can the various systems in Bronfenbrenner's model influence how school counselors or school counselors-in-training work with their students?

_____

_____

In working with students at various ages and grade levels, consider how each of these developmental theories and concepts impacts students and how change occurs. Further consideration should include your values and perspectives in relation to the values and perspectives held by the students you are counseling. For instance, consider Lawrence Kohlberg's (1976) theory of moral development (adapted from Piaget's work) to explain the development of moral reasoning as you work with children and adolescents.

Moral Development

Kohlberg (1976) extended Piaget's theory by describing moral development as a continual process occurring throughout the lifespan. Whereas Piaget described a two-stage process of moral development, Kohlberg's theory of moral development outlined six stages within three different levels. Preconventional, the first level, begins with making moral choices to avoid punishment, and progresses into a hedonistic stage, in which moral judgment is based on self-indulgence (i.e., if it feels good, it must be the right thing to do). Conventional, the second level, begins with interpreting the reactions of others and how they would view the person as a result of decisions made. As this stage progresses, values of honor and duty motivate conduct. Postconventional, the third level, moves away from social acceptance to the rights of individuals and the societal responsibility to uphold those rights as principles of justice for everyone (see Table 13.3).

Table 13.3 Kohlberg's stages of moral development chart.

Level 1: Preconventional
Stage 1: Obedience and punishment. No respect for the underlying social order that is supported by punishment and authority. There is a concentration on avoiding punishment.
Stage 2: Reward-seeking, self-benefit. Self-interest motivates any good deeds or favors provided to others.

Level 2: Conventional
Stage 3: Avoidance of disapproval. Recognition sought for being "good." Desire to please other people in order to gain their approval. One is concerned about the opinions of others.
Stage 4: Law and order. Belief in the value of society's rules, not just the avoidance of punishment. Law is enacted to protect the rights of the individual. Laws are important.

Level 3: Postconventional—Decisions Based on Personal Ethics
Stage 5: Contract fulfillment. A belief in the rights of individual. If laws are not good, they should be changed, as one need not obey a bad law. There is an awareness of personal opinions and values.
Stage 6: Individual principles, conscience. Reliance on abstract ethical principles with an emphasis on value of human life.

Conceptual Application Activity 13.7

Read and respond to the following scenario. Compare your answers with those of your peers.

Adhira is an 18-year old girl who is a senior at a private high school. Recently, she has gotten a facial piercing and a visible tattoo, although both are against school rules. Her parents, who immigrated from India when Adhira was 9, discouraged her from getting the piercing and tattoo because they knew it was against school policy, as well as against their personal beliefs about body art. Because Adhira is of legal age, however, she went ahead and got them anyway. She is currently suspended, and faces possible expulsion from school if she does not remove the piercing and cover the tattoo while at school. Adhira refuses to do either, and references the Constitution and its emphasis on "freedom of choice" as her justification.

- At which stage of Kohlberg's moral development theory is Adhira?
- What forces other than school policy might be at play here?
- How would you, as a school counselor-in-training, use Kohlberg's theory to assist you in addressing this situation?
- How might you apply ASCA (2014) Category 2 Behavior Standards B-SMS 1, B-SMS 2, and B-SS 8 to this situation?
- Are there other Mindset and Behavior standards that apply?

_____

_____

Basic Forces in Human Development

Developmental tasks are typically examined in terms of what is happening to the student biologically, physically, cognitively, and psychosocially. By considering and combining the effects of these variables, we can begin to better understand the development of the student. The interaction of these forces is referred to as a *bio-psycho-social framework*. Biological forces are defined as aspects of development pertaining to genetics and heredity, physical development, and overall health-related issues. Psychological forces include cognitive development, as well as emotional and affective issues and personality characteristics. Sociocultural forces describe the impact of social issues and culture on the person's development. By using the bio-psycho-social framework, each stage of development and age group can be understood better, helping you to apply these concepts in counseling.

Elementary School-Aged Children and Developmental Issues (Grades K–5)

Biological Development

Generally speaking, elementary school-aged children are typically healthy and self-reliant. Physical growth is fairly steady at this age, with the greatest growth occurring in the legs and trunk. Growth can be affected positively or negatively by nutrition, genetic factors, and gender. Brain size development reaches adult size by age 7, and both boys' and girls' brain sizes tend to be the same, although individual differences may exist based on contextual or environmental factors. Middle childhood is a period when chronic illness is less common than at any other time in life. Changes in fine and gross motor development become increasingly apparent. For girls, there is typically a focus on fine motor skills, with improvement in dexterity, flexibility, and balance. For boys, the focus is primarily on gross motor skills, with improvement in strength most emphasized.

Common and contemporary biological issues in early childhood include childhood obesity, asthma, autism spectrum disorder (ASD), ADHD, and learning disorders. The SCIT should be aware of physical concerns that can develop in childhood, have a basic understanding of their treatment, and know how to discuss these issues with parents when necessary.

Childhood Obesity

Childhood obesity is currently considered by the medical community as an epidemic in the United States (Betbeze, 2018). Children may either be considered overweight (20% above ideal weight for height) or obese (30% or more over ideal weight for height). According to the World Health Organization (2020), worldwide obesity has nearly tripled since 1975, and an estimated 38 million children under the age of 5 years are considered to be overweight and/or obese. Overweight children may face psychological, physical, and medical problems, experience low self-esteem, and have difficulty forming and/or maintaining healthy peer relationships (Fonvig et al., 2017). Childhood obesity can occur due to genetic factors; however, it may also occur due to environmental and/or contextual issues, such as food-centric cultural values, lack of exercise, lack of access to quality food, and the maintenance of a sedentary lifestyle (e.g., watching excessive television and playing video games with little regular physical activity).

Box 13.2

The obesity rate in the US has steadily risen over the past century, and has more than doubled over the past 35 years. Conventional wisdom states that obesity is a result of a sedentary lifestyle. However, recent research indicates that it is not just a matter of Americans eating higher-caloric foods, but also that less nutritious food is often cheaper and easier to obtain. Food is less expensive in our society today than at any other point in history, but there has been a 20% increase in caloric intake over the past 40 years. In addition, the prevalence of obesity among children between 2 and 4 years old from low-income families participating in Women, Infants, and Children (WIC) was 14.5% in 2014. These statistics illustrate that continued prevention methods (such as reducing the cost of healthy food items) are needed at the national, state, and local levels.

Sources: CDC (2016a); *The Week* (2014)

Asthma

Asthma, which is three times more prevalent today than 20 years ago, is defined as a chronic inflammatory disorder of the airways. It is the most common medical condition experienced by children, is one of the leading causes of school absences, and is the third leading cause of hospitalization among children under the age of 15 (American Lung Association, 2018). According to the Centers for Disease Control and Prevention's (CDC, 2017b) National Health Interview Survey, asthma affects 5,661,000 males and 3,902,000 females under the age of 18 in the United States. Although the school nurse will likely be the staff member who deals most directly with any medical concerns, the school counselor may be the entry point for students dealing with physical issues. School counselors can be aware of the early warning signs of either a child developing asthma or an asthmatic child being at risk of an attack. Children who appear or act differently from the norm, even with something relatively minor like asthma, may be teased or ostracized. As a SCIT, you can use your clinical experiences as opportunities to learn more about the social and emotional tolls a physical condition like asthma may take.

Autism Spectrum Disorder

In the fifth edition of the *Diagnostic and Statistical Manual of Mental Disorders* (*DSM-5*; American Psychiatric Association, 2013), autism spectrum disorder is defined as "persistent deficits in social communication and social interaction across multiple contexts" (p. 50). Autism spectrum disorder is characterized by persistent impairment in reciprocal social communication and social interaction (Criterion A), and restricted, repetitive patterns of behavior, interest, or activities (Criterion B). According to Autism Speaks (2018), data gathered by the CDC in 2014 projected that by 2018, 1 in 59 children were expected to be diagnosed with ASD, representing a 15% increase over a four-year span. ASD is four times more commonly diagnosed in males, and 31% of children living with ASD are also diagnosed with co-occurring intellectual disabilities. Developmental disorders such as ASD are less commonly diagnosed than other conditions, such as speech and language impairments, learning disabilities, and ADHD. Early intervention is key to helping children diagnosed with autism or other related genetic developmental disorders, such as Rett syndrome. Because symptoms can usually be observed by 18 months of age, children with autism may already be diagnosed by the time they enter school. However, as a SCIT, you can learn more about this disorder and hone the skills necessary to helping diagnosed children improve their social and communication skills, providing information to parents, and acting as a support for teachers of students with autism.

Box 13.3

Most children with autism are diagnosed after the age of 4, however, signs and symptoms have proven to lead to reliable diagnosis as early as age 2.

Source: Autism Speaks (2018).

Attention-Deficit Hyperactivity Disorder

According to the National Institute of Mental Health (n.d.), attention-deficit hyperactivity disorder is one of the most common disorders of childhood, often continuing through adolescence and into adulthood. The *DSM-5* (American Psychiatric Association, 2013) describes the essential feature of ADHD as "a persistent pattern of inattention and/or hyperactivity-impulsivity that interferes with functioning or development" (p. 61). In addition, the *DSM-5* describes three subtypes of ADHD. First, the predominantly inattentive type focuses primarily on inattentive behaviors such as not paying attention to details, poor listening and organizational skills, not following instructions, failing to complete work or chores, and so forth, avoiding tasks requiring mental effort (e.g., schoolwork, homework), losing items such as toys and school materials, and forgetting daily activities. Second, the predominantly hyperactive/impulsive type focuses on behaviors such as fidgeting, squirming, running, or climbing excessively when inappropriate, having difficulty focusing on leisure activities or playing, talking excessively, blurting out answers, difficulty awaiting turn, and often interrupting others. The ADHD combined type has criteria of both inattention and hyperactivity/impulsivity. Although the causes of ADHD are unknown, possibilities include neurological problems and genetic vulnerability. The primary treatment of ADHD includes medications such as Ritalin or Adderall. In some cases, the most appropriate treatment is a combination of medication and counseling to help the child develop coping skills for dealing with the impact the condition may have on school performance and learning. As a SCIT, you can learn about special accommodations that assist these individuals, provide individual and group counseling, consult with teachers, and observe, participate, and advocate for students with ADHD as part of their Individualized Education Plan team.

Learning Disabilities

In childhood, cognitive ability develops rapidly and is typically reflected in improved test scores, including aptitude and intelligence quotient (IQ, measuring the potential to learn or achieve in the future) and achievement (measuring what the child has already learned). Although the school psychologist may be the helping professional most likely to conduct intelligence testing, school counselors are often asked to participate in the testing process. While IQ testing is a common assessment in schools, this type of testing often comes with criticism because it does not consider achievement and the influence of other environmental factors such as culture, family, strength of school, and rate of development.

Figure 13.2 Reading is an example of automatization.
Source: Shutterstock.

One specific use of IQ testing is to determine whether a student has a learning deficiency. Some students experience learning disabilities that, if identified early, can be addressed to enhance the student's ability to be successful in school. A learning disability is defined as a marked delay in a particular area of learning that is not associated with any physical handicap, mental retardation, or any significant stress in the home environment. A common type of learning disability is dyslexia, which typically manifests in reading difficulties. Once a student has been identified as having a learning disability, schools are legally required to provide special accommodations for those students. Refer to Chapter 12 for more information on working with children who have exceptional needs.

Belsky (2019) offers information processing tips that are beneficial to all adults, including school counselors. Some of her tips for working with students in early and middle childhood include the following:

Younger (and Sometimes Older) Childhood

1. Don't expect boys and girls to remember, without prompting, regular chores such as feeding a pet.
2. Expect most children to have a good deal of trouble in situations that involve inhibiting a strong "prepotent impulse"—such as not touching desirable toys, following unpleasant rules, or doing homework.

Middle Childhood

1. Actively teach the child study skills (such as rehearsing information) and selective attention strategies (such as underlining important points) for tests.
2. Scaffold organizational strategies for school and life. For example, get the child to use a notebook for each class assignment, and keep important objects, such as pencils, in a specific place.
3. Expect situations that involve multiple tasks (such as getting ready for school) and activities that involve *ongoing* inhibition (such as refraining from watching TV before finishing homework) to be especially problematic. Build in a clear structure for mastering these difficult executive-functioning tasks: "At 8 or 9 p.m., it's time to get everything ready for school." "Homework must be completed by dinnertime, or immediately after you get home from school."
4. To promote selective attention (and inhibition), have a child do his/her homework, or any task that involves concentration in a room away from tempting distractions such as the TV or Internet (p. 171).

Psychosocial Development

Psychological and social development for elementary-aged children tends to focus primarily on establishing independence and developing stability for their future emotional lives. Much of a child's psychological development and socialization begins with his/her parents and cultural influences. Children, while trying to master abilities and cultural values, often judge themselves dichotomously as either competent or incompetent, productive or failing, winners or losers. Increases in competence are related to emotional regulation and one's understanding of self and others. However, this self-awareness also has consequences, which can include lowered self-esteem and increased self-criticism and experiences of self-consciousness, as well as the emergence of *social comparison* among peers. Social comparison is the tendency to assess one's abilities, achievements, social status, and other attributes in comparison to those of others, such as peers. Friendship-building and relating to peers are the most important aspects of the psychosocial developmental tasks at this age. Children begin to develop peer groups that are usually composed of the same age, ethnicity, and socioeconomic status (SES) and who play, work, or learn together. Children depend on each other for companionship, advice, and self-validation. Children who are willing to assume the best about other children are successful with friendship development and therefore are typically well-adjusted and prosocial. Well-adjusted children often display behaviors such as altruism, empathy, and sympathy. In contrast, children who have difficulty connecting with peers often feel rejected, which could lead to other psychological problems later in life.

Conceptual Application Activity 13.8

Read and respond to the following scenario. Compare your answer with those of your peers.

Logan, a fourth-grade student, often gets in trouble for fighting with his classmates at school. He claims they make comments to disrespect him and he is not going to let anyone run over him. Many of the students are scared of him and think he is a bully.

- As a school counselor-in-training, what strategies might you use to further explore Logan's reasons for fighting with his peers?
- How might you help Logan to learn more effective social skills?
- Which of the ASCA Category 2 Behavior Standards Social Skills apply to this situation?

_____

_____

Adolescents and Developmental Issues (Grades 6–12)

Biological Development

When discussing the biological development of adolescents, the first and most critical aspect to examine is puberty. Puberty is the time in life when children become more mature sexually, primarily based on hormonal and physical changes. Puberty is a period of rapid physical growth and sexual maturation, and is typically completed three to four years after the first visible signs.

Puberty cannot be discussed without acknowledging the extreme emotional reactions associated with biological changes that occur in adolescents during this time. Hall (1904) referred to the difficulty adolescents experience during puberty as *storm and stress*. Due to the rapidly increasing hormone levels characteristic of this developmental stage, extreme emotional shifts occur, and increased hormone levels produce visible signs of sexual maturation, which often leads adults to think of the adolescents as more adult-like, with an expectation of increased maturity. School counselors-in-training can help adolescents entering puberty by normalizing what is happening and helping them to recognize that they are not alone in what it is a universal developmental stage that happens to everyone.

Normally, body changes begin to appear between ages 8 and 14, a wide span of years. With puberty comes a growth spurt, defined as a rapid change in the size, shape, and proportions of the body. During this period, there is an average increase in height of about 8 inches in boys and about 4 inches in girls. Boys may gain an average of about 40 pounds, while girls may gain an average of about 35 pounds. Facial features change dramatically, with the nose and ears growing before the skull, causing disproportional facial features that are often corrected when head growth catches up to the rest of the face. This pattern may create emotional distress for youth who are already coming to grips with self-concept in relation to their peers. For girls, growth spurts typically begin about two years before they do for boys, with adult height often reached by age 12.

Although puberty is considered a universal developmental task, it is also context-specific, in that all individuals go through puberty (universal), but the timing of puberty can vary (context-specific) by person. Factors that can affect puberty include genetics, culture, ethnicity, nutrition, body weight, family stress, and SES.

The stress experienced by most adolescents in puberty can manifest in a variety of ways. Early-maturing girls may be embarrassed by their early development, while later-maturing girls can experience equal embarrassment due to their static, child-like appearance as their peers become more adult-like. Both ends of the spectrum can be subjected to teasing. Early-maturing boys often excel in sports, making them more popular than their later-maturing counterparts. Later-maturing boys may be shunned and ostracized, while early-maturing adolescents may experience unrealistic expectations from adults who expect them to demonstrate more adult-like thoughts and feelings than they are capable of. Early-maturing girls may begin to choose friends who are older, thereby exposing themselves to more risky behaviors, such as having sex and using drugs and alcohol. For both boys and girls, another problem that can cause stress is an overproduction of oil and sweat in the skin, often resulting in acne. Due to the tremendous changes in physical appearance during puberty, dissatisfaction with body image often constitutes a stressful part of adolescence. Many adolescents become very critical of their bodies, sometimes leading to them taking extreme measures involving dieting, exercising, or developing an eating disorder.

Helping the prepubescent adolescent, rather than focusing on the adolescent already experiencing puberty, is an ideal approach for you to take as a SCIT. The Guttmacher Institute (2019) reports that only 24 states and the District of Columbia mandate sex and HIV education in schools. For schools that do provide sex education classes, the focus is typically on identifying what to avoid (e.g., sexual contact, STDs, teen pregnancy), rather than on having an open discussion about strategies to help adolescents handle the significant changes they are experiencing or are about to experience. Educating parents about how to deal with their prepubescent adolescents and encouraging them to talk to their children about puberty can also be important school counselor functions. Specifically, it is important for parents to remember to avoid negatively discussing menstruation in front of their children (Rembeck & Gunnarsson, 2004), avoid teasing their children about their changing bodies, and to engage with their children in open, supportive communication about all that puberty entails (Triyanto & Iskandar, 2015).

Cognitive Development

During adolescence, many advances occur in intellectual, logical, and intuitive thinking. Brain maturation continues, helping in the areas of planning, analyzing, and being able to pursue goals. Language mastery also improves. According to Piaget (1972), adolescents find themselves in the fourth and final stage of his model—formal operations, which begins around 12 years of age. In this stage, Piaget believed that adolescents are able to think logically, abstractly, and hypothetically, and are better able to see the various aspects of a problem. Determining the cognitive level of the students with whom you work is helpful in determining a theoretical counseling approach and techniques that would work best for each individual student you counsel. For instance, a youth at the concrete cognitive level may benefit more from physical movement as opposed to theories that rely on higher-level cognition.

One of the positive aspects of this improved adolescent thinking is the ability to self-monitor and self-regulate; however, with this improved thinking also come other challenges that rival only puberty in terms of difficulty. Elkind (1978) applied Piaget's theory to understanding adolescent emotional states. He developed the term *adolescent egocentrism* to describe adolescents' focus on self to the exclusion of others and the belief that their personal thoughts, feelings, and experiences are unique. Elkind (1978) described three types of adolescent egocentrism: (a) invincibility fable, (b) personal fable, and (c) imaginary audience. The *invincibility fable* is defined as adolescents' belief that they are immune to the laws of mortality, probability, and nature. This belief may explain why adolescents tend to engage in risky behaviors without recognizing the consequences of their choices. The *personal fable* describes when adolescents imagine their own lives as unique, mythical, or heroic and destined for fame or fortune. The *imaginary audience* is characterized by adolescents fantasizing about how others will react to them. They tend to be very concerned about the opinions of onlookers, often assuming that others are judging their appearance.

Although adolescents may be able to think logically, they may often be challenged with decision-making; they tend to think about possibilities, not practicalities. Because of this, they may be less likely to consider important matters rationally. This may cause parents and other involved adults to spend a great deal of time and effort trying to protect teenagers from experiencing the consequences resulting from poor judgment.

School counselors can be influential when adolescents are learning to make thoughtful, wise, and healthy decisions. Adolescents will be challenged with many aspects of life. Some of these aspects that relate more closely to the school counselor include the school environment, decisions about sex, drugs, and alcohol, establishing a healthy independence, depression, and suicide.

Conceptual Application Activity 13.9

Read and respond to the following scenarios. Compare your answers with those of your peers.

While at a school-sponsored swimming party, Miguel decided to jump off the roof of the nearby pool house into the pool. Despite being cautioned of the risks by some partygoers, Miguel dismissed their concerns and listened to those who were encouraging his antics.

- How would you, as a future school counselor, work with Miguel and other individuals who exhibit these types of behaviors?
- What personal and systemic factors would be important to consider?
- How does the ASCA (2014) Category 1, Mindset Standard M1 apply to this scenario?

Naomi is a talented high school basketball player. Her coaches and others encourage her to pursue playing for a college basketball team. Although Naomi accepts this encouragement to pursue college basketball, she believes she is destined to play basketball in the major WNBA league and refuses to consider other options at this time.

- What are some strategies that you might utilize to help Naomi develop a realistic outlook on herself and her future?
- How can you support her ambition while simultaneously helping her plan for alternative paths after high school?

School Environment

Additional challenges that adolescents face involve making decisions about school, which, according to Christenson, Sinclair, Lehr, and Godber (as cited in Garrett-Peters, Mokrova, Carr, Vernon-Feagans, & The Family Life Project Key Investigators, 2019) are often made after long periods of disengagement and early indicators of risk. According to Tas, Selvitopu, Bora, and Demirkaya (2013), an estimated 12 million students will leave school before graduating over the next 10 years, with the National Center for Education Statistics (2018) reporting a 2016 status dropout rate of just over 6%. When adolescents succeed in graduating from high school, they are exposed to many benefits, including living healthier, longer lives, an increased likelihood of financial stability, and stronger possibilities associated with getting married and owning a home. However, there are also numerous reasons adolescents report for dropping out of high school. According to Bridgeland, DiIulio, and Morison (2006), adolescents across the country described reasons for dropping out that included classes being uninteresting, being unmotivated to work hard, getting a job instead, becoming a parent, or caring for a family member. In addition, some reported failing in school as a major factor. Another important factor Bridgeland et al. (2006) discovered was that 70% reported feeling confident they could have graduated, despite having low grades. A majority of teens reported they would have stayed in school if classes had helped prepare them for real-world experiences, if school personnel and parents had higher expectations, and if more supervision were provided.

Another interesting aspect of schools today is that the school schedule itself may create difficulties for the adolescent. According to Berger (2007), traditional school structure was established in the early 1900s, when only 8% of teens completed high school. Today, this structure may not effectively meet the needs of contemporary students. For example, particularly in very large schools, there is often little supervision, minimal interaction between teachers and students, and a schedule that does not match the changing needs of today's adolescent, who often requires close guidance and/or advisement, someone to speak with in confidence about personal matters, and scheduling that best supports his/her academic, career, and social/emotional development (American School Counselor Association, 2014).

Researchers have recently investigated developmental factors and other contextual contributions to delinquency; however, the amount of sleep adolescents get has not been thoroughly investigated. Sleep deprivation has been associated with lower stress management, deficiencies in problem-solving, and increased health problems. Furthermore, youth who have 6 hours of sleep or fewer also report greater violent tendencies (Clinkinbeard, Simi, Evans, & Anderson, 2011). As such, schools that begin in early hours may further contribute to such problems. Boergers, Gable, and Owens (2014) found that beginning school as few as 25 minutes later may more closely align with adolescents' sleep needs. Basically, the biological clock of teens is working against them, with alertness coming at night rather than during the day, when school is in session.

Decisions about Sex

Whether to engage in sexual activity is one of the most difficult decisions teens have to make. According to the CDC (2019), 40% of high school students surveyed in 2017 regarding their sexual activity reported that they had engaged in sexual intercourse. Along with decisions about sex come other risks such as STDs and teen pregnancy. Sexually active teenagers are at greater risk of getting an STD (e.g., gonorrhea, genital herpes, syphilis, and chlamydia) due to biological susceptibility, not obtaining recommended STD tests, not having health insurance or access to transportation, and experiencing difficulty in talking about sexual behaviors (CDC, 2019). Over the past several years, the definition of what teens consider sexual activity has changed because many teens do not believe that being sexually active includes sexual behaviors other than penile–vaginal penetration. For example, most teens believe that oral or anal sex is not considered sex.

The US teen pregnancy rate has decreased by 7% since 2016; however, it is substantially higher than that of other westernized nations (CDC, 2017a). School counselors can combat the negative experiences pregnant teenagers or young parents encounter by "demonstrating cultural competence, a socially just perspective, and by collaborating with student service professionals to ensure mental health wellness" (Dowden et al., 2018, p. 26).

Conceptual Application Activity 13.10

Read and respond to the following scenarios. Compare your response with those of your peers.

Eric is a 15-year old student who makes good grades and is well-liked by his teachers and peers. Recently, however, Eric has become increasingly quiet and withdrawn at school. One day, he makes an appointment with you, the school counselor, and in the midst of making small talk to explore what's brought him to your office, Eric blurts out that he recently had sexual intercourse for the first time and that he's felt ashamed ever since. He discloses that his partner now pressures him "almost daily" for sex and that he feels uncomfortable and confused. He says he's "just not sure where to go from here."

- What are some of the personal challenges Eric may have faced up to this point?
- What are some issues he might be experiencing in this moment?
- How will you assist him in reflecting on next steps he feels comfortable taking?

_____

_____

Drugs and Alcohol

Tobacco, alcohol, and marijuana are three substances often referred to as *gateway drugs*, due to their potential for abuse and addiction, as well as their contribution to other socially significant problems. Tobacco, the most physically addictive of the gateway drugs, can decrease food consumption, interfere with absorption of nutrients, and reduce fertility. Alcohol is harmful in adolescence due to its effects on a teenager's physical, sexual, and emotional development. Marijuana seriously slows cognitive processes related to memory and abstract reasoning, and can initiate a lack of motivation and indifference toward the future.

Distinguishing between the signs of typical developmental hardships associated with adolescence and issues associated with substance abuse can be challenging. The National Institute on Drug Abuse (2014) reports that signs and symptoms of personal substance abuse often include, but are not limited to, poor hygiene, academic remediation, and deteriorating interpersonal relationships with family and friends. Sudden loss of appetite, depression, and lack of maintaining school/work responsibilities are also strong indicators, and represent physical, social, emotional, and academic domains which school counselors can pay careful attention to and address should any abrupt changes be observed.

It is also important to be aware of indicators that a student may be living in a home setting where substance abuse and/or addiction are present. Students who live in such environments are at risk for negative academic, career, and social/emotional outcomes, as well as for eventually engaging in personal substance abuse as well (Epstein, Hill, Bailey, & Hawkins, 2013). According to Lipari and Van Horn (2017), 1 in 8 children aged 17 or younger live in households with at least one parent who has a substance use disorder. While it may not be readily apparent that a student is living in a home where substance use is occurring, students exposed to drugs and alcohol may demonstrate similar signs and symptoms to those who personally abuse substances, including decreased hygiene maintenance, sudden decline in academic performance, abrupt shifts in mood or demeanor, and/or noticeable withdrawal from peers.

Depression

The self-esteem of children tends to drop around age 12, and adolescents without support from family, friends, or school are more vulnerable to experiencing self-esteem issues than others. A loss of self-esteem may push the adolescent toward depression, which can affect 1 in 5 teenage girls and 1 in 10 teenage boys (Mental Health America, 2020). It is possible that hormonal changes may account in part for depression, but various stress factors experienced by adolescents can also play a role in teens experiencing internal and external emotional problems. Internalizing problems often manifests inward and can lead to the infliction of self-harm, while externalized problems are often "acted out" by injuring others, destroying property, or defying authority figures.

Suicide

According to the American Academy of Child and Adolescent Psychology (2017), suicide is the second leading cause of death in children, adolescents, and young adults between the ages of 5 and 24. Although suicidal ideation appears to be common enough among high school teens that it may be considered the norm, the act of completing suicide is rare in comparison. So why do we believe suicide is a common occurrence during this time? First, according to the CDC (2018), age-adjusted rates of suicide increased by 33% between 1999 and 2017. Second, although these figures may be alarming, it is important to note that these statistics include young adults (aged 20–24), who tend to have much higher rates of suicide than adolescents. Third, the media is more likely to focus attention on adolescent suicides than on adult suicides. Last, although suicide completion may not be common, suicide attempts are very common, thus affecting the perceptions held by the general public.

Establishing a Healthy Independence

The antithesis of establishing a healthy independence can be adolescent rebellion. As discussed previously, adolescents often do not have the cognitive ability to recognize what is considered to be risky behavior. According to the CDC (2016b), "motor vehicle crashes are the leading cause of death for U.S. teens. In 2012, seven teens ages 16 to 19 died every day from motor vehicle injuries" (para. 1). Excessive alcohol consumption is the third leading preventable cause of death in the United Stated, and is associated with approximately 88,000 deaths per year, with 1.3 million adolescents reporting "heavy alcohol use" within the past month (National Institute on Alcohol Abuse and Alcoholism (NIAAA), 2018). Additionally, according to David-Ferdon and Simon (as cited in Bushman et al., 2016), "More U.S. youth die from homicide each year than from cancer, heart disease, birth defects, flu and pneumonia, respiratory diseases, stroke, and diabetes combined" (p. 18).

Based on these alarming statistics, it is crucial that the adults involved in the lives of teenagers are aware of the risks and are prepared to help them make better decisions. You, as a SCIT, can be a strong voice to encourage teens to choose wisely. According to Belsky (2019), there are certain variables that can alert school counselors and others to adolescent risk factors, including those with emotional regulation problems, those with poor family relationships, and those who live in risk-prone environments. Falling into any of these categories does not mean the adolescent is destined to have problems, but the presence of any of these circumstances may serve as a guide when making decisions about teens who may need some type of intervention.

Psychosocial Development

The primary focus of psychosocial development for adolescents is based on developing senses of *self* and *identity*. The primary question they must answer is "Who am I?" According to Erikson (1968), the developmental struggle for the adolescent stage is identity versus role confusion. Identity can be defined as unique individual beliefs based on roles, attitudes, values, and aspirations. Erikson believed that unsuccessful teens develop *identity confusion*, marked by an inability to develop a positive path toward adulthood. Until they are able to integrate all aspects of their identity, they may try out *multiple or possible selves*, meaning various possibilities of who they are or who they wish to become in the future.

Through the process of engaging with multiple or possible selves, teens come closer to integrating all aspects of their identity, and they begin to reach identity achievement. This process occurs when they are successful in establishing their own identity by accepting or rejecting the values, beliefs, and goals they have been or will be exposed to through parents, community, and culture. However, this is a challenging process, with some adolescents achieving success and others not. Marcia (1966) developed four types of identities to help understand the process of identity development, with *identity achievement* being the first type that describes an adolescent experiencing an identity crisis and choosing to make a values-based commitment to forming his/her identity. *Identity foreclosure* describes an adolescent who adopts the values and goals of his/her parents and culture without question, basically ending the process of identity development before it actually begins. *Identity diffusion* describes the most troubled adolescent, who lacks commitment to goals or values and is apathetic about taking on any particular role. *Identity moratorium*, described as the healthiest approach to identity, characterizes an adolescent who experiments with different identities by trying them out in order to make decisions about his/her future.

One of the key aspects of successfully navigating adolescence is having a strong support system that consists of family and friends and is characterized by positive relationships. This support system helps the adolescent through both good and bad times, and you, as a school counselor-in-training, may be a significant part of that support system.

Considering the impact of developmental issues on children and adolescents is an important aspect of a school counselor's work. Because of the comprehensive nature of human growth and development, a tremendous amount of knowledge can be gained by understanding developmental concepts and how these can be applied in a school setting.

Conceptual Application Activity 13.11

Read and respond to the following scenario. Compare your response with those of your peers.

Suyin is a 16-year-old female who is failing her classes. In middle school, Suyin was an exceptional student and reported wanting to be a pediatrician when she grew up. She has recently begun associating with a new peer group that is not interested in school and spends most of its time at the local mall. Suyin has quickly followed suit. The school has reported to Suyin's parents that she has been absent from school multiple times for the past few weeks. Suyin appears content with following her new peer group rather than considering her future goals. She reports having no career goals or interest planning for life after high school at this time.

- What factors might be contributing to this abrupt shift in Suyin's perspective?
- How can you respect Suyin's individual autonomy and help her to develop a sense of who she is in relation to others?
- Which ASCA (2014) Mindsets and Behaviors apply to this scenario?

Impact of Culture on Development

Up to this point, this chapter has concentrated primarily on the developmental models and theories used to identify and address healthy and unhealthy developmental processes. When identifying factors that contribute to the development of a child or adolescent, however, it is also critical to consider the impact of cultural background and personal worldview. How much or how little one identifies with his/her race, SES, or gender, for example, needs to be understood and cultivated to make sense of a person's overall development. School counselors are in a unique position to bring students together to engage in dialogue about issues of diversity through their developmental lessons and small-group curriculum. Although culture is made up of innumerable nuances and identity markers, we address here five of what we consider to be the most salient aspects for today's youth: race and ethnicity, SES, gender, affectual orientation, and ability status.

Race and Ethnicity

Part of the lifespan experience for all individuals is the development of one's racial and ethnic identity. While there are various models of identity development, they generally include stages through which the individual must pass in order to achieve a healthy, integrated, and functional personal identity (Rowe, Bennett, & Atkinson, 1994). Individuals must first accept stereotypes associated with their race or ethnicity, often experiencing some sort of conflict where they begin to question these stereotypes. They then immerse themselves in the culture of the larger racial or ethnic group, and reject those outside the group with which they have identified. Finally, they come to a balance between accepting others and retaining a positive association with their own group.

To foster healthy racial and ethnic identity development, it is important to understand that one's awareness of racial and ethnic identity begins as early as 3–4 years old, when children are first able to differentiate individuals on the basis of racial characteristics such as skin color. Race-related messages from adults and feedback about behaviors and experiences contribute greatly to a child's racial and ethnic identity. Based on this racial socialization, children can potentially develop either ethnic pride or racial bias (Swanson, Cunningham, Youngblood, & Spencer, 2009).

Socioeconomic Status

Socioeconomic status has a significant impact on childhood development. Children from low-SES families are more likely to experience major health concerns (e.g., respiratory illness, higher blood lead levels, iron deficiency, sensory impairment) which can negatively impact their overall development (Bradley & Corwyn, 2002). These children often experience longer hospital stays than their more affluent counterparts, in addition to experiencing illnesses with more long-term consequences (Bradley & Corwyn, 2002).

In addition to contributing to significant health concerns, poverty impacts children's educational outcomes. Children and adolescents from low-SES families are at an increased risk of leaving school without graduating, perform at lower rates both cognitively and academically, and demonstrate more behavior problems than those from higher-SES families (Engle & Black, 2008). As a result, low-SES children are at a disadvantage in terms of both college- and career-readiness, with individuals from more financially secure families tending to have higher levels of education, higher occupational status, and increased access to resources with direct benefits related to educational outcomes (Bradley & Corwyn, 2002).

Gender Identity

Gender identity is a construct that involves not only one's biological sex, but also the gender with which a person most readily and personally identifies. Sometimes a person's assigned sex matches with his/her gender identity, resulting in a person who identifies as *cisgender*. Other times, a person's internal understanding of him/herself, and, at times, outward expression of gendered characteristics, is not aligned with the sex that was assigned at birth. This represents someone who identifies as *transgender*. There are also many other points along the gender spectrum with which a person can identify, resulting in a need for school counselors to be well versed not only in the language associated with gender identity, but also with the personal challenges encountered by children and adolescents at any point along the spectrum.

The fluidity of gender identity can quickly amplify the already difficult experience of navigating adolescence in today's world. For students who identify as anything but cisgender, the K–12 school experience can be lonely, hostile, and unsafe (Kosciw, Greytak, Giga, Villenas, & Danischewski, 2016). In the 2015 National School Climate Survey, middle school students reported higher rates of victimization and gender-based harassment than their high school counterparts, as well as less access to adult support networks, inclusive curriculum, and school-based Gay-Straight Alliance clubs (GSAs; Kosciw et al., 2016). Nearly half (48.9%) of school mental health professionals reported believing that transgender students felt unsafe in their schools, with 70% reporting perceptions of gender-based bullying among students (Kull, Greytak, & Kosciw, 2019).

School counselors can combat these statistics by ensuring their visibility as gender-supportive allies within the school setting. Advocating for the adoption of inclusive curriculum models and school policies, as well as the establishment of GSAs, provides a concrete way for school counselors to positively impact the developmental experiences of children and adolescents with non-conforming gender identities.

Affectual Orientation

Often confused with gender identity, affectual orientation refers not to someone's internal understanding and expression of self-identity, but rather to that person's emotional, physical, and intimate attraction to other individuals (Goodrich & Luke, 2015). For students navigating childhood and adolescent development, identifying, exploring, and/or accepting their affectual orientation can sometimes be a complicated and confusing process, fraught with simultaneous issues of hormone development, physical transformation, and personal maturation. School counselors are well positioned to support students who may be experiencing challenges associated with clarifying, understanding, and/or expressing their own affectual orientation. Particularly for students identifying as lesbian, gay, bisexual, queer, questioning, pansexual, or asexual, some of these challenges may include facing discrimination from peers and/or family members, navigating the coming out process, and/or feeling unsafe or unsupported at school (Goodrich & Luke, 2015).

Nearly half (49.2%) of the 10,528 students surveyed in the 2015 National School Climate Survey (Kosciw et al., 2016) identified as gay or lesbian. In the same survey, LGBTQI (lesbian, gay, bisexual, transgender, questioning or queer, intersex) students reported school-based experiences of discrimination that resulted in increased absences, decreased academic performance, lower rates of reported self-esteem, and higher rates of depression. Although students reported frequent instances of harassment and discrimination based on their affectual orientation, 57.6% chose not to report the incident based on a perception that school staff would not intervene effectively and/or that the harassment might become worse as a result. Of those who did report, 63.5% encountered school staff who either failed to intervene or told the student to ignore the bully (Kosciw et al., 2016).

It is important for school counselors to be aware of the negative experiences of LGBTQI students and the ways in which these experiences impact their development and their ability to succeed in school. In addition, however, it is equally important that they not "overfocus on the impact of the LGBTQI youth's identity and, in doing so, unintentionally ... and entirely miss [their] unique experience" (Goodrich & Luke, 2015, p. 50). As with all students, school counselors should attend to the holistic development and personal experiences of LGBTQI students, supporting the integration of their affectual orientation as one unique part of their overall personal identity.

Ability Status

Navigating childhood or adolescence with a physical, cognitive, and/or psychological disability can, at times, present unique developmental challenges. It is important that school counselors foster genuinely inclusive school environments (Marshak, Dandeneau, Prezant, & L'Amoreaux, 2010) for students with disabilities and work to help students positively integrate their disability into their overall self-concept. Part of this role involves educating the school community at large about specific disabilities and disability-relevant constructs, such as typecasting, inclusion, advocacy, and accommodations (Marshak et al., 2010).

One helpful tool for understanding the ways in which disability intersects with a student's development is Rodis, Garrod, and Boscardin's (as cited in Marshak et al., 2010) identity formation model. Although developed initially to represent the experiences of many students with learning disabilities, the model is applicable to the identity formation of those with other types of disabilities, as well. The model posits that students with disabilities experience a seven-stage process of "com[ing] to terms with a disorder that is stigmatizing" (Marshak et al., 2010, p. 172). The stages include experiencing the problem or disability without having a label for it, being diagnosed, feeling alienated from other students as a result of the diagnosis, hiding the disability in order to "pass" and avoid discrimination, encountering consequences resulting from the hidden disability, transitioning to taking ownership of the disability and integrating it into one's self-concept, and finally, transcending into viewing the disability as a fundamental part of one's personal identity (Rodis, Garrod, & Boscardin, as cited in Marshak et al., 2010). Using this model can help school counselors to better understand the experiences of students with disabilities and design interventions that ease their navigation of both lifespan development and identity formation processes during childhood and adolescence.

Conclusion

Throughout this chapter, you have reviewed many theories and concepts related to human development. Your task is to understand how developmental constructs influence your counseling relationships with students. Not all the students with whom you work will be at the same developmental stages biologically, cognitively, and/or socially. School counselors have the responsibility to work with all students in the school setting and to facilitate an understanding of developmental issues for other educators and parents/guardians so that each student will have the opportunity to develop his/her potential and become a contributing member of our society.

Websites

- "6-Year-Old Child Development Milestones": http://psychology.about.com/od/early-child-development/a/social-emotional-development-in-middle-childhood.htm

This website covers physical, cognitive, and social/emotional milestones of young elementary-aged children.

- "School Age Children Development & Parenting Tips (6–12)": https://childdevelopmentinfo.com/ages-stages/school-age-children-development-parenting-tips/

This website offers tips for dealing with physical, cognitive, and social/emotional milestones of middle childhood.

- "Developmental Milestones for High-Schoolers": www.understood.org/en/learning-attention-issues/signs-symptoms/developmental-milestones/developmental-milestones-for-typical-high-schoolers

This website describes physical, cognitive, and social/emotional milestones for typically developing high-schoolers.

- "Adolescents with Disabilities: Enhancing Resilience and Delivering Inclusive Development": www.odi.org/publications/11165-adolescents-disabilities-enhancing-resilience-and-delivering-inclusive-development

This website covers research about physical, cognitive, and social/emotional development for adolescents living with disabilities.

References

American Academy of Child & Adolescent Psychiatry. (2017). *Suicide in children and teens.* Retrieved from www.aacap.org/AACAP/Families_and_Youth/Facts_for_Families/FFF-Guide/Teen-Suicide-010.aspx

American Lung Association. (2018). *Asthma and children fact sheet.* Retrieved from www.lung.org/lung-health-and-diseases/lung-disease-lookup/asthma/learn-about-asthma/asthma-children-facts-sheet.html

American Psychiatric Association. (2013). *Diagnostic and statistical manual of mental disorders* (5th ed.). Washington, DC: American Psychiatric Association.

American School Counselor Association. (2014). *Mindsets and behaviors for student success: K-12 college-and career-readiness standards for every student.* Alexandria, VA: American School Counselor Association.

Autism Speaks. (2018). *CDC increases estimate of autism's prevalence by 15 percent, to 1 in 59 children.* Retrieved from www.autismspeaks.org/science-news/cdc-increases-estimate-autisms-prevalence-15-percent-1-59-children

Bandura, A. (1977). *Social learning theory.* Englewood Cliffs, NJ: Prentice Hall.

Bandura, A. (1986). *Social foundations of thought and action.* Englewood Cliffs, NJ: Prentice Hall.

Baumrind, D. (1971). Current patterns of parental authority. *Developmental Psychology, 4*(1), 1–103.

Belsky, J. (2019). *Experiencing the lifespan* (5th ed.). New York, NY: Worth.

Berger, K. S. (2007). *The developing person through the life span.* New York, NY: Worth.

Betbeze, P. (2018). The childhood obesity epidemic: Insights from claims plus EMR data. *HealthLeaders Magazine, 21*(4), 15–18.

Boergers, J., Gable, C. J., & Owens, J. A. (2014). Later school time is associated with improved sleep and daytime functioning in adolescents. *Journal of Developmental and Behavioral Pediatrics, 35,* 11–17.

Bradley, R. H., & Corwyn, R. F. (2002). Socioeconomic status and child development. *Annual Review of Psychology, 53,* 371–399.

Bridgeland, J. M., DiIulio, J. J., Jr, & Morison, K. B. (2006). *The silent epidemic: Perspectives of high school dropouts.* Retrieved from www.ignitelearning.com/pdf/TheSilentEpidemic3-06FINAL.pdf

Bronfenbrenner, U. (1979). *The ecology of human development.* Cambridge, MA: Harvard University Press.

Bushman, B. J., Calvert, S. L., Dredze, M., Jablonski, N. G., Morrill, C., Romer, D., . . . Webster, D. W. (2016). Youth violence: What we know and what we need to know. *American Psychologist, 71*(1), 17–39.

CDC. (2016a). *Childhood obesity facts.* Retrieved from www.cdc.gov/obesity/data/childhood.html

CDC. (2016b). *Motor vehicle crash deaths.* Retrieved from www.cdc.gov/vitalsigns/motor-vehicle-safety/index.html

CDC. (2017a). *About teen pregnancy.* Retrieved from www.cdc.gov/teenpregnancy/about/index.htm

CDC. (2017b). *National Health Interview Survey Data (NIHS): Lifetime asthma populations.* Retrieved from www.cdc.gov/asthma/nhis/2017/table1-1.htm

CDC. (2018). *Suicide mortality in the United States, 1999–2017.* Retrieved from www.cdc.gov/nchs/products/databriefs/db330.htm

CDC. (2019). *Sexual risk behaviors can lead to HIV, STDs, & teen pregnancy.* Retrieved from www.cdc.gov/healthyyouth/sexualbehaviors/index.htm

Clinkinbeard, S. S., Simi, P., Evans, M. K., & Anderson, A. L. (2011). Sleep and delinquency: Does the amount of sleep matter? *Journal of Youth Adolescence, 40,* 916–930. doi:10.1007/s10964-010-9594-6

Dowden, A., Gray, K., White, N., Ethridge, G., Spencer, N., & Boston, Q. (2018). A phenomenological analysis of the impact of teen pregnancy on education attainment: Implications for school counselors. *Journal of School Counseling, 16*(8), 1–25.

Elkind, D. (1978). Understanding the young adolescent. *Adolescence, 13,* 127–134.

Engle, P. L., & Black, M. M. (2008). The effect of poverty on child development and educational outcomes. *Annals of the New York Academy of Sciences, 1136,* 243–256.

Epstein, M., Hill, K., Bailey, J., & Hawkins, J. (2013). The effect of general and drug-specific family environments on comorbid and drug-specific problem behavior: A longitudinal examination. *Developmental Psychology, 49*(6), 1151–1164.

Erikson, E. (1950). *Childhood and society.* New York, NY: W. W. Norton & Co.

Erikson, E. (1968). *Identity: Youth and crisis.* New York, NY: W. W. Norton & Co.

Fonvig, C., Hamann, S., Nielsen, T., Johansen, M., Gronbaek, H., Mollerup, P., & Holm, J. (2017). Subjective evaluation of psychosocial well-being in children and youths with overweight or obesity: The impact of multidisciplinary obesity treatment. *Quality of Life Research, 26*(12), 3279–3288.

Garrett-Peters, P. T., Mokrova, I. L., Carr, R. C., Vernon-Feagans, L., & The Family Life Project Key Investigators (2019). Early student (dis)engagement: Contributions of household chaos, parenting, and self-regulatory skills. *Developmental Psychology, 55*(7), 1480–1492. doi:10.1037/dev0000720

Goodrich, K. M., & Luke, M. (2015). *Group counseling with LGBTQI persons.* Alexandria, VA: American Counseling Association.

Guttmacher Institute. (2019). *Sex and HIV education.* Retrieved from www.guttmacher.org/state-policy/explore/sex-and-hiv-education

Hall, G. S. (1904). *Adolescence.* New York, NY: Arno Press.

Kohlberg, L. (1976). Moral stages and moralization: The cognitive-developmental approach. In T. Lickona (Ed.), *Moral development and behavior* (pp. 31–55). New York, NY: Holt, Rinehart & Winston.

Kosciw, J. G., Greytak, E. A., Giga, N. M., Villenas, C., & Danischewski, D. J. (2016). *The 2015 National School Climate Survey: The experiences of lesbian, gay, bisexual, transgender, and queer youth in our nation's schools.* New York, NY: Gay, Lesbian, and Straight Education Network.

Kull, R. M., Greytak, E. A., & Kosciw, J. G. (2019). *Supporting safe and healthy schools for lesbian, gay, bisexual, transgender, and queer students: A national survey of school counselors, social workers, and psychologists.* New York, NY: Gay, Lesbian, and Straight Education Network.

Lefrancois, G. L. (1996). *The lifespan.* Belmont, CA: Wadsworth.

Lipari, R., & Van Horn, S. (2017). *Children living with parents who have a substance use disorder.* Retrieved from www.samhsa.gov/data/sites/default/files/report_3223/ShortReport-3223.html

Marcia, J. (1966). Development and validation of ego-identity status. *Journal of Personality and Social Psychology, 3,* 551–558.

Marshak, L. E., Dandeneau, C. J., Prezant, F. P., & L'Amoreaux, N. A. (2010). *The school counselor's guide to helping students with disabilities.* San Francisco, CA: Jossey-Bass.

Mental Health America. (2020). *Depression in teens.* Retrieved from https://www.mhanational.org/depression-teens-0

National Center for Education Statistics. (2018). Digest of education statistics: Table 219.70. Retrieved from https://nces.ed.gov/programs/digest/d17/tables/dt17_219.70.asp

National Institute of Mental Health. (n.d.). *Attention-deficit/hyperactivity disorder*. Retrieved from www.nimh.nih.gov/health/topics/attention-deficit-hyperactivity-disorder-adhd/index.shtml

National Institute on Alcohol Abuse and Alcoholism. (2018). *Alcohol facts and statistics*. Retrieved from www.niaaa.nih.gov/alcohol-health/overview-alcohol-consumption/alcohol-facts-and-statistics

National Institute on Drug Abuse. (2014, January). *Principles of adolescent substance use disorder treatment: A research-based guide*. Retrieved from www.drugabuse.gov/publications/principles-adolescent-substance-use-disorder-treatment-research-based-guide/frequently-asked-questions/what-are-signs-drug-use-in-adolescents-what-role-can-parents-play-in-getting-treatment

Piaget, J. (1926). *The language and thought of the child* (M. Worden, Trans.). New York, NY: Harcourt Brace Jovanovich.

Piaget, J. (1929). *The child's conception of the world*. (J. Tomlinson & A. Tomlinson, Trans.). New York, NY: Harcourt Brace Jovanovich.

Piaget, J. (1972). Intellectual evolution from adolescence to adulthood. *Human Development, 15*, 1–12.

Piaget, J., & Inhelder, B. (1969). *The psychology of the child*. New York, NY: Basic Books.

Rembeck, G. I., & Gunnarsson, R. K. (2004). Improving pre- and postmenarcheal 12-year-old girls' attitudes toward menstruation. *Health Care for Women International, 25*, 680–698.

Rowe, W., Bennett, S. K., & Atkinson, D. R. (1994). White racial identity models: A critique and alternative proposal. *The Counseling Psychologist, 22*, 129–146.

Santrock, J. W. (2012). *A topical approach to life-span development* (6th ed.). New York, NY: McGraw-Hill.

Seligman, L., & Reichenberg, L. W. (2014). *Theories of counseling and psychotherapy* (4th ed.). New York, NY: Pearson.

Swanson, D. P., Cunningham, M., Youngblood, J., & Spencer, M. B. (2009). Racial identity development during childhood. In H. A. Neville, B. M. Tynes, & S. O. Utsey (Eds.), *Handbook of African American psychology* (pp. 269–281). Thousand Oaks, CA: SAGE Publications.

Tas, A., Selvitopu, A., Bora, V., & Demirkaya, Y. (2013). Reasons for dropout for vocational high school students. *Educational Sciences: Theory and Practice, 13*(3), 1561–1565.

The Week. (2014, June 14). Health scare of the week. *The Week Magazine*, p. 18.

Triyanto, E., & Iskandar, A. (2015). Family support needed for adolescent puberty. *International Journal of Nursing Education, 7*(1), 106–110. doi:10.5958/0974-9357.2015.00021.5

Vygotsky, L. S. (1986). *Thought and language*. (A. Kozulin, Trans.). Cambridge, MA: MIT Press (original work published 1934).

Weaver, F. (2014, April 11). The mainstreaming of mindfulness meditation. *The Week*, p. 9. http://theweek.com/article/index/259351/the-mainstreaming-of-mindfulness-meditation

World Health Organization. (2020, April 1). *Obesity and overweight*. Retrieved from www.who.int/news-room/fact-sheets/detail/obesity-and-overweight

Part IV

Completing the Clinical Experiences

14 Transitioning from Clinical Experiences to a Professional School Counselor

Michael Bundy

CACREP Standards

Contextual

1. professional organizations, preparation standards, and credentials relevant to the practice of school counseling

Chapter Objectives:

*   terminating the clinical experiences
*   assessing one's own counselor skills
*   searching, applying, and interviewing for school counseling positions
*   comprehending the licensure processes
*   understanding professional memberships

Introduction

The time has come for you to plan how to leave your practicum or internship site. Your site supervisor has encouraged you, and has provided you with positive guidance. Teachers and administrators at your clinical sites gave you support and assistance when you needed it. Many students were changed by the individual and small-group sessions you held with them. By showing your appreciation to them, future school counselors-in-training who follow you to this school will be warmly received too. So give careful consideration to how you separate from your students, teachers, site supervisor, and others with whom you have worked closely.

Terminating Relationships with Students

The process of terminating a counseling relationship can be a stressful time for students, but it can also be an opportunity to affirm their growth and see the ending as a new beginning. Students who have received special attention from you may become uneasy when you begin to discuss terminating their counseling sessions. They may need help considering what it will be like to function without you as part of their support system. Seeing the end of one relationship or event as a natural time to redefine and begin new relationships and activities is a healthy way to perceive change. Here are a few tips on closing your relationships with students and some examples of what you can say to implement the suggestions in a session with them:

- *Give students advance notice.* You should begin talking with students about ending their counseling at least two sessions before their last one. *What to say:* "Jill, in two weeks my time at Jefferson School will end because my internship training with your school counselor Ms. Jones will be completed. I would like for us to talk a bit about what we have done together to help you with the goals you wanted to work on."

- *Have students self-assess their progress.* Allow students to express the progress they think they have made as a result of their relationship with you. You should help them acknowledge their accomplishments in terms of how they changed their behaviors, their thoughts, and/or their emotional responses. *What to say:* "I'd like to hear what changes you think you have made since we have been meeting. You had some goals you wanted to accomplish. What progress do you think you have made toward them?"

- *Offer your observations.* Be prepared to provide students with your assessment of their progress. Students often need to hear what you think of what they have done. This can be an encouraging and confidence-building time for them. The more specific your observations, the more powerful and meaningful they will be to your students. *What to say:* "Jill, would you like me to tell you what I think you have done these past few weeks toward achieving your counseling goals? I have noticed that you no longer say things like 'I must do what Bill tells me to do or he won't like me anymore.'"

- *Anticipate future challenges.* Help students identify potential stumbling blocks they may encounter. It is quite likely that students will continue to face challenges when their counseling sessions with you are over. Talk about those potential hurdles and how students might overcome them. This could be another confidence-builder for students as you help them realize how resourceful they have become. *What to say:* "Jill, what will you think if Bill says that he wants to spend time apart? What will you say to him? How will you control your emotions?"

- *Identify student resources.* Help students utilize resources within their support systems for times when they may need extra assistance to overcome difficulties. Those resources could be the adults they respect and with whom they have a good working relationship (e.g., school counselor, favorite teacher, trusted relative, youth minister). *What to say:* "Jill, should one of those 'stumbling blocks' begin to give you a big hassle, what can you do? Is there someone you can talk to about it?"

- *Create a picture of the future.* In order to help students feel confident and build resiliency to cope with the challenges to come, it is usually effective to have students think and talk about what they would like to have happen, new relationships they may want to develop, or activities they want to start. If this is too difficult, have students try to imagine how they would like things to be for them. This could give them a positive image and provide motivation to continue moving forward along the path of successful change they found in counseling with you. *What to say:* "Jill, where would you like to be in six months when it comes to having or not having boyfriends?"

- *Write notes to students.* Recording your goodbyes in handwritten notes can be powerful and can give meaningful messages to students. Students have been known to carry these treasured thoughts with them for months. Your note should express appreciation for what you have learned from them, and it should communicate encouragement to them to continue growing, learning, and moving forward. The following note was written by a school counseling intern to significant people at her internship site:

Janna,

You are truly a very special person. Your mom would be so proud of where you are. That first day, you made me feel at ease. I looked forward to seeing your smiling face every day. I will miss our talks. Remember to give your dad a break; he loves you very much and you are still his baby. Study hard in college and you will do well. People who deal with you will see that you are genuine and honest. You are a great role model. Watch over Vicki, and please continue your friendship with her. You have already changed lives . . . including mine . . . you will always have a place in my heart.

Debbi

Conceptual Application Activity 14.1

Think about one of your past or current students. To make this activity more challenging, think of a student with whom you had difficulty. Write a brief note to this student. In your note, review resources available and create a positive picture of the future.

Terminating counseling groups should be another growth experience for students, and can be a fun activity as well. Most school counselors-in-training give their groups 2 weeks' notice so the students have ample time to process their feelings and plan for the future. The following are a few suggestions school counselors-in-training have found to be effective closing activities:

- *Have refreshments at the last group session.* Food always makes for an enjoyable time. Be sure that your refreshments are consistent with any dietary restrictions of group members or school rules. Popcorn and juice boxes are usually safe for elementary students. Older students could be responsible for bringing their own tasty treats to the final group meeting. Put some limits on what can be brought; food can become a distraction to your final group agenda. Have some group process activities planned so that closure is focused and meaningful.
- *Have group members acknowledge their progress.* This would be a time for group members to proudly announce changes they have made as a result of group support. Expressive art activities or open letters written to the group provide structured approaches for sharing retrospective observations.
- *Give feedback to group members.* Upon terminating the group, give each group member your assessment of his/her progress in specific terms before you leave. Follow a similar approach to that which is given above for individual students; offer your observations to the group as a whole and/or to members in individual sessions.
- *Write notes to group members.* These notes should offer specific observations and encouragement. Your message could be to the whole group, allowing them time to respond, or you could give notes to individual members outside the group session. If the notes are read to the whole group, it could make a powerful closing session that

builds cohesiveness among group members or assists members to see their peers from a different perspective. If your note contains content to a specific student, provide that student with positive pragmatic feedback to help him/her continue improving upon the growth already started in the group. Imagine how a group member would be affected upon receiving the note below:

Emilie,

How can I ever put in words how proud I am of you? You never missed a group session, and always kept up with the other students. You now have the confidence to keep a smile on your face. I know how hard it is, but just remember that we talked about how we can control what we think and how we act, and as a result our feelings will follow. I have seen you do this for the past five weeks. Your teachers have noticed how much easier you are to get along with and how your anger doesn't boil over so quickly. YOU are the one who chooses these actions, you made your own decisions, and you can continue on. I will miss you, but know that all the lessons we talked about are still in your head and you can pull out your group notes and use them when you feel stressed. Please don't forget to be as proud of yourself as I am of you!!!

Debbi

Conceptual Application Activity 14.2

Consider the same student you identified in the previous activity, or think of a different student. Review the student's progress and provide feedback specific to him/her. Be encouraging, and be honest.

_____

_____

Terminating with Colleagues

Bringing relationships with your new colleagues to a close requires a heartfelt expression of appreciation for the mentorship and collaboration they provided. Throughout your experience, your site supervisor offered you wisdom and encouragement. Teachers in your school site worked with you to meet student needs, resulting in confidence in your counseling and consulting competencies. It may seem that a simple "thank you" note would be insufficient to communicate your feelings toward them, but it carries special meaning to those who receive one. Shortly, you expect to be employed as a professional school counselor, and when this dream becomes your reality, these folks who helped you during your training may now be meeting with you as new colleagues in professional meetings or conferences. The impression you leave them with will be carried over into new professional relationships. Give them something extraordinary to remember about you. Try writing a note similar to the following:

Bruce,

The words "Thank you" can hardly express how I feel about all I have learned and experienced in school counseling this semester. Your training has been exemplary, and I have learned so much. Seeing Choice Theory in action is so much more powerful than just reading about it. You taught me how to teach others, but never criticize them. You taught, by example, how to empower students to find the answers for themselves. You have shown me what school counselors are doing on a daily basis. You truly made a difference in so many lives; just add me to the list. Thank you so much for allowing me to be your student! I hope someday to make you proud. I will never forget this time and what a truly great mentor you are! You're really the best!

Debbi

Terminating with Administrators

You must not avoid saying or forget to say goodbye to administrators who approved your placement and supported your clinical activities. Central office supervisors and building-level principals may not have worked as closely with you as your site supervisor or the teachers, but their support was certainly critical to your success. Moreover, they will be important to your future job plans. When you apply for a counselor position, the employing principal will likely call the principal where you conducted your clinical experiences to ask about your performance. You will certainly want to leave the principal at your site with a positive impression of your maturity, independence, and competencies as a school counselor.

Here are two things you should consider doing: (1) make an appointment to debrief the principal about the things you accomplished before you leave, and (2) send a note of thanks to the principal and any central office personnel involved in your placement. The following is a note written by a school counseling intern to her site principal after she met with him before she left her internship experience in his building.

Mr. Schneitman:

Thank you so much for the opportunity of completing my internship at Jefferson County High School. You are a multi-talented administrator who has put together an awesome staff. I also know that I would not want your job for love or money.

Thank you for allowing me the pleasure to put together a program using the peer counselors already in place as mentors for special-needs children and helping them learn social and emotional skills. You allowed me time for group counseling during school and gave me a place in the media center to conduct my sessions. You have allowed our program to have some great successes, and for that I will be forever indebted. I wish you, your staff, and your students continued success.

Debbi

Conceptual Application Activity 14.3

Write a thank you termination note to either a colleague or an administrator. Express your sentiments, and provide specific examples of how this person assisted you. Keep in mind that this person may provide a reference or recommendation letter for you, or even be your future employer.

_____

_____

Self-Assessment as a Transition Activity

With your clinical experiences almost finished, and as you continue your transition from student to professional school counselor, it can be both an anxious and an exciting time for you. At this point, you should reflect upon the development of your competencies as a future school counselor. You will want to approach this new challenge with the same intensity and determination you exemplified during your training program. But where do you begin the process?

Because counselor preparation programs provide ample opportunities for students to examine themselves and to facilitate personal growth, most school counselors-in-training know themselves fairly well at this stage of their training. The information you have accumulated from your counseling coursework should be used to help you identify your strengths and areas that may need further development. Most recently, you have (or will have) feedback from your site supervisor and from your program supervisor. They have objectively assessed your readiness for assuming the responsibilities that come with organizing a comprehensive school counseling program as an appropriately credentialed professional. You should take these data and develop a plan to maximize your strength and overcome your relative weaknesses; however, a more systematic self-assessment would be most beneficial to your planning.

The American School Counselor Association has a long history of providing vigorous leadership in articulating a professional identity for counselors who work primarily in school settings. As needs of pre-K–12 students have changed and as society's expectations have changed for schools, the ASCA has been at the forefront in promoting standards for counseling training and for the practice of counselors. As you have already learned, the ASCA developed the *School Counselor Professional Standards and Competencies* document that lists the knowledge, abilities and skills, and attitudes counselors should possess in order to implement a comprehensive school counseling program. In addition, school counseling program faculty can use these competencies to assess how well their school counselors-in-training are meeting identified proficiencies. These competencies can be revisited each year to identify knowledge, abilities and skills, and attitudes that you still need to attain. With this information, develop a self-improvement plan that includes long-term goals and short-term goals that reflect the degree to which you need to acquire certain competencies. For example, suppose you expect to be employed as an elementary school counselor and you consider that you need more experience in classroom management. If so, then this is a high priority, and you will need to identify short-term goals to gain competency in this area. Completing this self-assessment will also give some points to consider when preparing to apply for an interview for a counseling position. Interviewees will certainly wish to highlight their strong points and acknowledge a plan to address relative weaknesses. For example, in completing an application or during an interview, prospective employees are often asked what they consider to be their strengths for the job and what they believe are weaknesses. The self-assessment provides an informed position from which you can confidently respond.

Box 14.1

The Occupational Outlook Handbook (US Bureau of Labor Statistics, 2019) predicted that the job outlook for school counselors would increase by 8% over that year, a faster than average growth.

The Application Process

Searching for a job as a professional school counselor can be a daunting process. Here are a few tips to assist you with this journey.

Searching and Applying for Job Openings

- *Use technology to accelerate the search.* As the old commercial said, "Let your fingers do the walking." Using the Internet, research all of the school systems where you wish to apply. Go to the Human Resources link and complete the online application. You will find that almost all school systems now prefer applicants to submit electronic applications. Even though surrounding area school systems may not currently have a school counseling position posted, it is advisable to complete an application for each of your desired locations anyway. You will soon learn that school principals know of their staff vacancies long before they are announced and generally begin a search to fill the opening long before the position is officially posted. Therefore, it is better to have your application on file for principals to review as soon as they begin their search.
- *Proofread online applications.* A word of caution: It would be prudent for you to complete a hard copy of the application before you enter it online. Before you hit the "submit" key, you should make a copy of your online application and proofread it. Proper grammar and spelling are essential!
- *Attend monthly meetings of the local counselor association.* You should attend these meetings, especially during your clinical experiences. It is here that you will develop your professional network and hear of potential job openings. This will give you advance notice to begin developing your strategy for applying. You can "pick the brains" of your new colleagues to assess the counseling needs of the schools where vacancies will be. You can begin to shape your application and start to prepare for the interview for those schools.
- *Request letters of recommendation.* Ask professors who know the quality of your work best, especially internship and practicum professors, as well as your school site supervisors, to write a recommendation. Give them something in writing that describes some points about yourself and some activities you conducted well at your sites (such as a résumé). Express your passion for school counseling, but do not use too much hyperbole. You could also provide them with a list of your strengths and skills (see your self-assessment results) for them to use.
- *Prepare a portfolio.* This professional portfolio can be taken to a job interview to show examples of your class work applicable to developing a school counseling program. For

William Robert Woods
46 Volunteer St.
Big Orange, TN 37830
(865) 326-3333
woodswr@utk.edu

Career Goal
To develop, implement, and lead a comprehensive school counseling program aligned with ASCA National Model.

Education
The University of Tennessee-Knoxville
MS in School Couseling (2014)
GPA (4.0 Scale): 3.95
BS in Psychology (2012)
GPA (4.0 Scale): 3.825
Dean's List, Phi Beta Kappa

Professional Association Membership
American School Counselor Association
Tennessee School Counselor Association
Smoky Mountain Counseling Association

Experiences
School Counseling Practicum at Modesto Middle School, Modesto, CA

- 60 hours of providing individual counseling
- 20 hours of conducting group counseling
- 10 hours of teaching classroom guidance lessons
- 15 hours of supervision

School Counseling Internship at Excel Elementary School and at Above Average High School, Oak Ridge, TN 37830

- Completed over 600 hours
- Counseled students individually and in small groups
- Cousulted with teachers and parents
- Collaborated in IEP & RtI meetings and parent–teacher conferences
- Taught classroom guidance lessons

Volunteer at GREAT KIDS Summer Program, High Achievers School, Oak Ridge, TN

- Worked with special needs students in small group as teacher assistant

Accomplishments

- Created a career information webpage for middle school students
- Presented research paper at Smoky Mountain Counseling Association conference, entitled "Effective use of peer counselors in high school"

Skills

- Computer Skills: Proficient in word procesing and data management, multimedia production, webpage development
- Foreign Language Skills: Spanish

Figure 14.1 Sample résumé.

example, you could include a career lesson plan you wrote for one of your classes. Your practicum and internship will also provide excellent opportunities to add to your port-folio. Include counseling activities, group lesson plans, pictures of students, notes from people you helped, and the like. Make it well organized and visually attractive. Or you may prefer electronic portfolios that contain artifacts of your work. A link to this elec-tronic portfolio can be sent to the building principal in advance of your interview. For more information about electronic portfolios, go to "How to Create Your Online Port-folio" at www.format.com/how-to/create-online-portfolio.

* *Develop a strong résumé.* Prepare a one- or two-page résumé that is concise, organized, and professional. It must present you as the outstanding candidate you are! See Figure 14.1. Email it to principals who have or will have counselor positions available.

* *Have others review your materials.* Ask your classmates, professors, site supervisors, and others to review your résumé and portfolio. They may have some great suggestions to add or other changes to materials that will enhance your image.

Conceptual Application Activity 14.4

Prepare or revise your résumé. Give it to three people, and request written feedback. Make revisions based on this feedback. Be prepared to continue to update and revise your résumé on an ongoing basis.

Preparing for an Interview

Once you have received an appointment for an interview, you want to be overprepared. Visit that school's website and thoroughly research the school. Also, visit websites of the school district and the state department of education. Analyze the school's testing results and its Every Student Succeeds Act (ESSA) status. Pay particular attention to the disaggre-gated data of subgroups. Ask yourself, "What can I do as a school counselor to support the academic development of *all* students in this school? What special challenges does this stu-dent population have that I as a school counselor can address?" Note any special successes this school announces on its homepage. Take time to visit websites of teachers that are linked from the school's homepage. What feelings about the school climate, its staff, and students do you glean from the homepage? This information can provide you with possible issues within this school that may indicate questions you could be asked during the inter-view. They could also indicate questions you wish to raise with your interviewer.

Box 14.2

"I am wondering if anyone has any suggestions for getting hired as a school counselor?"
  This question was recently asked by one of my student trainees at a local counselor's meeting. Practitioners offered the following answers:

a. Continue to attend the professional development meetings, in order to network.
b. Substitute-teach or volunteer in the schools. This helps make you visible, and school personnel will have an opportunity to get to know who you are.

    c. Work with as many different populations as you can. When I applied for a job, I was asked about my work with "at risk" youth.

    d. Always follow up interviews with a phone call or email thanking administrators for the interview. If you don't get the job, don't be shy about calling the interviewers to ask how you can improve your interviewing skills.

A drop-in visit to your interview school may be a turn-off for the busy principal and staff; however, it could be beneficial for you to drive around the community it serves. If you get a chance to talk with parents or students, you might gather information that you may be able to use during your interview (Mindsets and Behaviors). For example, what are some needs of this school's student population? What are some strengths of this teaching staff? How does (or could) the counselor contribute?

With the data you have collected about this school, you are now ready to prepare for your interview. Think about the questions that may be asked and consider your responses. Figure 14.2 lists actual questions asked during a school counselor interview.

School Counselor Interview Questions

1. Tell us about yourself—what experiences have prepared you for the position of professional school counselor?
2. Explain Behaviors and Mindsets in school counseling and how you would use them to plan your counseling program?
3. Talk about how you would develop the classroom curriculum component of your school counseling program.
4. How will you establish relationships with outside school resources?
5. Tell us about a small-group counseling series you have conducted.
6. Our school population is unique—what strengths do you have to work with our students and their families?
7. We have kindergartners who cry every day for weeks into the school year. How would you help beginning kindergartners and parents adjust to school?
8. Tell us how you would help a teacher who is highly frustrated and feeling overwhelmed by the behavior of a student.
9. What are some of the best practices in school counseling you have come across?
10. How can you help us analyze and interpret test data to guide our instruction and curriculum decisions?
11. As a school counselor, how would you facilitate parent involvement in our school and in our classrooms?
12. How would you use technology as part of your counseling program?
13. What do you love about school counseling?
14. How would you show that what you are doing is effective?
15. Do you have any questions for us?

Figure 14.2 Interview questions.

Figure 14.3 School counselor applicant discussing her educational background and her portfolio with the school principal.

Source: Shutterstock.

Many administrators are unaware of a comprehensive school counseling programs and do not understand best practices for school counselors (Lowery, Quick, Boyland, Geesa, & Mayes, 2018). Therefore, during the interview process you can be instrumental in informing these personnel as to how school counselors are key to improving student academic, career, and social/emotional growth. Principals who wish to be better informed about the school counselor can visit the ASCA website, where they will find a link tab especially for "Administrators." Information regarding school counselors' role is available as well, along with a link labeled "Interviewing School Counselors." As a counselor applicant, you may also wish to review these questions.

Conceptual Application Activity 14.5

After you have considered other questions that may be asked during your interview and you have considered your responses, role-play an interview with your classmates. They may have other questions and suggestions on how to respond. While practice may not make you "perfect," in this instance, practice will certainly help you fill gaps and build your confidence.

The Interview

The following are some tips on conducting yourself during the interview. By now, you should be fully prepared, and you want to make an outstanding impression that will remain with interview committee members long after you have departed the meeting.

- *Dress appropriately.* Business professional is considered clothing du jour.
- *Arrive early for your interview.* You might have an opportunity to chat with staff members before you go into the interview room.
- *Have several copies of your résumé printed on quality paper.* An intern who interviewed for a job made a good impression when she was able to distribute a copy of her résumé to each committee member.
- *Bring an attractive portfolio.* Have it available to show illustrations of your work during your training. For example, in response to a question, you might mention that you have an example in your portfolio of something similar you did during your practicum and internship. Or you may provide a link to your electronic portfolio.
- *Remember to use good non-verbal skills.* Lean forward slightly and maintain good eye contact with *each* committee member when answering each question. Don't just focus on one person or the committee member asking the question. This shows confidence.
- *Speak clearly and confidently.* Use a strong voice that reflects your assurance in what you say. Talk at your normal pace to show comfort and command of a comprehensive school counseling program.
- *Answer the questions directly and succinctly.* Principals like interviewees to keep their answers to the point. However, you want to ensure that you demonstrate sufficient knowledge and enthusiasm for school counseling.
- *Relax and believe in yourself.* Rely upon your training in human relationships and your preparation. You will do well!

Professional Credentials

Professional credentials are required at the state and district levels in order to be employed to practice school counseling. They are also a way of promoting professional identity and of demonstrating a higher level of counseling competency. Three areas of professional identity are presented in this chapter: (1) the basic requirements for employment, (2) ways to continue professional development, and (3) paths to obtain national credentials.

Qualifications Vary by State

Requirements for credentialing professional school counselors differ from state to state. Some states issue a license to practice school counseling, while other states issue a certificate. In addition, states change their criteria for issuing credentials from time to time. You likely already know the qualifications to practice as a school counselor in the state where you are receiving your training, but if you wish to apply for a school counseling position in another state, you will need to know the requirements in that state. Some states have a reciprocity agreement with neighboring states to allow a counselor with credentials in one state to practice in another state. Another resource is the ASCA homepage, www.schoolcounselor.org, where you can conduct a search at the "State Certification Requirements" link, or call the ASCA at (703) 683-ASCA if you need further assistance. A state-by-state description of requirements and a link to the department of education of each state will have more specific information.

The Praxis Exams

Most states require the Praxis II: Professional School Counselor (5421) in order to earn licensure or certification. Test code 0421 is a 2-hour, 120 multiple-choice paper and pencil test, whereas the 5421 is a 2-hour, 120 multiple-choice computer-based exam. The Praxis Exams are developed and administered by the Educational Testing Service (ETS). The exam covers your knowledge of the ASCA National Model, history and role of the school counselor, knowledge of human development, and ethical/legal principles. For more information, see www.ets.org/s/praxis/pdf/0421-5421.pdf.

To register for Praxis, go to its website at www.ets.org/praxis/ or call ETS at 1-800-772-9476. You can purchase study guides from ETS to help you prepare for the exam.

Continuing Education Requirements

Once you obtain your state certificate or license, you will be required to renew it periodically. Each state has a specific time frame in which school counselors and teachers must apply for renewal of their credentials. To renew state credentials, successful completion of a given amount of continuing education activities is required. This continuing education requirement could be called continuing education units (CEUs), professional development, in-service education, professional growth activities, or accredited institution credits. Ongoing professional training may be in-service programs hosted by your school district, or it could include professional conferences held by your local, state, or national counseling association. The amount and type of continuing education you must complete within the given period varies from state to state. Check with your state department of education or your school district's human resources director for the specific requirements of re-credentialing. On its website, the ASCA has a general overview of each state's requirements and contact information.

National Credentials

Once you have fulfilled the requirements for a school counselor credential at the state level, you may wish to seek additional qualifications. There are two organizations at the national level where you can obtain additional credentials: the National Board of Certified Counselors (NBCC) and the National Board of Professional Teaching Standards (NBPTS). The benefits of national certification are threefold: by participating in the certification process, you will be acknowledged for your competencies and accomplishments as a nationally certificated counselor; you will be elevating your professional identity, which could be important to your building principal and your community stakeholders; and you may receive financial incentives from your state and/or local school board.

National Certified School Counselor

The NBCC was founded in 1982 to develop an examination of counseling competencies for practitioners to obtain national certification. In the late 1980s, working with the American School Counselor Association and the American Counseling Association (ACA), the NBCC developed a specialty credential for school counselors called National Certified School Counselor (NCSC). All applicants for the NCSC must hold the National Certified Counselor (NCC) designation (NBPTS, 2012).

The application process involves holding accreditation as a National Certified Counselor in addition to coursework that includes a course in Foundations of School Counseling and additional courses in designated areas. Furthermore, supervision in school field experiences, two academic years of full-time post-graduate work as a school counselor, and a passing score on the National School Counselor Examination (NCSCE) are required. More information about the NCSC application process and the NCSCE test is available by visiting the NBCC website at www.nbcc.org.

Credentials are issued for a period of 5 years, during which you must complete 100 clock hours of counseling-related continuing education, of which 25 hours must be in the area of school counseling. Check the NBCC website for current costs of exams and annual maintenance fees.

Some states provide financial incentives to NCSC-certified counselors. In addition, some local school districts award salary supplements to school counselors with NCSC certification. For more information about NCC/NCSC advantages and the application process, see the National Board for Certified Counselors website at www.nbcc.org/certification or call 1-336-547-0607.

National Board for Professional Teaching Standards

Founded in 1987, the National Board for Professional Teaching Standards is dedicated to advancing quality instruction by recognizing teachers, school counselors, and others who distinguish themselves through accomplishing certain performance standards. There are 11 standards which school counselors must show evidence of meeting: School Counseling Programs; School Counseling and Student Competencies; Human Growth and Development; Counseling Theories and Techniques; Equity, Fairness, and Diversity; School Climate; Collaboration with Family and Community; Informational Resources and Technology; Student Assessment; Leadership, Advocacy, and Professional Identity; and Reflective Practice. These are very similar to the School Counselor Competencies as identified by the ASCA.

Applicants for NBPTS must hold a state school counselor credential and have practiced school counseling for at least 3 years. Interestingly, a master's degree is not required for this credential. The application process for NBPTS involves a performance-based assessment with two key components: a portfolio of counseling practice and an examination of counseling knowledge. The portfolio includes student work, video recordings, and other counseling examples.

NBPTS certification for accomplished school counselors is for a 10-year period. Check the NBPTS website (www.nbpts.org) for current application and re-certification fees. There is no annual fee to maintain the certification, but the Profile of Professional Growth must be completed within the 10-year period. The Profile of Professional Growth documents the three areas of continuing education that accomplished school counselors have completed. The re-certification process involves a video recording of performance.

All 50 states offer some financial incentives to offset the application costs involved in the NBPTS certification process; however, those funds are limited. Each state has specific guidelines and deadlines, so counselors seeking to request these funds to help with the cost of NBPTS should contact their respective state departments of education as soon as possible. An increasing number of local school districts are electing to provide increased pay to accomplished school counselors certified by NBPTS. You should check with your local human resources director and/or your state's department of education for details *before* you begin the application process. For more information about the application process and possible financial support available to assist with the application costs, visit the National Board for Professional Teaching Standards website at www.nbpts.org or call 1-800-228-3224.

Comparison of NCC/NCSC and NBPTS

Both the NCC and the NBPTS offer opportunities for school counselors to grow and be acknowledged professionally through the demonstration of competencies beyond state creden-tialing requirements. Both afford school counselors a higher level of professionalism when they earn national credentials, and both require additional assessment of knowledge and skill in implementing comprehensive school counseling programs (Milsom & Akos, 2007).

Each approach has advantages and limitations, as you can see in Table 14.1. Should you prepare yourself to earn national certification? If so, which path to national certification should you choose? Both require 3 years of experience before one can obtain national certification, which gives a beginning counselor ample time to prepare for the rigors of an evaluation based upon national standards. The NBPTS assessment is heavily weighted in performance and writ-ten measures, while NCC/NCSC is rooted in a multiple-choice examination. While NBPTS is initially more expensive, limited financial assistance is available from some local districts, state departments of education, and national resources.

It is believed that pursuing either one or both certifications will make one a better school counselor (Milsom & Akos, 2007). Nationally certified counselors are perceived as more professional and competent and are likely to be more respected by their principals. This typ-ically means more support for their counseling programs. The bottom line is that a growing number of states and local school districts are providing additional compensation to nation-ally certified teachers and counselors.

Membership in Professional Organizations

As you complete your final preparations to become a professional school counselor, it would be prudent for you to consider membership in professional organizations. Associating with other counselors will help you to maintain your enthusiasm and your passion for your work and will provide opportunities to engage in professional activities and resources specific to the field.

Table 14.1 NCC/NCSC versus NBPTS.

	NCC/NCSC	NBPTS
Minimum educational requirement	Master's degree	Bachelor's degree w/state license
Supervision experience requirement	100 hours over 3 years	3 years
Written examination	Yes	Yes
Portfolio of work	No	Yes
Period of certification	5 years	10 years
Required continuing education	100 clock hours	Complete *Profile of Professional Growth*
Salary supplements	Yes	Yes

At the present time, ASCA membership of professional, practicing school counselors is 24,000, or 21.6% of the total number of 111,278 practicing school counselors (A. Hickman, personal communication, September 17, 2019). This is unfortunate, in that many school counselors are missing out on the personal and professional growth activities the ASCA promotes through its many workshops and conferences and the tremendous resources available to *members only* at its website. The following are some professional materials and information members can access at the ASCA website:

- *ASCA Resource Center*—contains links, publications, sample articles, sample documents, and journal articles on almost 50 topics, ranging from abuse to war/deployment
- *ASCA Ethical Standards for School Counselors*—includes the ASCA's Ethical Standards for School Counselors, journal archives on legal and ethical issues, and a forum where members can submit ethical questions
- *Publications and Position Statements*—enables members to search the archives of ASCA publications such as *Professional School Counseling, ASCA School Counselor*, position statements on counseling related topics, and *ASCA Aspects*
- *Professional Development*—provides a comprehensive listing of state conferences, site-based training, upcoming conferences, and training opportunities on the ASCA National Model
- *Online Store*—offers professional books and materials at discounted prices to members
- *ASCA National Model*—gives detailed information about the four quadrants of the model and how to become a RAMP recognized program
- *ASCA Scene*—a social networking site that gives school counselors a method to connect and to communicate using blogging, discussion forums, and the like; this is an excellent service for soliciting suggestions to issues and concerns school counselors typically face
- *ASCA on Air*—a podcast service to provide members with information about school counseling issues, trends, and interviews; you can hear relevant information presented in a timely and portable manner

As education reformers rapidly revise the educational landscape on which school counselors must tread, it is important to be astute about proposed changes. The combined numbers of school counselors and other counseling professionals can have an impact on state laws and regulations that affect our counseling practice and professional image. It would be important for beginning school counselors to join forces with others to provide new approaches and fresh energy to association work. Collaboration with counseling colleagues can be highly rewarding work for new school counselors who wish to use their leadership and advocacy skills to make a difference on a larger scale.

Conclusion

This chapter began with a few suggestions on how to conclude your counseling and collaborating work at your clinical school sites in a manner that is both personal and professional. Taking a little extra time to plan positive closure activities with students and staff will not only help establish effective future behavior patterns, but will enhance your professional reputation as well.

As you prepare to leave your counselor training program and begin the transition into the world of a professional school counselor, you will want to improve your emerging knowledge and skills. Use the conceptual application activities provided in this chapter to monitor your professional development annually in order to focus on your career goals and provide reassurance in what you do.

Be mindful of your identity as a professional school counselor. You possess unique knowledge and skills that are greatly needed in schools today. The vision you have for developing a comprehensive school counseling program requires the support of significant others in your school, community, and state, but you will want to follow the advice of the Chinese philosopher Lao-tzu, who wisely stated: "The journey of a thousand miles begins beneath your feet." Build your school's counseling program component by component, and let data guide your journey.

This is the best time in history to be a well-trained and well-prepared school counselor. Whether you are hired in an elementary school, a middle school, or a high school, challenging and rewarding work awaits you there. What better calling can there be than to have a dream to build a comprehensive school counseling program and to have the abilities to design and deliver it for our nation's future generation?

Websites

- Microsoft Office Online provides various templates that you can use to build your résumé: http://office.microsoft.com/en-us/templates/CT101448941033.aspx
- "Best Techniques for a Successful Job Interview": http://jobsearch.about.com/od/interviews/tp/jobinterviewtips.htm

References

Lowery, K., Quick, M., Boyland, L., Geesa, R. L., & Mayes, R. D. (2018). "It wasn't mentioned and should have been": Principals' preparation to support comprehensive school counseling. *Journal of Organization and Educational Leadership.* EJ1180120.

Milsom, A., & Akos, P. (2007). National certification: Evidence of a professional school counselor? *Professional School Counseling, 10,* 346–351.

NBPTS. (2012). *School Counseling Standards,* 1st ed. Retrieved from www.nbpts.org/wp-content/uploads/ECYA-SC.pdf

US Bureau of Labor Statistics (2019). School and Career counselors. *Occupational Outlook Handbook.* Retrieved from www.bls.gov/ooh/community-and-social-service/school-and-career-counselors.htm

Index

Page numbers in *italics* refer to figures; page numbers in **bold** refer to tables.